SCIENCE 5
FOR YOUNG CATHOLICS

EDITS BY
SETON STAFF

SETON PRESS
FRONT ROYAL, VA

Executive Editor: Dr. Mary Kay Clark
Editors: Seton Staff

Seton Press
1350 Progress Drive
Front Royal, VA 22630
Phone: (540) 636-9990
Fax: (540) 636-1602

For more information, visit us on the web at www.setonpress.com
Contact us by e-mail at info@setonpress.com

ISBN: 978-1-60704-147-4

Cover Top Left: *Creation of Adam* by Michelangelo
       Top Right: Lion by shutterstock.com
       Lower Left: Dolphin by shutterstock.com
       Lower Right: Toucan by dollarphotoclub.com

DEDICATED TO THE SACRED HEART OF JESUS

Table of Contents

Introduction to Science 5 for Young Catholics

Science 5 for Young Catholics was written by a Catholic who is teaching science in a private Catholic school. We believe this book is not only a great presentation of science concepts, but also that the book is designed for Catholic students in 5th grade. In fact, the most important aspect of this book is a continuing theme of appreciation for God as the Creator of His amazing world, and a realization of the incredible enormity of His intellect which is beyond anything we could ever imagine!

Science 5 for Young Catholics is practical for the student and for the family to understanding the human body. The chapters show how God in His infinite Wisdom designed not only several intricate systems, but also designed the human body to be able to heal itself!

Please take time to look over the chapter outlines in the beginning of the book and at the front of each chapter. The rather extensive outline for each chapter is provided at the request of parents. These outlines should be helpful for students and for parents as a basic design for a Study Guide.

Notice that the paragraphs within each chapter are numbered or lettered according to the chapter outline. We hope this not only helps the student to relate the specific sections to the overall topic, but also that it helps the student to develop study skills in general. Each chapter outline functions as a broad study guide for certain words and phrases which the teacher believes the student should emphasize in the basic study of the chapter ideas.

Our technical department found clear and substantial photos to enhance the understanding of the lessons. While we encourage parents to locate videos on the Internet which would be helpful to increase understanding, the number and quality of the photos in the text should be sufficient for understanding the concepts.

The Review Questions at the end of each section are important for your child to reinforce the ideas that will be necessary to answer the questions at the end of each chapter, and which serve as a study guide for the chapter tests.

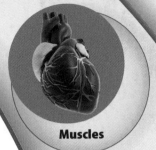

Muscles

Action

Exercise

Support

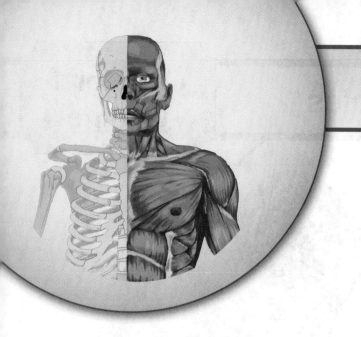

Bones and Muscles

are going to get a little scientific here, and learn something really special about our bones. The **axial** bones make up our head, neck, and trunk (chest and back bones). These are the bones that are along the *axis* of the human skeleton. The **appendicular** bones make up our limbs (that is, our arms and legs), as well as the shoulder blades and the pelvis. Thus, these bones include our *appendages* and those parts (shoulder blades and pelvis) that connect them to the axial part of the skeleton.

I. The Skeletal System

Every building structure has a foundation to give it support and strength. The human body is no different. God created the human body with a strong bone foundation. Unlike a building, though, the body's bone foundation can move, grow, and even heal itself! The amazing foundation that God has designed for the human body we call the skeletal system.

Perhaps you think of a Halloween costume when you think of a skeleton. The skeleton is supposed to be something fun, or funny, and in the dark, a little scary! If you have seen a model of a human skeleton in a museum, it may have looked like an elaborate, three-dimensional puzzle, maybe something you would rather avoid.

Actually, your own body's skeleton is much more than anything we can imagine. The human skeleton is totally miraculous, as any doctor who has studied the human skeleton will tell you. The adult human skeleton is made up of about **206 bones!** That in itself is hard to believe. Each bone God has designed to serve a specific function. God has an important purpose for each part of our skeleton.

The bones of the human skeleton are classified as either axial (AX-ee-uhl) or appendicular (app-en-DICK-you-lar). Now we

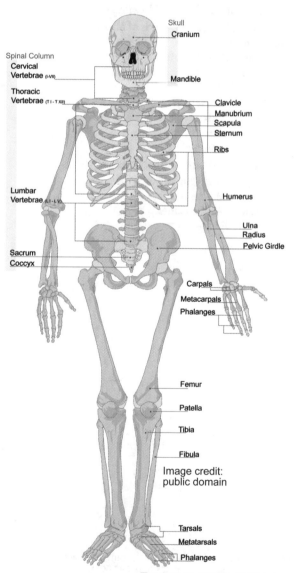

Skull
Cranium

Spinal Column
Cervical Vertebrae (I-VII)

Thoracic Vertebrae (T I - T XII)

Mandible

Clavicle
Manubrium
Scapula
Sternum

Ribs

Lumbar Vertebrae (L I - L V)

Humerus

Ulna
Radius
Pelvic Girdle

Sacrum
Coccyx

Carpals
Metacarpals
Phalanges

Femur

Patella

Tibia

Fibula

Image credit: public domain

Tarsals
Metatarsals
Phalanges

Top image credit: public domain

2

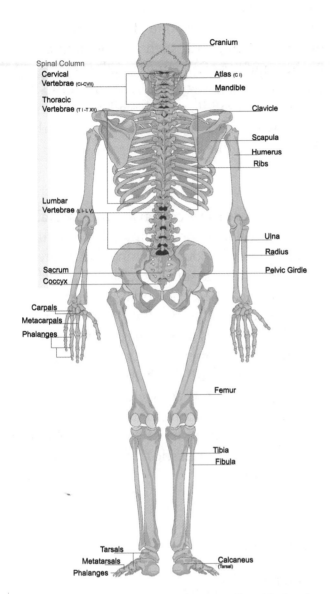

Spinal Column
Cervical
Vertebrae (CI-CVII)
Thoracic
Vertebrae (T I - T XII)
Lumbar
Vertebrae (LI - L V)
Sacrum
Coccyx
Carpals
Metacarpals
Phalanges
Tarsals
Metatarsals
Phalanges

Cranium
Atlas (C I)
Mandible
Clavicle
Scapula
Humerus
Ribs
Ulna
Radius
Pelvic Girdle
Femur
Tibia
Fibula
Calcaneus
(Tarsal)

Image credit: public domain

Axial and appendicular may be new words for you, but this is a science book, so we are going to discuss scientific terms. If you write those words down in a notebook, as well as any new vocabulary words you find in this book, your brain and your fingers will help you to remember the spelling and the pronunciation of new scientific words.

II. Primary Functions of Skeletal System

Much like the stem of a plant, one of the **primary functions of our bones** is to **support** our body and **give shape** to our body. Many bones, such as the skull and rib cage, are vital

for **protecting** fragile organs like the brain and the heart. In addition, the bones work together with the muscles to give us the **power** to move. One thing we often forget is that our bones **create blood cells** and **store minerals** our body needs. Most of us forget that the tiny bones in our ears allow us **to hear!** If you have grandparents who have trouble hearing, you should be able to appreciate the importance of those tiny bones in your ears!

III. Helping Bones Move

A. Joints, Ligaments, Tendons

The most important function of the skeletal system is to help people move their bodies. However, most bones are stiff and inflexible; they cannot move by themselves. God has given our bodies helps to move our bones. Joints are strong connections that join a bone to another bone; without joints, we could not move our bones at all! Ligaments are tough bands of tissue that fasten bones together. Tendons are connective tissues that connect bones to muscles.

B. Kinds of Joints

There are numerous types of joints in the human body that facilitate movement, known as synovial (sih-NOH-vee-uhl) joints. Three well-known types of synovial joints are hinge joints, pivot joints, and ball-and-socket joints. Our bodies also have fixed joints that do not move, such as many joints in our skulls.

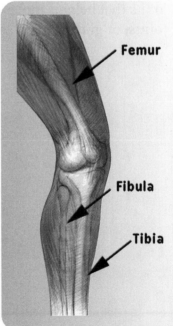

Femur
Fibula
Tibia

The bones of the upper and lower leg come together at the knee in a hinge joint.

Hinge joints allow movement only along one plane. Examples of hinge joints are the knee and elbow joints, which allow the arms and legs to bend back and forth in one direction.

Pivot joints allow for rotation. An example of a pivot joint is at the top of your spine, where it meets the skull. It allows you to rotate your head from side to side.

Ball-and-socket joints allow for a much wider range of movement. In a ball-and-socket joint, a rounded part of one bone fits into the hollow part of another bone. Move your shoulder around slowly in as many directions as you can. It has a much greater range of movement than your knee or elbow. The shoulder is an example of a ball-and-socket joint.

C. Other Types of Synovial Joints

There are three other types of synovial joints that help us move our bones. **Plane joints**, or gliding joints, allow for gliding or sliding movements. Most of these allow for movement only along one plane. **Condyloid (KON-dil-oyd) joints**, such as those found in the knuckles of our fingers, allow for movement along two planes. **Saddle joints** are shaped like a saddle and also allow movement along two planes. The joint at the base of the thumb is a saddle joint.

Joints are a critical part of the skeletal system. With 206 bones connecting to make up the "puzzle" of our skeleton, God created our joints with the same precision He used to create our bones. Each bone and joint is specially designed to fulfill its specific purpose. Our skeleton gives us an amazing ability for all kinds of movement; it is truly a testimony to God's love for us! Think about acrobats and their amazing ability to stretch their joints to the utmost. Think about your own gymnastic tricks and how so many of your joints help you to do amazing gymnastic tricks as well as play various sports.

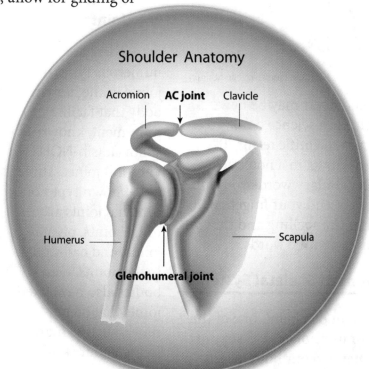

Shoulder Anatomy

Acromion   **AC joint**   Clavicle

Humerus

Scapula

Glenohumeral joint

Image credit: shutterstock.com

Review Questions

1. How many bones make up the skeletal system?

_____

2. In what two groups are bones classified?

_____

3. Name three functions of the skeletal system.

_____

_____

4. What are joints?

_____

5. What are the three main types of synovial joints that allow movement?

_____

_____

Optional: How do you use your bones and muscle and joints for any sports activities?

_____

_____

IV. Bones in General

As mentioned in the last section, the skeletal system is primarily made up of bones. What are the different kinds of bones. What exactly are bones? What are they made of? How do they grow? What are their different shapes?

A. Kinds of Bones: Compact Bones and Cancellous Bones

Bones are the hard parts of the skeleton of the body. The bones of the human body contain two layers. **Compact bone** is the dense outer layer of a bone, and **cancellous bone** is the spongy inner layer of a bone. Bones are made up mostly of two materials: collagen and calcium phosphate. The **collagen** gives the bone a soft framework, while the **calcium phosphate** gives it strength and hardness. Bones are actually an important source of calcium for the whole body. Bones release calcium into the blood stream whenever it is needed. We often don't think about the importance of milk. Milk provides the calcium needed not only for strong bones, but also for the calcium needed in our blood which is provided by our bones.

B. Inner Part of Large Bones

The inner part of larger bones also contains **bone marrow**. This jelly-like bone marrow is where most of the body's blood cells are made. There are two types of bone marrow: red and yellow. The **red marrow** produces the blood cells, while the **yellow marrow** consists mainly of fat cells. When a person is born, most of the bone marrow is red, but as a person ages, the bone marrow begins to be converted to yellow marrow.

C. Bone Development

A person's bones begin to form very early in life, approximately six months before a person is even born! When still just a tiny baby in his or her mother's womb, a child begins to develop bones. However, these bones will not be fully developed for nearly 20 years, until the person is a young adult.

You have probably heard about the importance of being careful with babies, and the "soft spots" on their heads. This is because our bones actually start out as a soft material called **cartilage**. Much of a baby's skull is still made of cartilage. As a child grows, the cartilage grows, and then begins a process called ossification (AH-suh-fuh-KAY-shun). **Ossification** is the process by which cartilage is replaced with collagen and calcium, and becomes bone. Infants are said to have nearly 300 bones because when they are born, parts of some of their bones are separated. However, they fuse together as they grow.

Even when we are grown, we still have some cartilage. It can be found in our joints, where cartilage supports bones and protects bones where they rub against each other. Other parts of our bodies, such as our nose and outer ears, are made of cartilage.

D. Four Categories of Bones

There are four **categories of bones**, classified by their shape. **Long bones**, such as those in the arms and legs, are tubular in shape. **Short bones** tend to be the shape of cubes, and are found in the wrists and ankles. **Flat bones**, such as the ribs and the bones of the cranium, usually have a protective function. If a bone cannot be classified as long, short, or flat, it is considered an **Irregular Bone**.

Our skeletal system continues to develop until late adolescence or early young adulthood, but actually, because our skeleton is always repairing itself, it never really stops changing.

Review Questions

1. What are the two layers of bones called?

_____

2. Where is bone marrow found, and what is its function?

_____

3. What is ossification?

_____

4. How are bones classified?

_____

5. What are the four categories of bones?

_____

V. Major Bones

Now that you know what bones are, and what they are for, we will explore some of the major bones in the human body. Something one quickly discovers when studying the human body is that God has left nothing to chance. Every bone has been created perfectly to serve an important specific function, whether it is protection of organs, or an attachment point for tendons and ligaments, or support for the shape of the human body.

Some of the major **axial bones** are the skull, the spinal column, and the rib cage. Let's explore these in more detail.

A. The Skull

The skull is actually made up of 22 bones! Eight of the bones in the skull form the cranium. These cranium bones fuse together during ossification to form a protective helmet for the brain. The cranium "helmet" is about a quarter of an inch thick. Besides serving as an all-important protection for the brain, the skull also houses our eyes, our nasal cavity, our ear canals, our teeth, and our tongue, giving it an essential role in the exercise of our five senses.

Even though the skull protects the brain, it is still important to be careful about severe blows to the head. A concussion can result when a blow to the head causes the brain to bruise by striking against the skull. Other serious injuries can result from head trauma, which is why it is always important to wear a helmet when riding a bike or a skateboard.

Some of the tiniest bones in the skull are the three bones of our inner ear: the stirrup, the hammer, and the anvil. These three bones in the ear are created and situated so intricately that different sound waves cause them to vibrate in ways that allow us to hear the wide variety of sounds we enjoy, from speech to beautiful music. It is amazing to think that God could provide us the wide array of sounds we experience using the vibrations of just these three little bones.

Connected to our **brain** are nerves coming from every part of our body. These nerves send messages back and forth between the brain and the rest of the body. Most of these nerves are connected to the brain

Image credits: public domain

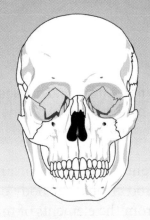

Some of the bones of the skull are fused together to form the cranium, a protective "helmet" for the brain.

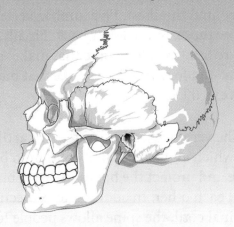

The human jaw is an example of both a hinging joint and a sliding joint.

through our spinal cord. Protecting these nerves in the spinal cord is vital to our ability to move and experience our five senses.

B. The Spinal Column

The bones that God has designed for this essential job of protecting the nerves in the spinal cord make up our **spinal column**. The spinal column is made up of 33 bones called **vertebrae** (VER-tuh-bray). The vertebrae bones have holes in the middle, almost like a donut, allowing the spinal cord to run the length of the vertebrae, while still providing strong protection.

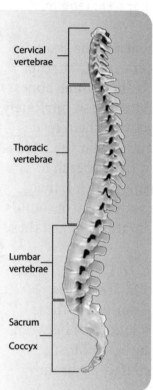

Image credit: Kisco 3

The top seven vertebrae, found in the neck area, are called **cervical** (SIR-vick-uhl) vertebrae. Below them are 12 **thoracic** (thoe-RASS-ick) vertebrae, found in the upper back, behind the chest. Five **lumbar** vertebrae sit below those, in the lower back. Finally, there are five fused vertebrae that make up the **sacrum**, and four fused vertebrae that make up the **coccyx** (KOCK-six).

The vertebrae are separated by **cartilage discs**, which allow the spinal column to be flexible and protect the bones from rubbing against each other. In addition to protecting our spinal cord, the spine allows people to stand upright and bend their bodies in various ways.

C. The Rib Cage

In the trunk of our bodies, between the neck and the pelvis, there are many vital organs. Some of these are protected by a series of bones called the **rib cage**. The rib cage is located in the chest and is made up of 24 long, curved bones called ribs, connected to the sternum (the breastbone) and the spine, forming a "cage" that protects our heart and lungs.

The 24 ribs in the human body form pairs, with 12 on the left side and 12 on the right. The first seven ribs on each side connect with cartilage directly to the sternum. The next three ribs connect to the sternum indirectly; their cartilage connects with that of the rib immediately above. The last two ribs are called floating ribs because they do not connect to the sternum at all.

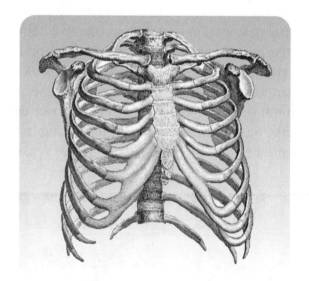

The ribs form a kind of cage
that protect the vital organs.
Image credit: unknown

The rib bone holds an important place in Scripture. God created the body of the first man, Adam, from the elements of material creation, the "dust of the Earth," as Genesis puts it. Eve, however, was created from the rib of Adam. The words of Scripture tell us that God fashioned Eve out of one of Adam's ribs.

"Then the Lord God cast a deep sleep upon Adam; and when he was fast asleep, he took one of his ribs and filled up flesh for it. And the Lord God built the rib which He took from Adam into a woman, and brought her to Adam. And Adam said, 'This now is bone of my bones and flesh of my flesh; she shall be called woman because she was taken out of man'" Genesis 2:21-23.

This is an important image God has given us, that of Adam's bride coming from his side, because as Jesus was hanging on the cross, He was pierced in His side by a lance. Blood and water came from His side. Blood and water are often recognized as symbols of the Church. Many saints and theologians believe that when Jesus died on the Cross, when the blood and water came from His side, it was meant as a symbol that His Church was established and came from Jesus as He died on the Cross. (Of course, Jesus gave Peter the keys of the Church, even saying, "Upon this rock, I will build My Church.")

D. The Appendicular Bones

The **appendicular bones** make up our limbs (that is, our arms and legs), as well as theshoulder blades and the pelvis. The bones in our arms and legs are long, sturdy bones, such as the **femur** and **humerus**, and also small bones like those in our hands and feet.

The longest bone in the human body is the **femur**, which is the bone in the upper part of each leg. The knee joint contains cartilage. This cartilage is especially important because it gives us the ability to bend the knee. The cartilage provides cushioning for our leg

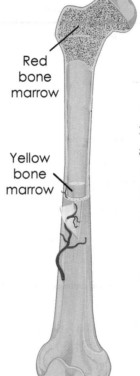

Red bone marrow

Yellow bone marrow

Image credit: Public Domain

bones, which bear the full weight of our bodies when we stand.

Below the knee are two bones that run from the knee to the ankle. The larger bone is called the **tibia**, and the smaller is called the **fibula**. Each foot is made up of 26 bones called tarsals, metatarsals (**met**-a-tar-sals), and phalanges (fa-lan-jees).

Our hands and arms are similarly designed. The large bone of our upper arm is the **humerus**. Below the elbow are two bones, the radius and the ulna, which connect to the wrist and hands. These are made up of 27 bones called carpals, metacarpals, and phalanges.

Another important bone that is vital to the use of our arms is the **scapula**, also known as the shoulder blade. We have one scapula on each side of our body, located in the upper back. The movement of the scapula allows us a wide range of movement for our arms.

The **pelvis** in the human body is a series of six bones (three fused bones on each side) just below the waist. The pelvis gives stability to the body and (with the sacrum and the coccyx) is a connection point for many muscles and tendons that allow us to stand and walk.

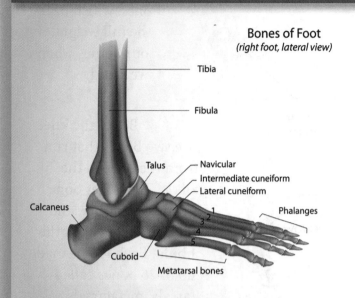

Bones of Foot
(right foot, lateral view)

Tibia

Fibula

Talus

Navicular

Intermediate cuneiform

Lateral cuneiform

Calcaneus

Phalanges

Cuboid

Metatarsal bones

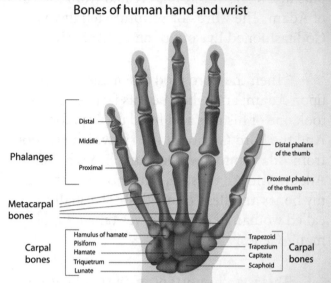

Bones of human hand and wrist

Distal

Middle

Phalanges

Proximal

Distal phalanx of the thumb

Proximal phalanx of the thumb

Metacarpal bones

Hamulus of hamate
Pisiform
Hamate
Triquetrum
Lunate

Carpal bones

Trapezoid
Trapezium
Capitate
Scaphoid

Carpal bones

Image credits: shutters

The pelvis also protects vital organs, such as the bladder and the lower part of the large intestine.

These bones, along with the others that make up the human body's 206 bones, are an amazing foundation for God's special material creations: our bodies!

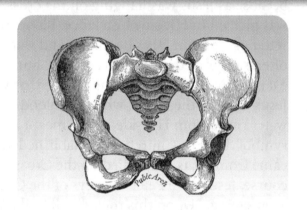

The pelvis helps to protect the vital organs and gives stability to the body.
Image credit: unknown

Review Questions

1. What is the name for the 8 bones in the skull that fuse together to form a protective helmet for the brain?

_____

2. How do the bones of the inner ear help us to hear?

_____

_____

3. What are the bones called that make up the spinal column? How many of them are there?

_____

_____

4. Which organs does the rib cage primarily protect?

_____

_____

5. What is the longest bone in the human body?

_____

VI. Bone Health and Natural Healing with Vitamin D

You're familiar with the stories of Jesus giving sight to the blind and speech to the dumb, healing the lame and the deaf. These are great miracles of healing. These show that Jesus, as God, was not bound by the laws of nature. Sometimes, however, we don't think about the gift of **natural healing** God has given to all our bodies. We often overlook the wonderful, **natural healing** way God has designed our bodies to heal themselves. This is a God-given gift that should make us realize how very much Jesus loves us.

God has given our body an incredible capacity for healing itself when it is injured. Our bones are no different. Perhaps you have broken a bone, or have known someone who has. A broken bone has the ability to fuse back together! For it to heal properly, however, the bones must fuse in the right place. This is why a doctor often has to "set" the broken bone in the right place, to line up the broken parts correctly so they fuse correctly and smoothly. Once that is done, a person usually must wear a cast to make sure that the bone stays in the proper position as it is healing. After a number of weeks, the bone should be healed, at which point the cast can be taken off.

Broken bones are not the only threat to our skeletal system, however. It is important that we take good care of our skeletal system to maintain our long-term health.

One common and painful problem is **back injury**. The bony vertebrae in our backs protect our spinal cord, a vital and vulnerable nerve center. Cartilage discs between the vertebrae cushion and protect the vertebrae from rubbing together, which causes serious pain.

A **hernia**, or **herniated disc**, is a bulge in one of the cartilage discs. A hernia can cause pain and instability in the back, and can pinch nerves that run along the spinal column, causing dramatic pain in other parts of the body. When a disc ruptures or breaks, the gelatinous (jelly-like) center flows out. Often these types of injuries require long periods of physical therapy or even surgery to be treated.

Some important things people can do to protect their backs are to sit correctly in chairs, maintain a healthy weight, and take care when lifting heavy things. It is important not to lift anything that is too heavy. It is also important not to lift it improperly. Too much strain on the back from heavy lifting is a common cause of back injuries.

Our **joints** also can be susceptible to injury. **Arthritis** is inflammation of the joints. Arthritis causes pain and stiffness, and can seriously limit a person's mobility. Proper diet, exercise, and stretching can help prevent arthritis. Arthritis is a common disease among older people.

The most common bone disease is **osteoporosis (OS-tee-o-po-RO-sis)**. This happens to many older women. This is when **bones lose density**, meaning the amount of calcium in the bones is low. **Lack of calcium** causes bones to be brittle and break more easily. Although there are many risk factors for osteoporosis, there are many things people can do to protect their bone health.

One of the most important things to do to protect bones is **exercise**. It is important for children and adults alike to get plenty of exercise, preferably every day.

Another key component to bone health is a **healthy diet**. Because osteoporosis is a lack of calcium in bones, a diet that provides plenty of **calcium protects bone health**. Calcium can be found in foods such as almonds, leafy green vegetables, and dairy products, like milk, cheese, and yogurt.

Vitamin D is also important for bone health. **Vitamin D** helps the body absorb calcium, which is why many dairy products are fortified with vitamin D. Surprisingly, we can obtain vitamin D from sunlight! Often older people who stay inside during the winter begin to suffer from a lack of Vitamin D. Some people take a multivitamin every day to obtain the proper amount of Vitamin D for good health.

To protect our bones, it is important to **wear protective equipment**, such as helmets and knee pads, when we are doing activities that can put our bones at risk for injury. These are important tools to keep us safe and healthy.

If we exercise every day, eat a healthy diet with calcium and vitamin D, wear proper safety equipment, and maintain a healthy posture, we are giving our bones what they need to remain healthy and strong.

St. Stanislaus Kostka

Did you know there is a patron saint who has been known to help people with broken bones? His name is St. Stanislaus Kostka. St. Stanislaus is a Polish saint who was born in the year 1550. He had great devotion to God from childhood. Once when he was gravely ill, St. Stanislaus Kostka had a vision of St. Barbara, who appeared to him with two angels, who brought him Holy Communion. Stanislaus recovered from his illness and was told by Our Lady to become a Jesuit priest. Stanislaus never became a priest, though. He died at the age of only 17 when he was still a novice, learning about how to become a priest. We can ask St. Stanislaus to pray for the strength and health of our bones. His feast day is November 13.

Review Questions

1. Why do people wear casts when they have a broken bone?

_____

_____

2. What injury can occur when lifting something that is too heavy?

_____

_____

3. What is osteoporosis?

_____

_____

4. Name the vitamin and mineral that are important for bone health.

_____

5. Name two sources of calcium in food.

_____

_____

VII. The Muscular System: Kinds of Muscles

You know that the skeletal system allows you to move. You probably know that your bones can't move alone. The **system that really causes movement for bones is the muscular system.** Move your arm back and forth in front of your face. It took multiple muscles to make that simple movement. Even focusing your eyes to read this book requires muscles. Even when you feel like you are not actually doing anything, your muscular system is still hard at work. The muscles of your stomach, for instance, may be digesting food, and your heart muscle is beating. All of this and more shows that your muscular system is in constant action.

When God created our muscular system, He left nothing to chance. Have you ever thought about how many muscles you have in your body? There are over **650 muscles** in the human body! Each one has a specific purpose. Like our bones, our muscles grow, and even can heal themselves when they get injured. Of course, God made muscles in such a way they heal themselves. Did you know that muscles typically make up about half a person's body weight?

There are three main kinds of muscles in our bodies: skeletal, smooth, and cardiac.

A. Skeletal Muscles

Most **skeletal muscles** are connected to our bones by fibrous tissue called **tendons**. Some skeletal muscles connect directly to organs, such as those muscles that connect to the eyes. These muscles are sometimes called voluntary muscles because they are muscles

Skeletal Muscle

We can control the movement of skeletal muscles.

Smooth Muscle

Smooth muscles move involuntarily.

Cardiac Muscle

Cardiac muscles move involuntarily to pump blood throughout the body.

Image credits: unknown

that we move intentionally. They produce our external bodily movements, such as walking, bending, or throwing a ball.

B. Smooth Muscles

Smooth muscles are found in the walls of many of our inner organs. Smooth muscles move involuntarily. For example, the last time you ate a meal, you did not concentrate on moving the muscles you needed to digest it; those smooth muscles just started digesting your food automatically.

C. Cardiac Muscles

The third type of muscle, **cardiac muscle**, also moves involuntarily. This is the very important muscle that makes up the heart. Your cardiac muscle pumps rhythmically to move blood throughout your body, even before you were born. The heart beats about 100,000 times a day! Sometime, you might try feeling your pulse and figuring out how many times your heart beats in one minute.

Although your muscles are growing now, your muscular system began functioning very early in your life when you were very small, before you were even born. If you have ever seen the ultrasound of a baby before he or she is born, you may have seen him or her moving inside his or her mother. Often, a pregnant woman can feel her baby's muscular system working from the inside. We can detect a baby's heartbeat when he is only three weeks old, more than eight months before he is born!

The muscular system is truly an important and amazing part of the human body.

D. St. Sebastian

There is no patron saint specifically in relation to muscles, but St. Sebastian is the patron saint of athletes. To participate

in athletics requires the use of all types of muscles. Performing even the simplest athletic activity uses numerous skeletal muscles. The cardiac muscles of the heart must be healthy for an athlete to have endurance. Also, the functioning of the smooth muscles of the internal organs is important for our bodies to function properly as we play.

St. Sebastian was a Roman soldier who converted to Catholicism secretly. He lived during the reign of the Emperor Diocletian, who persecuted Christians terribly. When Sebastian was found to be a Catholic, he was sentenced to death by being shot with arrows. Amazingly, he survived his wounds and was nursed back to health. Sebastian later confronted the emperor and then won a martyr's crown when he was killed by the emperor's soldiers.

St. Sebastian's feast day is January 20. He is a good saint to ask for intercession that our muscles will be healthy and allow us to participate fully in good health, particularly when we play sports and other games.

Saint Sebastian is the patron
saint of athletes.
Image credit: Raffaello Sanzio

Review Questions

1. What are the three types of muscles?

_____

_____

_____

2. Which type of muscle is considered "voluntary"?

_____

3. Which type of muscle is found in the heart?

_____

4. Which type of muscle is found in other organs of the body?

_____

5. How many muscles are in the human body?

_____

VIII. How the Muscular System Works

You know the importance of the muscular system. But what are muscles? How do they work? Did you know that muscles are organs? Muscle tissues are made up of bundles of fibers that cause movement by contracting. To contract means to shorten. Even when you extend a part of your body, it is caused by one or more muscles actually shortening or contracting! How is that possible?

A. Skeletal Muscles

Skeletal muscles are muscles that attach to bone. These muscles generally work in pairs. One muscle contracts, while its opposing muscle relaxes, to move a body part in one way or in one direction. To move the other way, in the opposite direction, the muscles switch roles. For example, to bend at the elbow and bring your hand toward your face, your biceps muscle, on the top of your upper arm, contracts. To extend your arm out again, your biceps relaxes, while your triceps, on the back of your upper arm contracts, pulling your hand down, away from your face.

Sometimes both of the muscles in a working pair must contract at the same time. This is called **cocontraction**. This occurs when the body needs to provide additional stability to a particular joint. For example, when landing after a jump, the ankle joint may need additional stability to keep the landing safe and under control. It this case the muscles in the calf and the muscles in the shin, which normally work in opposite directions, will all contract at once to make the foot and ankle more stable during the high stress of landing from a jump.

Muscle tissue also has the characteristic of **elasticity**. This means muscles can be stretched and then returned to their usual resting length without damage, like a rubber band.

Skeletal muscles serve to hold the skeleton bones together and give form to our bodies. Skeletal muscle is called **striated** (STRY-ate-ed) (meaning "striped") muscle. Because muscles are made up of fibers containing parallel bands of different material, muscles appear striped under a microscope.

One of the primary functions of skeletal muscle is to produce voluntary movement of the body. There are skeletal muscles up and down the body that first, help maintain your posture, second, allow you to move your head, and third, even cause your chest to rise and fall as you breathe.

Skeletal muscle fibers can be divided into two groups: slow-twitch and fast-twitch fibers. **Slow-twitch muscle fibers** can contract for a long time without much effort. An example would be the muscles on either side of the spine, which hold the trunk upright for long periods while sitting or standing. **Fast-twitch muscle fibers**, on the other hand, can contract quickly with a lot of power, but they cannot hold their contraction for very long. Strenuous lifting, for example, uses fast-twitch fibers.

Skeletal muscles can contain very few to several hundred **muscle fibers**. Large muscles, such as those in the trunk and the thighs, contain hundreds of muscle fibers. Small muscles responsible for very precise movements, such as those that move the eye, contain only a few muscle fibers.

Another important function of skeletal muscle is the **production of heat**. The heat that skeletal muscles generate helps people maintain their body temperature.

B. Smooth Muscles

Smooth muscles, as their name suggests, are not striated or striped. Smooth muscles are found in the walls of organs and even in blood vessels. These involuntary muscles help our bodies perform basic functions like digestion and circulation. The smooth muscles in blood vessels help maintain a healthy blood pressure. These muscles can stretch and maintain tension for a long time.

C. Cardiac Muscles

Cardiac muscle is striated, but much less noticeably than skeletal muscle. Heart muscle tissue works constantly with twitch contractions that pump blood throughout the body. The heart has an internal pacemaker that causes the muscle to pump in the right way and with the appropriate regular rhythm.

Although each type of muscle is different, they are all necessary to enable our bodies to move in many different ways. Although we cannot always see all these muscles at work, we can thank God that they always are performing vital functions to keep us alive, and allowing us to move around in many different ways. As we think about our muscles in relation to our prayers, let's not hesitate to kneel in church when we should at Mass, during Benediction, in Confession, and perhaps when saying the Rosary with our family or in church. Kneeling is an "exercise" to show our devotion. Kneeling has always been a part of our Catholic prayer life and culture.

Review Questions

1. What action do muscle fibers perform to move body parts?

_____

_____

2. Which type of muscle is not striated at all?

_____

3. What is the difference between fast-twitch and slow-twitch fibers?

_____

_____

4. What is the main function of cardiac muscle?

_____

_____

5. What does it mean to say muscle has the characteristic of elasticity?

_____

_____

IX. Muscle Shapes and Contractions

Most of our muscle tissue is skeletal muscle. Skeletal muscles come in different shapes. There are **five main shapes of skeletal muscles**. Some are **flat** muscles, such as the muscles in the abdomen (the front of the belly). Some are **pennate** muscles which usually have a feather-like shape and allow for greater force production. The shapes of pennate muscles can be varied, however. A couple of examples are the deltoid muscle in the shoulder and the quadriceps at the front of the thigh. **Fusiform** muscles are spindle-shaped, meaning they have a round, thick middle, but taper at the ends. The biceps is a fusiform muscle. A **quadrate** muscle, such as that of the lower back, has four relatively equal sides on the muscle. Finally,

credits: unknown

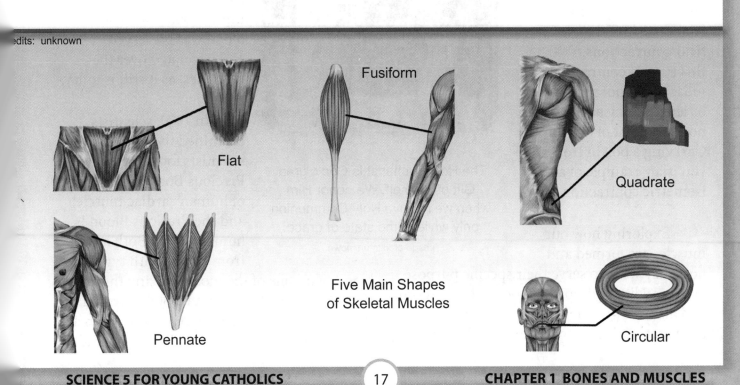

Flat

Fusiform

Quadrate

Pennate

Five Main Shapes
of Skeletal Muscles

Circular

there are **circular** muscles, which can be found around body openings, such as the mouth and the eyes.

Not only do skeletal muscles come in different shapes, they perform three different types of contractions. **Concentric contractions** are when muscle fibers shorten to move a body part, as when you raise your hand toward your face. **Eccentric contractions** occur when muscle fibers contract, but an external force pulls in the opposite direction. In this case, the contraction may serve to slow down movement in an opposing direction. For example, imagine you are taking a heavy box off a shelf and lowering it slowly to the ground. The box would come crashing down, except your muscles are performing eccentric contractions that slow the descent of the box, even though it does eventually reach the ground. Physical therapists often use eccentric contraction exercises to treat injured patients.

The final type of contraction is called **isometric (EYE-soh-MET-rick) contractions**. With this type of contraction, the muscles are not shortening or lengthening and there is no movement of any joint. Carrying a box in front of you is an example of an isometric contraction.

Exploring how our muscles are formed and how they work to serve their specific purpose gives us a little glimpse at God's great wisdom, and also His great love. Our Father in Heaven has taken such care to create us with bodies that are truly wonderful gifts. "I praise you, for I am fearfully and wonderfully made" (Psalm 139:14).

Eucharistic Miracle of Lanciano

Have you heard of the Eucharistic miracle of Lanciano, Italy? In this incredible event, God used heart muscle to demonstrate one of His greatest gifts to us. You know that at every Mass, the bread and wine become the Body and Blood of Christ. However, although they become the Eucharist, they still look like bread and wine. The characteristics called the "accidents" (the touch, taste, and feel) do not change, even though the substance does change.

The Holy Eucharist is God's great Gift of Himself. We honor Him when we receive Holy Communion only while in the state of grace.

Image credit: unknown

In the early eighth century in Italy, God gave us a great gift. During Mass, at the Consecration, the accidents or characteristics of the Eucharist changed as well. The Host no longer looked like bread, but became human flesh; and the Blood is real human blood. This miracle, this miraculous heart and blood was preserved and venerated over the centuries, as it still is today.

In 1970, scientists examined the miracle. The scientists found that the Precious Body is composed of human cardiac muscle, and the Precious Blood is human blood. Both are from a male with type AB blood. And one of the most amazing things is that, even though it is about 1,300 years old, the heart tissue was found to be Flesh from a living Heart! The Blood had also not degraded.

In the miracle of Lanciano, God used cardiac muscle. That makes sense, considering it was Jesus's Heart that was pierced by a lance as He hung on the Cross. Also, we often poetically speak of the heart as the source of love, and the Eucharist is God's great Gift of love to us.

Review Questions

1. What are the five muscle shapes?

_____

_____

_____

2. Where are circular muscles found?

_____

_____

3. Give an example of a fusiform muscle.

_____

_____

4. Contrast the three types of muscle contractions.

_____

_____

_____

_____

5. Which type of muscle was present in the miracle of Lanciano?

_____

X. Muscles: Healthy and Otherwise

In order to get the most out of our bodies, it is essential to maintain healthy muscles. With proper treatment, broken bones often heal completely and afterward are no weaker than bones that have never broken. Muscles are different, however. After a muscle is injured, it is often repaired with scar tissue, making it permanently weaker and more prone to further injury. So keeping your muscles healthy is extremely important.

A. Keeping Muscles Healthy

With all the risks to the muscular system, it is important to do what is necessary to maintain healthy muscles. As with bones, **nutrition** is a key ingredient in maintaining healthy muscles. Muscles use protein to grow, so it is important for people to get enough healthy **protein** in their diets. Young people, pregnant mothers, and the elderly especially need good sources of protein. Muscles also need **calcium** and **sodium** to contract. Another key ingredient to muscle health, as with bone health, **is vitamin D**.

It is also important to drink plenty of **water** to prevent cramps in muscles, and to keep our muscles functioning properly. Doctors recommend drinking 6 to 8 glasses of water every day.

What we don't eat is as important as what we do eat. Junk food should be kept to a minimum, and trans fats should be avoided completely if possible. This is important for the health of all types of muscles.

Exercise is important for muscle health. Aerobic exercise, such as running, swimming, or brisk walking, is important to maintain a healthy body weight and keep muscles healthy, particularly cardiac muscles. Muscles also need resistance exercises. Resistance exercises include pushups, pullups, and crunches.

Strenuous exercise helps
to keep muscles healthy.
Image credit: shutterstock.com

It is important to stretch our muscles to prevent injury and maintain flexibility. Most athletes do stretch exercises at the beginning of a practice or a workout. This is very wise. It is important to stretch before, during, and after exercise, and even on a regular basis, outside of exercises.

Stretching before play helps to
protect muscles from injuries.
Image credit: shutterstock.com

Finally, to keep our muscles healthy, it is important to get enough sleep. This is a key component of allowing our muscles to rest and repair themselves, particularly after a strenuous workout.

B. Skeletal Muscle Injuries

There are many different types of skeletal muscle injuries. Some of the more common are: strains, contusions, cramps, and ruptures.

1. Strains

A muscle **strain** occurs when a muscle is pulled too far and one or more fibers in the muscle are torn. Mild strains can be treated with rest, ice, and compression, while severe strains may require surgery.

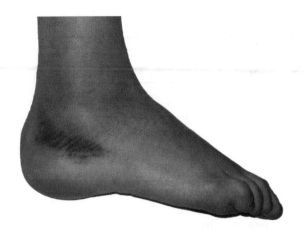

A sprained foot caused by movement beyond what is normal.
Image credit: public domain

2. Contusions

A **contusion** is simply a bruise to a muscle. It is usually caused by being hit.

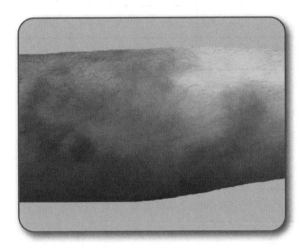

This bruised arm was caused by falling on a solid object.
Image credit: public domain

3. Cramps

A **cramp** occurs when a muscle forcibly contracts and will not relax. Older people are known to have leg muscle cramps at night, which some doctors believe result from a lack of calcium and other minerals. It can be very painful, but it usually only lasts for a few seconds or for a few minutes. Being sure to eat a variety of foods with a variety of vitamins and minerals is the best cure for muscle cramps.

4. Ruptures

A much more serious injury is a muscle **rupture**. Ruptures occur when a muscle tears completely. This is not common because it takes a lot of force to rupture a muscle. When a muscle does rupture, surgery is usually required, and this injury can leave much scar tissue and a weakened muscle.

C. Muscle Disease

People can have trouble with their muscular systems because of disease.

A. Muscular dystrophy is a genetic disease, often inherited, in which muscles grow steadily weaker. It causes the muscle tissue to break down and be replaced by fatty deposits.

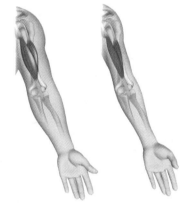

Normal biceps   Muscular dystrophy

Notice the muscle on the right side is getting smaller and weaker.
Image credit: shutterstock.com

B. Sarcopenia is loss of muscle mass due to aging. It can cause a real lack of mobility among elderly people.

Review Questions

1. What is the difference between a muscle strain and a rupture?

_____

_____

_____

2. Why are injured muscles sometimes more prone to future injuries?

_____

_____

_____

3. Name three nutritional substances important for muscle health.

_____

_____

_____

4. What is one disease that can cause muscle problems?

_____

_____

_____

5. Resistance exercises include the following three:

_____

_____

_____

Chapter Review Activity

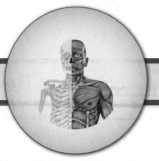

SECTION A

Use the words and phrases in the word box to complete the sentences:

axial	appendicular	ball-and-socket	cardiac
elasticity	hinge	ligaments	ossification
pivot	skeletal	smooth	tendons

1. _____ bones make up the head, neck, and trunk.

2. The bones of the arms and legs are called _____.

3. Bones are connected to other bones by _____.

4. _____ joints, like that of the elbow, move along one plane.

5. _____ connect bones to muscle.

6. _____ joints allow for rotation.

7. _____ is the process by which cartilage is replaced by collagen and calcium, and becomes bone.

8. _____ is the trait of muscle meaning it can be stretched and then return to its usual resting length without damage.

9. _____ muscle, which produces our external bodily movements, is voluntary muscle.

10. The muscle found on the walls of many organs is _____ muscle.

11. _____ muscle makes up the heart.

12. _____ joints, like those of the shoulders, contain a rounded part of one bone that fits into the hollow of another bone, and allow for wide range of motion.

Chapter Review Activity

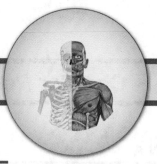

SECTION B

Label the following bones "axial" or "appendicular".

NAME OF BONE	
Skull	13.
Ribs	14.
Humerus	15.
Femur	16.
Tibia	17.
Pelvis	18.

SECTION C

Fill in the blank (#19-22):

19. The two layers of bone are _____ and _____.

20. There are _____ bones in the adult human body. (How many?)

21. The _____ _____ consists of 33 vertebrae and protects the spinal cord.

22. Most of the body's blood cells are made in the _____ _____.

23. What is the difference between fast-twitch and slow-twitch muscle fibers?

24. What are concentric, eccentric, and isometric muscle contractions?

25. What did scientists discover about the Body and Blood when they investigated the miracle of Lanciano?

Heart and Blood

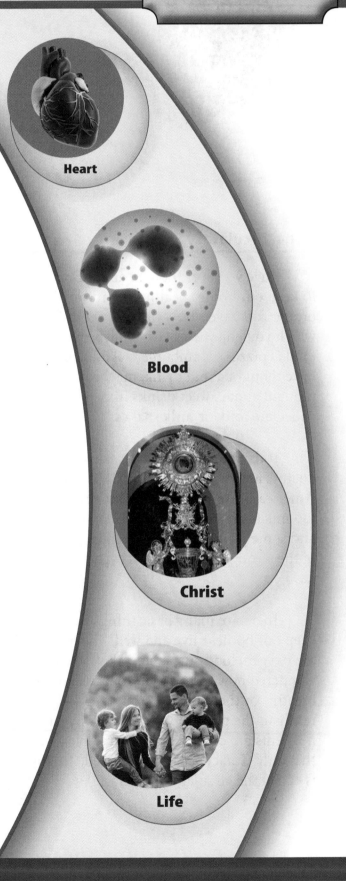

Heart

Blood

Christ

Life

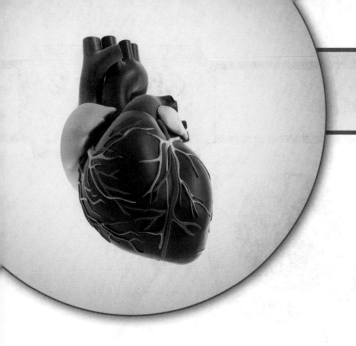

Heart and Blood

The circulatory system is made up of the heart, the blood, and the blood vessels that run throughout the body. You can almost imagine the circulatory system as God's system of human blood highways, with a moving truck's blood delivery system, right inside your body.

The blood is the part of the human body circulatory system that makes deliveries and later picks up deliveries. The blood carries oxygen and nutrients and delivers them to all the cells in the body. The blood also picks up wastes from the cells in the body. Blood is constantly flowing through your body because it is being pumped by your heart. The blood travels through an intricate (detailed) system of blood vessels to reach all the parts of the body. Blood vessels form the paths for blood to travel.

In this chapter, you will learn how the heart is constructed and how it works. You will learn what blood is, and how it works to deliver nutrients to your body. You will learn the different types of blood cells. You will learn about the different types of blood vessels and their different functions. You will learn about the diseases that can endanger the circulatory system, and about how to keep your circulatory system healthy.

For a little historical background, think about this: to the ancient Jewish people, a person's blood or animal's blood was considered its fountain of life. They believed this before there were any modern scientific experiments. This is one of the reasons their Jewish dietary laws forbid eating blood. It is also why some Jewish people stopped following Jesus when He taught that they should eat His Flesh and "drink His Blood."

I. The Circulatory System

Have you ever thought about God's plan to keep our bodies healthy and in working order? You have surely thought about food, which you enjoy every day. Maybe your favorite food is pizza or hamburgers. And while you have thought about drink, maybe you have thought about sweet drinks like soda pop or chocolate milk or milk shakes.

Today there is a big concern among doctors about the food and drinks that all Americans are consuming. Our drinks have too much sugar. Many people are overweight, and some people suffer from eating too much of the wrong kind of fat and sugary food every day.

There are many basic things we need to keep our bodies alive and well. The most basic are oxygen, food, and water. Have you ever wondered how the oxygen from the air you breathe, or the nutrients from the food you eat, reach all the parts of your body? Oxygen and nutrients are carried by an incredible system that only God could have designed. This system is called the circulatory system.

Jesus freed his followers, however, from the restrictions of Jewish dietary guidelines. We praise God for His wonderful gift of the Holy Eucharist, by which He feeds us with His own Body and His own Blood, in fact, His own life. Nonetheless, by associating blood with life, God had given the ancient Jewish people real insight into the truth about blood. Blood is the essential ingredient that keeps all our body cells and organs functioning. A healthy circulatory system is essential for a healthy life. Blood is necessary for life.

Review Questions

1. What part of the circulatory system brings oxygen and nutrients to cells?

_____

_____

2. What part of the circulatory system takes waste away from cells?

_____

_____

3. What organ is the pump that keeps blood flowing through the circulatory system?

_____

_____

4. What do we call the parts of the circulatory system that form the paths for blood to travel throughout the body?

_____

_____

II. The Heart

When you are sitting in a car, and your mom or dad starts the car, you feel the motor start up. Men and women have developed various kinds of motors for all kinds of things to make them run. Many things have motors besides cars, such as airplanes, but even many things around the house have motors, such as a washing machine or a cake mixer or a blender. But no motor anyone ever invented compares to the one "motor" that God created to keep the human body running: the heart. The heart is the "motor" of the human body. And it runs by God's Will!

A. Heart Beats

Think about this fact: Your heart beats all by itself, all day, every day, up to 100,000 times a day! For your whole life! That is incredible! Of course, God is the Person Who keeps your heart beating, just as He keeps all of creation in existence.

Your heart beats while you are sitting, your heart beats while you are standing, your heart beats while you are exercising, your heart beats even while you are sleeping! And you did nothing at all to keep it beating. Your parents did nothing at all to keep it beating.

Your amazing heart keeps beating and keeps life-giving blood pumping through your body all the time, twenty-four hours a day, week after week, month after month, year after year—because it is God's Will to keep your heart beating!

But how does your heart work?

You already know that the heart is made of muscle, a unique kind of muscle called **cardiac muscle**. The contractions, or squeezing of the heart or cardiac muscle, pump blood throughout the body in rhythmic spurts. This constant contracting and expanding of the heart muscle is called the **heartbeat**. You can feel your heartbeat, or pulse, by holding your fingers against your neck or against the inside of your wrist. If you've ever used a doctor's stethoscope, you've also heard your heartbeat.

Your heart beats faster when you are exercising and more slowly when you are at rest in bed at night. A healthy resting heart rate for a ten-year-old is about **90 beats per minute**, although it varies a little from person to person. Take a moment to check your heart rate. Usually people count how many times their heart beats in ten seconds, and then multiply by six to figure out their heart rate for a full sixty seconds or one minute.

There are specialized cells in the heart that use electrical impulses to make the heart beat, usually at a regular rate or regular pace.

These electrical impulses are sometimes called the heart's natural pacemaker. If a person's heart doesn't beat properly, doctors can insert a medical pacemaker to control the heartbeat so it beats properly.

Babies have faster heart rates than older children and adults. Did you know that doctors can begin to hear a baby's heartbeat more than eight months before it is even born? A baby's normal heartbeat can be as high as 160 beats per minute! God is keeping a baby's blood running more quickly to deliver important nutrients through his tiny body to keep him healthy and growing.

B. Heart Chambers

The human heart is made of **four main parts called chambers**. The top two chambers are called **atria** (singular: atrium). Blood enters the heart from the body through the atria. The bottom two chambers are called **ventricles**. Blood is pumped out of the heart to the whole body through the ventricles.

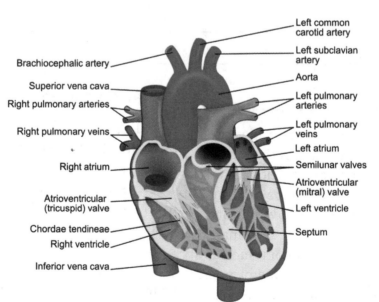

Blood flows in only one direction in the heart. There are four valves that snap shut after blood passes through them, keeping the blood from passing back the other way.

The blood from both the upper and lower parts of the body enters the heart through the right atrium. Then the blood passes down to the right ventricle through the tricuspid valve. From there, the blood goes through the pulmonary valve to the lungs, where the blood collects oxygen. <u>The oxygenated blood then returns to the heart, into the left atrium</u>. It passes through the mitral valve to the left ventricle, and then out to the rest of the body through the aortic valve.

C. The Sacred Heart

God has taken advantage of the human poetic understanding of the heart to give us one of our most beautiful devotions. In the seventeenth century, Jesus appeared to St. Margaret Mary Alacoque (AL-uh-coke), a French nun. Jesus asked her to spread devotion to His Sacred Heart. Devotion to the Sacred Heart of Jesus is a great way to honor His immense love for us. Jesus once said to St. Margaret Mary: "Behold the Heart that has so loved men ... instead of gratitude, I receive from the greater part of mankind only ingratitude."

We can honor the Sacred Heart of Jesus through special prayers or by practicing the First Friday devotion. In this devotion, people receive Holy Communion on the first Friday of nine consecutive months, specifically with the intention of honoring the Sacred Heart of Jesus, and in reparation for offenses against the Blessed Sacrament.

Another important method of honoring the Sacred Heart is as a family. The image of the Sacred Heart is displayed in the home, and the family is consecrated to the Sacred Heart of Jesus. The Sacred Heart image is a picture of Jesus showing us His Sacred Heart, crowned with thorns and with flames on the top of the Heart. The fire represents Jesus' burning love for us, and the thorns represent His suffering. Some families say a daily Litany of the Sacred Heart of Jesus, an extremely popular devotion said in front of the image of the Sacred Heart. Many churches have statues or images of the

May the Heart of Jesus in the Most Blessed Sacrament be praised, adored, and loved, with grateful affection, at every moment, in all of the tabernacles of the world, even to the end of time. Amen.

Image credit: unknown

Sacred Heart of Jesus. St. Margaret Mary, St. Madeleine Sophie Barat, and Josefa Menendez are all known for their devotion to the Sacred Heart.

Pope Clement XIII officially recognized and approved devotion to the Sacred Heart in 1765. In 1856, Pope Pius IX extended the Feast of the Sacred Heart to the universal Church. On June 11, 1899, Pope Leo XIII consecrated all mankind to the Sacred Heart of Jesus. The Feast of the Sacred Heart is celebrated now on the Friday following the Feast of Corpus Christi in the month of June.

Review questions

1. What are the names of the four chambers of the heart?

_____

_____

2. Which two chambers receive the blood into the heart, and which two discharge it to the rest of the body?

_____

_____

3. Explain why the valves in the heart are important.

_____

_____

III. Blood Vessels

A. Arteries

The body has three main types of **blood vessels**: **arteries**, **veins**, and **capillaries**. Each type of blood vessel is perfectly created to perform its function, the function God planned when He designed the human body.

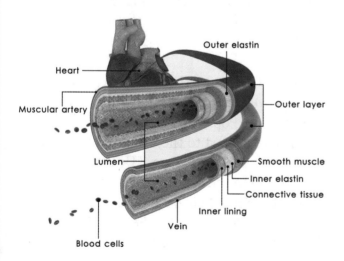

These tiny highways of the body, if placed end to end, would span a distance of about 60,000 miles!
Image credit: dollarphotoclub.com

This is hard to believe, but if you laid out all the three types of very tiny blood vessels in an adult human body in a straight line, they would stretch about 60,000 miles! This is possible because most of the blood vessels are so small, so very, very tiny, that they can be seen only under an excellent microscope.

Let's study **arteries** first. Arteries, like miniature highways, carry blood away from the heart and to the rest of the whole body. A large artery, called the **aorta**, connects to the left ventricle of the heart and runs over the top of the heart. The aorta is the path that oxygenated blood, blood which is carrying oxygen, takes away from the heart to the system of other arteries that then will carry the blood to all the parts of the body. The aorta is an **elastic artery**. Elastic arteries can expand and then return to normal, smaller size as the heart beats. The largest arteries in the body are elastic arteries.

Some arteries are called **muscular arteries** because their walls contain a thick layer of smooth muscle. Muscular arteries regulate the flow of blood to different parts of the body. The smallest arteries are called arterioles (ar-TEER-ee-olz). The firmness of the arterioles' walls controls the pressure in the system. This is commonly called **blood pressure**. It is important not to let the walls of these arteries harden or become less elastic. This can happen if a person eats a lot of unhealthy food or does not exercise. If that happens, a person can develop **high blood pressure** which is dangerous and can cause a heart attack. While children do not usually have high blood pressure, it is important for children to eat healthy food, so they will develop good eating habits and not develop high blood pressure. Children should get plenty of exercise riding their bikes, running races, or playing baseball, football, or other sports. It is important for people of all ages to keep a healthy heart to stay active.

B. Veins

Veins are blood vessels that bring blood back to the heart. After the blood has done its work, delivering nutrients and oxygen to the many cells of the body, the blood travels the system of veins back to the heart. This is when the blood will "stock up" on the nutrients or vitamins and minerals essential for its next trip. Most of the blood that the veins carry as they return to the heart is not well-oxygenated. The exceptions are the veins that carry blood from the **lungs** to the heart before it is distributed to the rest of the body.

Veins can be small, medium, or large. Veins that carry blood up the body, especially from the legs, against gravity, are medium-sized veins. These veins that move up have special valves that keep the blood from flowing backwards, back down the legs. However, when these veins lose their elasticity, as happens in older people, these veins become weakened and their valves often stop working properly. When this happens, the veins appear swollen and twisted. These swollen veins are called **varicose veins**, and they are most often seen in the legs, especially of older women.

C. Capillaries

Finally, there are very tiny blood vessels known as **capillaries**. The capillaries are arranged in networks, and they connect the artery and vein systems. Capillaries are the place where oxygen and nutrients are passed over to the body's cells and waste products are taken away from the body's cells.

Amazingly, capillary walls are only one cell thick! Can you believe it? Talk about teeny tiny: only one cell thick! Because their walls are so thin, capillaries allow water, oxygen, nutrients, and waste products to pass through them. Blood passes from the arteries, through the capillaries, where the blood delivers the oxygen and nutrients, and then the blood moves to the veins, which carry it back to the heart. On the way, the blood deposits cell wastes to the liver and kidneys, which finally filter the cell wastes out of the body.

CAPILLARY

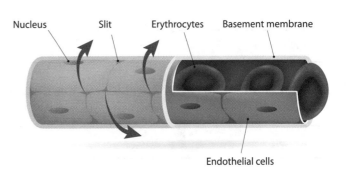

The smallest blood vessels in the human body are capillaries, which are only one cell thick!
Image credit: shutterstock.com

D. Passion of Jesus

Do you remember when Jesus was praying in the garden, immediately after the Last Supper, and right before He was arrested? As He was praying, He began to sweat Blood. This is a condition called hematidrosis (HEE-muh-tih-DRO-sis). This is very unusual, but can occur when a person is under tremendous strain and suffering. What happens is that some of the capillaries under the skin actually burst, and the blood seeps through the skin like sweat.

When this occurs, a person is much more sensitive to touch, so being hit hurts much more than usual. We must remember that when we meditate on Our Lord's Passion. After His agony in the garden when He was sweating Blood, His Body was much more sensitive to the pain when He was whipped by the soldiers. Then, of course, He suffered beatings, the scourging, and the crucifixion. Jesus loves us so much that He was willing to suffer all this in order to open the gates of Heaven for us.

Jesus loves us so much that he paid the ultimate price of crucifixion to save us from our sins.
Image credit: Diego Velázquez

Review Questions

1. Which system of blood vessels carries blood away from the heart?

_____

_____

2. What is the major artery that leaves the heart called?

_____

_____

3. Which system of blood vessels carries blood back to the heart?

_____

_____

4. What are capillaries and what do they do?

_____

_____

_____

_____

5. Name something that can cause high blood pressure.

_____

_____

IV. Heart Health

The heart is the most critically important part of the body, as you already know. The heart's proper functioning is necessary for a healthy life. There are many risks that can endanger the heart. Everyone is born with a unique genetic make-up, but a healthy lifestyle can play a big role in protecting your heart.

A. Heart Attack

One of the biggest risks to heart health is a **heart attack**. A heart attack occurs when cells in the heart die because they do not get proper blood flow. This usually occurs due to a condition called coronary artery disease. "Coronary" means *relating to the heart*, so coronary arteries are arteries that supply blood to the heart. A heart attack occurs because of a condition, coronary artery disease, that has been building up over a period of time.

B. Coronary Artery Disease

Coronary artery disease develops when a person's arteries become too narrow because plaque has built up inside of them. This causes a certain amount of blockage in the heart and makes it difficult for the blood to flow freely. **Plaque** is a fatty material that tends to stick to the inside of the arteries. If the plaque nearly or completely blocks an artery, or ruptures and

forms a blood clot, the plaque will cut off the flow of blood to a part of the heart. The cells in that part of the heart begin to die almost immediately without proper blood supply. This is called a heart attack. Children seldom if ever have a heart attack, but adults need to see a doctor regularly to make sure plaque is not building up in their hearts.

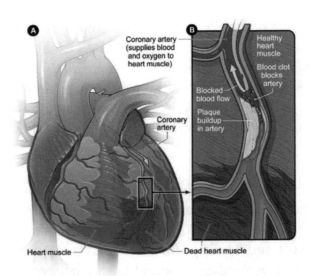

When plaque builds up in an artery, it can block the flow of blood, causing some heart muscle to die. This is a heart attack.
Image credit: Coronary Artery Disease NIH

Heart attacks can be deadly, but if medical help is found immediately, they often are not deadly. Like other muscle tissue, the damaged part of the heart will automatically repair itself! Remember that God designed the body with the ability to heal itself in order to help people stay healthy. However, a scar will develop at the damaged part, and this can weaken the ability of the heart to adequately pump the blood past the damaged part.

C. Keeping Cholesterol Low

The plaque that causes coronary artery disease is usually caused by too much **cholesterol** (kuh-LES-ter-all) in the person's diet. You may have heard that there is "good" cholesterol and "bad" cholesterol. This is true. The "bad" cholesterol is called low-density lipoprotein (lip-o-PRO-teen), or LDL cholesterol. It is important not to eat foods that contain this substance. We should avoid things with trans fats and hydrogenated oils, for example. Your parents can help you to avoid these foods.

Another key factor in keeping your LDL cholesterol levels low is **exercise**. As usual, plenty of good exercise is an important part of keeping the body healthy. Most 5th graders like to get plenty of exercise, but some may sit too long playing games on the computer or other devices.

The "good" cholesterol can remove bad cholesterol from dangerous spots. We can raise our good cholesterol levels by eating foods like **fruits and whole grain bread**, and by getting plenty of good exercise, outdoors whenever possible, to get oxygen from the fresh air into our blood.

D. Cardiac Arrest

Another dangerous heart condition is called **cardiac arrest**. Cardiac arrest is when a person's heart stops beating. Cardiac arrest occurs when the heart's electrical system malfunctions, causing the heart to

stop working. **CPR** is an exercise procedure someone else can perform to make someone's heart start beating again. Also, the use of a **defibrillator machine** can shock the heart back into a normal rhythm. Because CPR can save a person's life, everyone should learn how to do CPR. Many hospitals and fire stations offer CPR classes for adults and children.

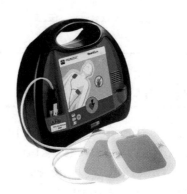

An automatic external defibrillator can be used during CPR to shock the heart back into a normal rhythm.
Image credit: Hborkyb

E. Abnormal Heart Rhythms and Scarring

Malfunctions of the heart sometimes are caused by abnormal heart rhythms. People can be born with **abnormal heart rhythms**, and usually these are not a problem. Other risk factors, however, include **scarring** from a previous heart attack.

Some people are careless and don't think about the consequences on their heart when they frequently take **dangerous drugs**. Drugs put people at risk for a heart attack; never take any drug, even medicine, without your parents' permission.

Some people can have bad reactions on their heart from too much **caffeine**. Children especially must not continually be drinking soda pop, drinking coffee, and/or eating chocolate, all of which contain caffeine. Too much caffeine can put children at risk for a heart attack. Children should not drink coffee or some teas until they are older.

F. High Blood Pressure

A disease associated with the heart, which you have read a little about already, is hypertension, or **high blood pressure**. High blood pressure occurs when there is too much pressure in the arteries. It makes the heart need to work harder, sometimes too hard. High blood pressure is a risk factor leading to a heart attack and/or heart disease.

Blood pressure is measured with two numbers. For example, a healthy blood pressure for most people is considered 120/80. The first number is called the systolic (sih-STOL-ik) pressure. The <u>systolic number</u> measures the pressure in the arteries when

the heart contracts. The second number is the diastolic (die-uh-STOL-ik) pressure. The <u>diastolic number</u> measures the pressure in the arteries when the heart relaxes.

Although there can be <u>genetic factors</u> involved in high blood pressure, people can work to control their blood pressure by eating wisely. Too much salt, for instance, is one main cause of high blood pressure.

<u>Lack of exercise</u> and <u>being seriously overweight</u>, called obesity, contribute to high blood pressure.

In conclusion, if you want to have a healthy heart, you must <u>eat properly</u> and get plenty of <u>exercise</u> every day! And <u>don't let yourself get overweight</u>! Stay healthy while you are young, and it will be easier to stay healthy when you are older.

Review Questions

1. What causes a heart attack?

_____

_____

2. Explain the difference between a heart attack and cardiac arrest.

_____

_____

_____

3. Name three risk factors for high blood pressure.

_____

_____

4. Why is high blood pressure dangerous?

_____

_____

5. What can you do to have a healthy heart?

_____

_____

6. If a person's blood pressure is 120 over 80 (120/80), what is the top number called?

_____

_____

V. Blood Composition

You've already learned that blood carries and delivers nutrients and oxygen to all the cells of your body, and then blood picks up wastes from those cells. You've learned that it is the job of the heart to pump blood throughout your body.

What is blood? What is it made of? In this section, you will find out more about this amazing gift God has given us.

A. Plasma

The liquid part of blood is called **plasma**. Plasma is made mostly of water, but it also carries the nutrients that blood distributes throughout the body. Besides plasma, blood also contains three main types of blood cells: red blood cells, white blood cells, and platelets.

COMPOSITION OF THE BLOOD

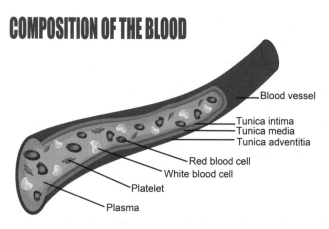

Image credit: shutterstock.com

B. Red Blood Cells

Red blood cells are produced in the bone marrow, which is the tissue inside the bones. Red blood cells are responsible for carrying oxygen throughout the body. Red blood cells contain an iron compound called **hemoglobin** (HEE-mo-gloh-bin), which allows the cells to carry oxygen.

Red blood cells are responsible for the nourishment of the body.
Image credit: Database Center for Life Science

C. White Blood Cells

White blood cells fight infection. When you are injured, or when disease-causing germs enter your body, white blood cells spring into action to heal. White blood cells are not confined to blood vessels, but travel naturally to wherever they are needed in the body. God has created white blood cells to be able to fight specific dangers in specific ways. White blood cells remind us of a general practice doctor who takes care of a variety of illnesses, rather than being a doctor who is a specialist in one disease.

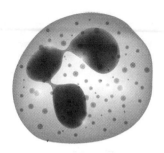

The nutrophil is one type of white blood cell.
Image credit: dollarphotoclub.com

Platelets form clots that can stop the flow of blood coming from a wound.
Image credit: shutterstock.com

D. Platelets

Platelets also are contained in the blood. **Platelets** are truly amazing cells in the blood. Have you noticed that when you cut yourself, the bleeding doesn't go on forever? That is really important because you wouldn't want a simple cut to cause you to lose an unsafe amount of blood.

When there is a cut in the body, the amazing platelets in the blood produce very tiny threads called **fibrin** (FY-brin) that actually trap the blood cells. The fibrin acts like a mesh or a screen to catch the blood cells. As the fibrin and blood hardens, it forms a clot over the cut, and stops the bleeding. Blood clotting is like a God-given bandage for a

cut. Obviously, a tight bandage also helps the wound to heal by applying pressure to the wound.

As you can see, the blood in our bodies is truly wonderful. We should thank God for taking such care in creating our bodies so they can heal quickly, even if a doctor is not around. When we are sick or have a cut, we can remember that Jesus suffered as well. We can offer our suffering, united to His, as a powerful prayer. We can remember that God will one day, at the end of time, raise the bodies of those who have tried to be good. He will reunite our glorified bodies with our souls in Heaven. All of us pray that we will have the reward to live in total, incredible happiness with those we love on this Earth as well as with our loving Jesus, forever and ever and ever!

Review Questions

1. What is the main function of red blood cells?

_____

_____

2. What does hemoglobin do?

_____

_____

3. What is the main function of white blood cells?

_____

_____

4. What is the main function of platelets?

_____

_____

VI. Blood Types

A. Blood Types

Has anyone ever asked you what is your **blood type**? If so, that person was asking you about your red blood cells.

A person's blood type refers to certain sugar molecules called **antigens** (AN-tih-jenz) that can be attached to the membranes of red blood cells. These antigens are labeled "A" or "B" antigens. A person who has only "A" antigens is said to have **Type A blood**. A person with only "B" antigens has **Type B blood**. If someone has both types of antigens, his or her blood type is **AB**. A person with neither type of antigen has **Type O blood**.

Type O blood is the most common type. About 45% of the people in the United States have type O blood. About 40% of people have type A; about 10% have type B; and only about 5% have type AB.

However, <u>blood types vary based on ethnicity</u>. For example, type A blood is most common in people of European heritage. A person from Africa or Asia has a greater than normal chance of having type B blood. Type O is most common in people with a Hispanic ethnicity. In fact, its prevalence is over 50% in that population. Type AB blood is very rare in all ethnicities.

B. Eucharistic Blood

What is so amazing is that the Eucharistic Blood in the miracle of Lanciano, in Italy, which you read about earlier, is the very rare blood <u>type AB</u>. Until the twentieth century, scientists and medical people did not even know about different blood types. The public is still welcome to visit and see the Eucharistic miracle at the church in Lanciano.

The Church has two other Eucharistic relics that many people believe to be the burial cloths of Jesus Christ: the Shroud of Turin and the Sudarium.

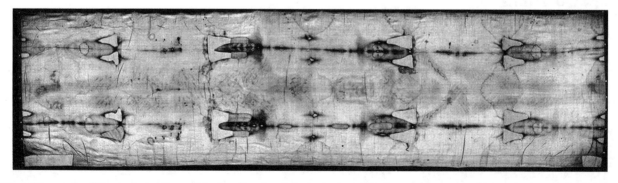

The Shroud of Turin is believed to be the burial cloth that Christ was wrapped in after His Passion.
Image credit: public domain

The Sudarium is believed to be the cloth that had been wrapped around Christ's Head in the tomb. It was then removed and Jesus was buried in a full-body cloth, which many people believe is the Shroud of Turin. Although the Church hasn't officially ruled on the authenticity of these relics, there is very strong evidence that supports both of them being authentic.

Both the Shroud and the Sudarium have blood on them. Like the blood in Lanciano, the blood type on both relics is AB. Considering the rarity of type AB, and that

An enhanced view of the face of Christ from the Shroud of Turin.
Image credit: public domain

these three relics have the same blood type, it is convincing that these are relics of the suffering of Jesus.

C. The D Antigen Protein

A person's blood type can have a protein called a "D" antigen. About 90% of people have a D antigen. This blood is said to be "positive." The 10% of people who do not have the D antigen are said to have "negative" blood. So,

if a person's blood type is B positive, it means that person's blood contains the B and D antigens. Scientists have determined that the blood of the Lanciano miracle, the blood of the Shroud, and the blood of the Sudarium is type AB positive.

D. Blood Transfusion

Sometimes a person may need a blood transfusion. A blood transfusion is when someone's blood is pumped into another person's body, usually due to an accident that caused the wounded person to lose a large amount of blood. When people donate blood, they are giving their blood to a blood bank, where it is carefully stored, usually in a hospital, until someone needs it. Because blood cells multiply so quickly, the person who donated blood has the volume replaced in his body in one day, but it takes four to eight weeks for complete replacement of red cells. Blood donors must wait eight weeks before donating blood again.

When people receive a blood transfusion, they generally need to receive the same type of blood that they already have. For example, a person with type A blood needs to receive type A blood. There are some exceptions to this rule, though. Type O negative blood is considered a universal donor, meaning a person with type O negative blood can donate to anyone. Type AB positive blood is the universal receiver, meaning a person with this blood type can receive any type of blood.

It is a wonderful gift that people who are in desperate need because of loss of blood can be helped by other people willing and generous to donate some of their blood. Charitable works are in God's plan so that in many situations, when someone is in need, we can help each other, whether it be by giving food or a home or even blood!

Review Questions

1. What are the four main blood types?

_____

_____

2. What is the difference between blood that is "positive" and blood that is "negative"?

_____

_____

3. What type of blood was found in the miracle of Lanciano, the Shroud of Turin, and the Sudarium?

_____

_____

VII. Blood and Health

You know that blood carries many important things throughout the body, such as oxygen and nutrients carried to the cells, and waste carried away from cells. Blood also can carry **viruses** and **bacteria** which can cause diseases. Many diseases can be transmitted by exposure to diseased blood. This is why if anyone wants to donate blood for someone who is sick in the hospital, the blood needs to be tested first.

Blood that is collected at a blood bank must be tested before it can be donated to anyone. If you see spilled blood, you should not try to clean it up or touch it, unless it is from someone in your family who is not sick. It is best to tell someone who can clean it properly, using the correct safety equipment. Strange as it may seem, diseases can survive in blood even outside the body, from a few hours to a few days!

A. Diseases Affecting Blood

1. Anemia

There are some diseases that directly affect the blood. One is **anemia**. Anemia is a condition in which the red blood cells do not provide enough oxygen for the person to be healthy. A person with anemia gets tired very easily. One reason a person can have anemia is that the person has too few red blood cells. This condition can be caused by a diet that does not contain enough iron. Iron can be found in foods such as leafy green vegetables and red meats. It is healthy to eat lean red meat, such as steak, but we should not eat too much of it. We should eat at least two or three servings of vegetables every day to stay healthy.

2. Sickle Cell Anemia

A person can have **sickle cell anemia**. Sickle cell anemia is not a condition that can develop; a person is born with it. Sickle cell anemia is a disease in which the red blood cells have an irregular shape. The red blood cells do not contain enough **hemoglobin**, the substance that allows red blood cells to carry oxygen. Sickle cell anemia must be treated by a doctor.

3. Hemophilia

Another disease of the blood is called **hemophilia** (HEE-moe-FEEL-ee-uh). With hemophilia, a person's blood does not clot properly. Someone with hemophilia must be very careful every time he gets cut because, even with a small cut, the blood will not clot and form a scab. Hemophilia is not a disease a person can catch; anyone who has it was born with it.

4. Leukemia

You may have heard the term **leukemia** (loo-KEE-me-uh). Leukemia is cancer of the blood. Like most cancers, there are different types of leukemia. Some can be treated easily, but some cannot. People who have leukemia must be treated by a medical specialist.

B. St. Januarius

Once blood is out of a body, if it is not properly stored and preserved, it breaks down very quickly. It dries out and, even if it is collected in a container, it will clot and become solid. The blood does not naturally liquefy again. If someone uses equipment to break up the clot, it is impossible to make it clot again. This is a normal fact of nature.

God, however, created nature and is therefore not bound by its rules. Miracles are phenomena that are outside the realm of nature, and thus have no natural, scientific explanation, such as the miracle of Lanciano. For many years, God has been working another miracle in Italy.

St. Januarius was the bishop of Benevento, in Italy, during the reign of the Roman emperor Diocletian, who persecuted and murdered Catholics. Bishop Januarius was eventually arrested and killed for his faith. Some bishops, however, were able to recover some of his blood, and his blood has been saved for over 1,700 years as a miraculous relic. The dried blood is kept in a small glass container in a church in Naples, Italy.

An amazing thing happens to the dried blood of St. Januarius. At different times throughout the year, his blood becomes liquid. Thousands of people have visited the church and have seen the blood actually moving, flowing in the container. At times, the blood has even bubbled! Over many years, people have come to see and to pray in front of the container of the blood. When the miracle is over, it dries again and re-clots, which is another miracle.

Scientists have studied the blood of St. Januarius many times, but no one can explain how the phenomenon happens. God has chosen to use this relic from this holy bishop and saint, St. Januarius, as a sign of His goodness. The miracle also reminds us that God is the Lord of life, and that He has power over death. We can see in this miracle a little glimpse of the Power that Jesus has to raise up to Heaven all God's holy ones on the last day of the Earthly world.

Traditional image of St. Januarius, bishop and martyr, whose blood miraculously liquefies and then becomes solid again.
Image credit: unknown

Review Questions

1. What is anemia and how can we avoid it with a healthy lifestyle?

_____

_____

2. What is hemophilia?

_____

_____

3. What is blood cancer called?

_____

4. Explain the miracle of St. Januarius.

_____

_____

VIII. Amazing Medical Treatments

The circulatory system is one of the true marvels of God's creation. In addition, God has also given us incredible brains so we can learn about and understand His creation. That is what science and medicine are all about. Over the centuries, we have used the gift of our intelligence to develop remarkable medical treatments. These medical treatments may not be as impressive as God's workmanship, but when people suffer disease or injury, these medical treatments have saved lives.

Dr. James Blundell began experiments giving human blood to other humans in the early 1800s with mixed results. When the different blood types were discovered in the early 1900s, blood transfusions became much safer and more common. The practice of setting up blood banks to store donated blood grew rapidly due to the great need caused by World War I (1914 to 1918). Today, many people donate blood to hospitals and blood banks on a regular basis to help those in need.

A. Transfusions

You have read about blood transfusions, a process in which one person's blood is donated to another person who has lost blood. The earliest experiments with blood transfusions date back to the mid-1600s, about 400 years ago. Back then, however, people knew nothing about different blood types. They experimented with giving blood to people, but those early transfusions were very dangerous and were soon stopped.

B. Stents

There are other impressive treatments of the heart and blood. One is a **stent**. A stent is a very very thin mesh tube, made of metal or fabric, which is implanted in a person's narrow or weak artery anywhere in the body. Think about having a water hose with a hole or a tear in it. If you can stick a tube into the hose and cover the hole with a rubber piece the size and shape of your little finger, the water will continue to run through the hose.

A stent is a thin tube which is inserted into the artery, strengthening the artery and improving blood flow. This is quite amazing! God gave medical doctors the ability to think of the idea, and then be able to perform an operation to insert a stent wherever the artery is located. Thousands of people are living healthy lives today because they have a stent implanted in an artery!

C. Bypass Surgery

Sometimes people need **bypass surgery** because one or more of their coronary arteries are blocked. In a bypass surgery, a blood vessel is removed from one part of the body, such as from an arm or leg, and placed in the area next to the blocked artery. This allows blood to "bypass" a problem blood vessel by traveling through the new one, so the heart is supplied with enough blood. Of course, the blood vessel must be removed from an area that would continue to receive less but sufficient blood flow without it. Although this surgery sounds very complicated, bypass surgery is one of the most common surgeries in the United States.

D. Artificial Heart

In 1982, a patient received an incredible invention, created by Dr. Robert Jarvik: the **artificial heart**. This mechanical artificial heart device could be implanted in a person to perform the functions of the heart. It was powered by a large air compressor, which meant the patient was always tethered to a big machine. Unfortunately, the artificial heart did not work as well as the one God designed, and patients usually did not live very long after receiving one. However, the patients did live a little longer than if they had not had the artificial heart.

In 1999, a **battery-powered artificial heart** was first implanted in a patient. It allowed people to move about without being attached to a large machine. However, this device also is not as effective as a natural heart. It is often used as a temporary solution.

These and many other medical inventions are good and helpful for many people. As we continue to learn, good doctors, including many faithful Catholics, are working hard to provide morally good ways to perform many important treatments. The Church is always studying advances in medical knowledge. We must continue to look to the guidance of the Catholic Church in these important moral matters. Doing what is right and pleasing to God should always be our top priority.

Review Questions

1. What is a stent?

_____

2. Describe bypass surgery.

_____

_____

3. What world event led to the rapid establishment of blood banks?

_____

_____

Chapter Review Activity

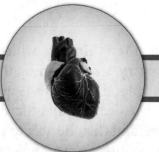

Use the words and phrases in the word box to complete the sentences:

anemia	arteries	atria	blood pressure
capillaries	cardiac arrest	cholesterol	heart attack
plasma	platelets	veins	ventricles

1. The _____ are blood vessels that take blood away from the heart.

2. The _____ are blood vessels that carry blood back to the heart.

3. The _____ are the blood vessels with very thin walls. Oxygen and nutrients pass through these walls to the body's cells.

4. The liquid part of the blood is called _____.

5. _____ are blood cells that allow the blood to clot.

6. A _____ _____ occurs when cells in the heart die because they do not get proper blood flow.

7. _____ _____ occurs when a malfunction with the heart's electrical system causes the heart to stop working.

8. The two chambers that receive blood into the heart are called _____.

9. The two chambers that pump blood out of the heart are called _____.

10. LDL, or "bad" _____, can build up in the arteries and put someone at risk for a heart attack.

11. _____ _____ consists of two numbers, the diastolic and the systolic.

12. If someone does not get enough iron, he can develop _____, a condition in which red blood cells do not provide enough oxygen.

Chapter Review Activity

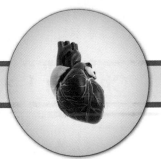

SECTION B

Fill in the table below

BLOOD TYPE	DESCRIPTION
13. _____	Contains 'A' and 'D' antigens
AB negative	14. Contains _____ and _____ antigens
15. _____	Contains 'A,' 'B,' and 'D' antigens
16. _____	Contains no antigens
B positive	17. Contains _____ and _____ antigens
18. _____	Universal donor
AB positive	19. Universal _____
20. _____	Blood type of the miracle of Lanciano

SECTION C

Write the letter of the correct answer on the line provided.

21. Which cells deliver oxygen to the rest of the body? _____
    A. White blood cells
    B. Cardiac cells
    C. Red blood cells
    D. Platelets

22. Which cells fight infection? _____
    A. White blood cells
    B. Red blood cells
    C. Platelets
    D. Capillaries

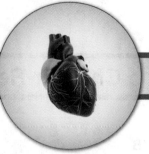

23. What parts of the heart snap shut to keep blood from flowing in the wrong direction? _____

    A. The atria

    B. The ventricles

    C. The coronary arteries

    D. The valves

24. What does hemoglobin do? _____

    A. Allows red blood cells to carry oxygen

    B. Fights infection

    C. Builds up in the arteries, leading to heart attacks

    D. Increases a person's risk for high blood pressure

SECTION D

Complete the following exercises using the lines provided.

25. What is a stent?

_____

_____

26. Describe bypass surgery.

_____

_____

_____

Lungs and Air

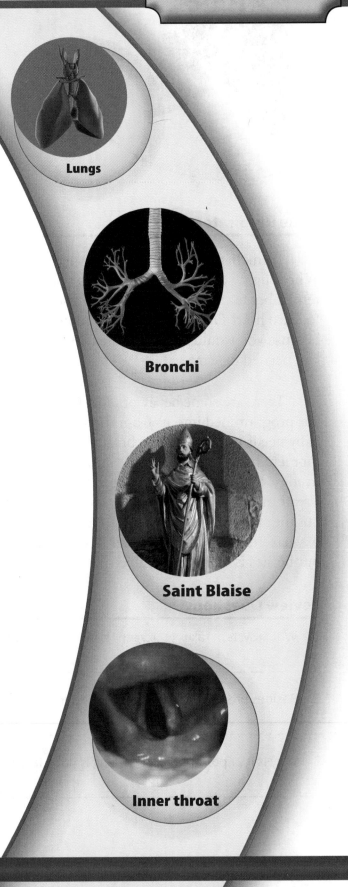

Lungs

Bronchi

Saint Blaise

Inner throat

Image credits (from top): shutterstock.com, shutterstock.com, Père Igor, Welleschik

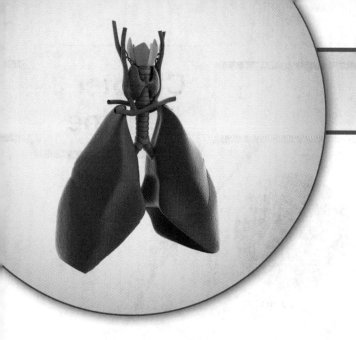

The body system with which we breathe is called the **respiratory system**. The respiratory system consists of a few main parts. The mouth and nose are responsible for taking air into the body. Air travels down the trachea (TRAY-kee-uh), or windpipe, which is a tube that connects to the lungs, the organs responsible for getting oxygen from the air into the blood so it can be carried throughout the body. Besides breathing, the respiratory system also allows us to speak!

Did you know there is a patron saint of the respiratory system? Saint Bernardine of Siena is the saint most commonly invoked against respiratory problems. Saint Bernardine was a Franciscan friar, a monk, born in 1380 in Italy. Bernardine was born with a respiratory defect that left him with a very weak voice. However, God healed the saint, and he became a powerful preacher. He was known as a peacemaker. He helped bring a peaceful solution to many groups that had been fighting. Saint Bernardine also helped lay people learn how to live holy lives.

I. The Respiratory System

Think back to when you were very small. Who taught you how to breathe? Do you remember taking lessons, or going to school to learn how? Of course not! It's a good thing, because you would not have lasted long if you had needed to learn.

There are some behaviors that God has programmed into us from the start. A baby needs to know how to breathe from the moment he or she is born. The human body needs a constant supply of oxygen from the air. Breathing may seem like a very simple activity, but the system God has designed to take oxygen from the air and deliver it to each cell in our bodies is truly remarkable.

Review Questions

1. Which system takes in oxygen from the air so it can be delivered to the cells throughout the body?

2. Besides breathing, what does the respiratory system allow us to do?

3. Why is it important that breathing is not a learned behavior?

Top image credit: shutterstock.com

II. Upper Respiratory System

A. Nose and Mouth

The nose and mouth make up the main part of the upper respiratory system. Air enters the body through the nose or mouth, passes through the <u>larynx</u>, and travels down the <u>trachea</u> to reach the lungs. These essential parts of the respiratory system do more than just take in air, however. They also work hard to <u>purify the air</u> as it enters our system.

You probably know that the air we breathe contains more than just oxygen and the other gases naturally found in the air. Often air is filled with dirt, germs, dust, exhaust fumes from trucks, household cleaning sprays, or other materials that we do not want in our lungs. The upper respiratory system of the human body contains <u>numerous filters</u> that help clean the air we breathe before it reaches our lungs.

Usually, air enters the body through the nose. The nose is divided into two cavities (often referred to as nostrils) by the **nasal septum**. Each cavity has two specific areas: an **olfactory** area for smelling, and a **respiratory** area for breathing. Inside the nose are many tiny hairs, which serve a very important purpose. These tiny hairs filter out dust and dirt particles so they cannot continue down through the respiratory system. The nose also has a mucus lining, a sticky liquid that traps unwanted materials, such as dust, and removes these materials from the air as we breathe.

B. Trachea

Part of the respiratory system is the **trachea**, often referred to as the windpipe. The trachea is the airway tube that lies beneath the larynx (LAIR-inks), or voicebox, and connects to the lungs.

The trachea or windpipe is also filled with hairs and mucus. Unlike the hairs in the nose, the hairs in the trachea, called **cilia** (SIH-lee-uh), are microscopic, that is, they are so tiny that they can be seen only under a microscope. However, the tiny cilia help with the same task, purifying the air. The cilia push mucus up through the trachea into the nasal passage, where it can exit the body, along with dust, through the nose or mouth. The cilia also help to warm and moisten the air we breathe before it reaches down to the lungs.

The Respiratory System

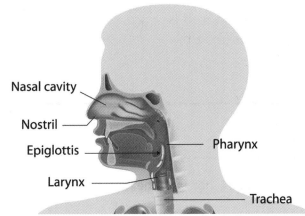

Nasal cavity

Nostril

Epiglottis

Pharynx

Larynx

Trachea

Image credit: shutterstock.com

C. Pharynx

Another incredibly important part of the respiratory system is the **pharynx** (FAIR-inks). Before air reaches the larynx and the trachea, air passes through the pharynx. The pharynx is sometimes referred to simply as the throat, but it is actually an organ that sits at the back of the mouth and nose, and connects to the nasal passages. The key role of the pharynx is to ensure that the air and the food go down in the right direction. The pharynx directs the air we breathe through our mouth so it goes down to the lungs, and also directs the food we eat so it goes down to the stomach.

The pharynx is an interesting organ that is divided into three main parts. The **nasopharynx** (nay-zo-FAIR-inks) is at the back of the nasal cavities. The **oropharynx** (or-oh-FAIR-inks) connects to the back of the mouth. The third part is the **laryngopharynx** (luh-RING-go-FAIR-inks). Both food and air pass through the laryngopharynx. From there, food is directed down the **esophagus** (ih-SOF-uh-gus), the tube that connects to the stomach. Air, on the other hand, goes from the laryngopharynx to the larynx, or voicebox, then to the trachea, and finally down to the lungs.

You might wonder, how does the pharynx keep food and air separated and going to the correct places? Well, at the back of the mouth is a flap of cartilage called the **epiglottis** (ep-uh-GLOT-iss). The epiglottis automatically covers the trachea when we eat so that the food does not go down the trachea to the lungs.

D. Conclusion

It is easy to not think much about the eating process and how very well the parts of our mouth and nose and throat all work together. After all, we all started breathing the moment we were born, and starting eating, most likely, only a few moments after that. So God made our tiny baby body just automatically start doing the right thing. However, when we take the time to examine the various parts of the human body, we need to say that it is truly a gift that is "wonderfully made" because of the love God has for each one of us.

Review Questions

1. Through what does air enter the body?

2. Compare and contrast the cilia in the trachea with the hairs in the nose.

3. What are the key roles of the pharynx?

4. Why is the epiglottis important?

5. Name and describe the functions of the parts of the upper respiratory system.

_____

_____

_____

_____

III. Lower Respiratory System

The lower respiratory system is the part of the system in which oxygen is taken from the air we breathe and given to the blood to be carried throughout the body. There are many parts that make up the lower respiratory system.

A. Bronchi and Capillaries

As air travels down the trachea or windpipe, the air reaches the **bronchi** (BRON-kee; singular: bronchus), which are two tubes leading from the base of the trachea into each of the lungs. These two main tubes break off into other, smaller bronchi and even smaller tubes called **bronchioles** (BRON-kee-oles) that are within the lungs. At the end of the bronchioles are tiny air sacs called **alveoli** (al-VEE-o-lie; singular: alveolus), which are surrounded by small blood vessels called **capillaries** (KAP-uh-lair-ees).

You already know that capillaries have very thin membranes that allow for the reception or intake of oxygen and nutrients. Alveoli, tiny air sacs, also have very thin membranes, and it is here that the transfer of

gases takes place. Oxygen passes through the thin membrane walls of the alveoli into the capillaries, where red blood cells pick up and carry the oxygen throughout the whole body.

At the same time, gas transfers **from** the capillaries, into the alveoli, to be breathed out of the body! This gas we breathe out is primarily carbon dioxide, as well as water vapor. So as we breathe in, the primary gas we need is oxygen. When we breathe out, we are giving off carbon dioxide and water vapor.

B. The Lungs

The lungs themselves are soft, spongy organs located in the chest and protected by the rib cage. Each lung is encased in a pleural (PLUR-al) sac. This pleural sac is a covering made of two membranes called **pleurae** (PLUR-eye; singular: pleura). The inside of the chest cavity is also covered by pleurae. There is a thin layer of fluid between the pleurae. The pleurae protect the lungs by allowing them to move without friction in the chest as a person breathes.

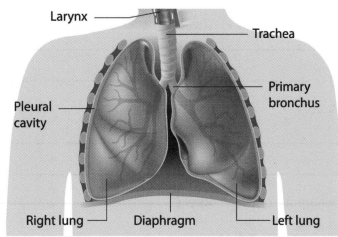

Larynx

Trachea

Primary bronchus

Pleural cavity

Right lung

Diaphragm

Left lung

Image credit: shutterstock.com

Although the two lungs are similar, they are not exactly identical. The right lung is divided into three lobes or rounded projections, while the left is divided into only two lobes. Both lungs have a superior lobe (on top) and an inferior lobe (on bottom), but the right lung also has a middle lobe.

The work of inhaling and exhaling is primarily done with the **diaphragm** (DIE-uh-fram), a muscle located at the base of the lungs. When we inhale, the diaphragm contracts and moves down, thus creating more space in the chest cavity and drawing air into the lungs. When we exhale, the diaphragm relaxes and moves up, forcing air out of the lungs.

C. Jesus Breathing on the Cross

Do you remember when Jesus was hanging on the Cross, and the soldiers came to break the legs of the men crucified with Jesus so they would die quickly? This is because that for a crucified person to breathe, he would need to push up on his legs to allow the chest cavity to expand and take in oxygen. If the leg bones were broken, the men would not be able to push up, and they would suffocate.

Jesus, though, had already died, and thus the soldier did not break His legs. Jesus wanted people of all time to know that He Himself was the ultimate sacrifice to God the Father. Jesus replaced the sacrifice God had given the Jews long before in the Old Testament. The Old Testament Jews were commanded to sacrifice an innocent lamb. A lamb that was sacrificed to God could not have any broken bones. Jesus was the perfect Lamb of God, Who was sacrificing His life for the sins of mankind; therefore, He too would not have any broken bones. Instead, His Heart was pierced by a lance, and blood and water poured forth.

Review Questions

1. What are the bronchi?

_____

_____

2. Why are the alveoli important?

_____

_____

3. Why are pleurae important?

_____

_____

4. How are the two lungs different from each other?

_____

_____

5. What does the diaphragm do?

_____

_____

IV. Speaking

There are a few instances recorded in Scripture in which Jesus heals a person who is mute, that is, unable to speak. Being mute is a terrible burden, especially if a person does not know sign language. Imagine not being able to speak or sing or communicate your thoughts and needs to any other person!

When was the last time we even thought about *how* we speak? It is safe to assume that the people whom Jesus healed of being mute were very thankful for the miracle to be able to speak. Have we ever thought about thanking God for our respiratory system, which allows us to be able to speak as well as to breathe?

A. The Larynx

The organ primarily associated with speaking is the **larynx** (LAR-inks), or voice box. The larynx is located in the neck, between the pharynx and the trachea. The larynx is connected to the epiglottis, the cartilage that prevents food and drink from entering the trachea.

The larynx contains the **vocal cords**, which are bands of muscle separated by a triangular opening called the **glottis**. When we breathe normally, air passes through easily. When the glottis narrows, passing air causes the vocal cords to vibrate, causing sound.

B. Volume and Pitch

Many things affect the volume and pitch of the sound that we make when speaking. For example, *longer*, more massive vocal cords produce a *lower* pitch. Men have *larger* vocal cords than women, which is why men usually have *deeper* voices. The tension of the vocal cords and the amount of air passing through also affect the sound produced.

Muscles in the larynx can adjust the cartilage, with which it is made up, into approximately 170 different positions, producing many different sounds! It is really incredible that the cartilage can adjust to 170 different positions! In addition, the placement of the lips and tongue are important in the formation of words.

C. Losing Your Voice

Have you ever "lost your voice"? A person can be mute because of damage to the larynx, but usually people lose their voice only temporarily, perhaps after prolonged yelling, singing, or screaming at a football game, or persistent coughing because of a cold or sore throat.

"Losing your voice" is sometimes caused by inflammation of the vocal cords. Sometimes small tissue growth forms after excessive strain on the vocal cords. There was a famous opera singer, Mario Lanza, and another famous singer from Hollywood, both of whom "lost" their voices for a time because of so much strain from their constant singing. Since both were professional singers, they both had great concern for their futures. After resting and not speaking for several months, both singers regained their voices. Most of the time, all that is needed for recovery is resting the voice.

Review Questions

1. Which organ is sometimes called the voice box?

_____

2. How do the vocal cords create sound?

_____

_____

_____

_____

3. Why do men usually have deeper voices than women?

_____

_____

V. Coughing, Sneezing, and Yawning

You have learned a lot about your respiratory system. You know the different parts and how they work. There are other things about the respiratory system you may still be wondering about. For example, when you cough, sneeze, or yawn, your respiratory system is involved. Why do we do those things? What causes coughs, sneezes, and yawns, and what purpose do they serve? Those are the topics we will be exploring in this lesson.

A. Coughing

A cough is the body's way of removing substances from the lungs or upper airway passages. If you have ever had something stuck in your throat, for example, you may have had to "cough it out." However, you may cough for other reasons. Coughing results when the cells of the lungs or airways are irritated. Coughing

can be involuntary, when you did not decide to cough, or voluntary, when you cough on purpose, such as when you feel the need to "cough up" something in your throat.

Often it is an illness that causes people to cough. Being sick can cause mucus to build up, or a respiratory infection can cause cell irritation, which leads to coughing. Asthma

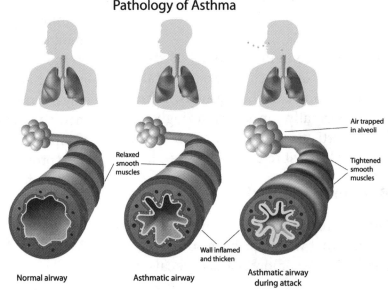

Pathology of Asthma

Relaxed smooth muscles

Air trapped in alveoli

Tightened smooth muscles

Wall inflamed and thicken

Normal airway

Asthmatic airway

Asthmatic airway during attack

Image credit: shutterstock.com

(AZ-muh) and bronchitis (brong-KITE-iss) are just two of the conditions that can cause involuntary coughing.

1. Asthma is a chronic long-term disease which often starts in childhood and continues for a lifetime. Although asthma symptoms can flare up at any time, when a person is exposed to smoke or dust or other things which could cause difficult breathing, there are likely to be difficulties. There is no cure for asthma, but people learn to avoid threatening situations, and learn how to control the disease when it flares up.

Asthma happens when the person's air passages become swollen and narrow. This makes it difficult for enough air to reach the lungs. Sometimes the airways produce more mucus, which makes the situation worse. Sometimes there is a wheezing or whistling sound as the person tries to breathe. Doctors give asthma medicine which helps reduce the swelling.

2. Bronchitis is an inflammation in the bronchi, the tubes that connect the trachea to the lungs. It is recognized by a "hacking cough." Bronchitis is most often caused by a virus, but usually doctors can give medication for a recovery or a lessening of the symptoms. Usually people recover in a few weeks. However, some people are susceptible to bronchitis, which means they are likely to get the condition fairly frequently, even every year. There is such a condition as chronic bronchitis, which means the person must work to keep the condition under control.

Chronic or frequent coughing can be annoying and even painful. Coughing can be helpful in clearing mucus from your airways, and can be essential to keeping your respiratory system clear. However, **chronic**

coughing is a time to contact a doctor. If a person has shortness of breath or chest pain, a doctor should be called immediately.

B. Sneezing

Sneezing is another function your body has for dealing with respiratory irritation. Sneezing is caused when something is irritating your nose. It may seem like a very simple, involuntary activity, but actually, your body must coordinate a wide range of muscles to produce a sneeze! For example, often when a person sneezes, he or she can "feel it" in the abdomen. That is because abdominal muscles are part of the sneezing process, along with muscles of the chest, throat, and face. This coordination is all controlled by the "sneezing center" in your brain.

All sorts of irritating things can make a person sneeze, such as dust, or allergens like certain perfumes, or certain foods. Sneezing can be caused by bacteria or viruses in the nose. This is why we often sneeze when we are sick. You may not realize it, but sneezing is important to help keep us healthy!

One interesting fact about sneezes is that they are fast. During a sneeze, particles can exit the nose at up to 100 miles per hour! It is also interesting that humans are not the only creatures that sneeze. You may have seen a pet dog or cat sneeze, for example. Studies suggest that iguanas are actually the "sneeziest" animals!

C. Yawning

Yawning is another action you may often do and wonder about. Coughing and sneezing may make sense, but why do we yawn? Are yawns truly contagious? Is there a difference between yawning due to tiredness and yawning due to boredom?

If you have some of these questions, you are not alone. The truth is that medical professionals do not have all the answers when it comes to yawning. We know that animals yawn. So do unborn babies! But why? There are numerous theories on the subject.

It has long been thought that yawning is caused by the body's need for more oxygen, but studies have called this theory into question. Other doctors believe that yawning stretches the lungs in a healthful way. One recent study suggests that yawning actually cools the surfaces of the brain! That is a stretch of the brain!

One thing about yawning is for sure, however. It is contagious. Data show that when people see others yawn, they are more likely to yawn themselves. Even thinking about yawning can cause a person to yawn! How many times have you yawned while reading this lesson about yawning? That might be an interesting science project!

How many times have you yawned while reading this lesson about yawning?
Image credit: public domain

Review Questions

1. What important function does coughing serve?

_____

_____

2. What causes people to sneeze?

_____

_____

3. How can sneezing help keep people healthy?

_____

_____

4. Name three theories about why people yawn.

_____

_____

VI. Respiration

A. Introduction

It is obvious that the respiratory system is critically important to a person's life and health. Human beings cannot live more than a very few minutes without oxygen. Lack of oxygen for even a few minutes can damage brain cells. So what happens if a person is unable to breathe sufficiently on his own, due to choking, drowning, poisoning, lung disease, or some other cause? If a person cannot supply his body with enough oxygen, he can be aided with artificial respiration.

B. Artificial Respiration

Artificial respiration is a term that refers to any method that supplies air to a person who cannot breathe effectively on his own. This can be done with a medical device, or by another person through cardio-pulmonary resuscitation (CPR). Technically speaking, artificial respiration is really artificial ventilation. Ventilation refers to the movement of air into and out of the lungs; respiration refers to the exchange of gases, which is necessary for survival. However, respiration cannot occur without ventilation, which is why ventilation is so critical.

1. "Rescue breaths," delivered as part of cardio-pulmonary resuscitation or CPR, are the simplest form of artificial respiration. This occurs when one person supplies another with oxygen by blowing into the mouth (or nose). The rescuer forces air into the lungs of the recipient.

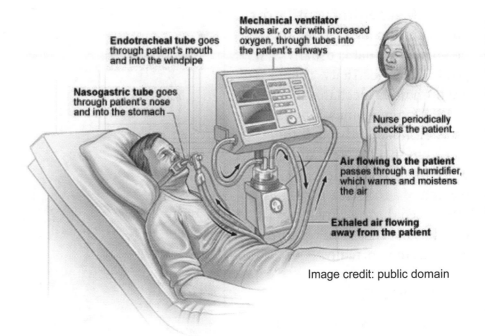

Endotracheal tube goes through patient's mouth and into the windpipe

Mechanical ventilator blows air, or air with increased oxygen, through tubes into the patient's airways

Nasogastric tube goes through patient's nose and into the stomach

Nurse periodically checks the patient.

Air flowing to the patient passes through a humidifier, which warms and moistens the air

Exhaled air flowing away from the patient

Image credit: public domain

Remember that respiration is about gas exchange. The air is made of many gases. Our bodies use the oxygen in the air, and give off carbon dioxide as waste when we exhale. However, carbon dioxide is not the only gas in our breath. The air we breathe out still has some oxygen in it. Though it is less efficient in terms of oxygen levels than regular breathing, providing rescue breaths can supply someone with enough oxygen to preserve life and protect vulnerable brain cells.

2. Ventilator — Artificial respiration can be provided through a medical device called a ventilator. These ventilators work on one of two principles: positive pressure or negative pressure. Positive pressure ventilators "push" air into the lungs and can be either manual or mechanical. Negative pressure ventilators will be discussed a little further on.

3. Manual ventilators are hand-held devices through which air is pushed when it is squeezed. Generally, a mask is placed over the patient, and a bag on the device is squeezed, forcing air into the airways, much like air might be forced out of an inflatable toy when the valve is opened.

4. Mechanical ventilators pump air into a patient by use of a machine that is usually powered by electricity. There are numerous mechanical ventilation machines. Often, air is pumped in through tubes placed in the nose or mouth of a patient. Intubation, the placing of a tube in a person, is often used during surgery as a precaution even when breathing is occurring normally.

C. Surgery

Sometimes providing air through the nose or mouth is impossible and doctors need to perform a **tracheostomy** (tray-kee-OSS-tuh-me). In this procedure, doctors are able to supply air directly to a person's trachea through a surgically cut hole at the base of the throat.

D. Negative Pressure Ventilators

Negative pressure ventilators work on a different principle than positive pressure ventilators. Negative pressure ventilators control the air pressure around a person's chest. As the air pressure decreases, it causes the chest cavity to expand, drawing air into

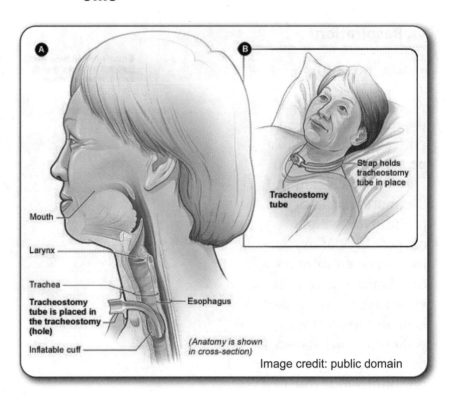

Mouth
Larynx
Trachea
Tracheostomy tube is placed in the tracheostomy (hole)
Inflatable cuff
Esophagus
(Anatomy is shown in cross-section)

Strap holds tracheostomy tube in place
Tracheostomy tube

Image credit: public domain

the lungs. Then, as the machine increases the pressure surrounding the patient, it forces air out of the lungs.

The most famous negative pressure ventilator is popularly called the **iron lung**, and was developed in 1929. The patient lay inside an iron tank, sealed off and covering his entire body except the head. The pressure changes were controlled within the tank, which caused the ventilation. Today, smaller versions are still in use. These smaller ones resemble a shell that a person wears on the upper body to control air pressure around his chest.

Review Questions

1. What is the difference between ventilation and respiration?

_____

_____

2. What are "rescue breaths"?

_____

_____

3. Compare and contrast positive pressure and negative pressure ventilators.

_____

_____

_____

_____

VII. Lung Diseases

There are many different types of diseases that affect the lungs and respiratory system. One group consists of diseases that affect the airways, such as the trachea or bronchi. Asthma and bronchitis are diseases that affect the airways.

A. Cystic fibrosis is another airway disease. This is a genetic disease that children sometimes inherit from their parents. With cystic fibrosis, mucus builds up in the airways. This can lead to blocked air passages and frequent infections.

B. Chronic Obstructive Pulmonary Disease (COPD) refers to a <u>group</u> of diseases that consistently or chronically cause breathing difficulties. **Chronic bronchitis** would fall in this category, as would emphysema (em-fuh-ZEE-muh). **Emphysema** is a disease in which the alveoli are damaged, restricting the capacity of gas transfer in the lungs. The primary cause of emphysema is smoking.

C. Lung Cancer and Pneumonia are two common lung diseases. These diseases affect the lungs themselves, either the lung tissue or the blood vessels in the lungs. As with most cancers, lung cancer can be caused by many different things, but the most dangerous risk factor is smoking. Lung cancer can be difficult to treat, depending on how advanced it is when it is diagnosed.

Pneumonia, however, usually goes away within two to three weeks and usually does not require a stay in a hospital. It can be very dangerous, though, and even deadly to the very young, the elderly, or those sick with something else.

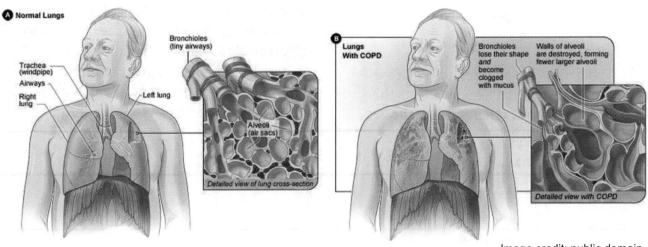

Image credit: public domain

Pneumonia is usually caused by bacteria or a virus, and is caught when the germs are breathed into the lungs. Pneumonia causes coughing, shortness of breath, fever, chest pain, and nausea. Pneumonia can be treated with rest and fluids. If it is bacterial pneumonia, it can be cured with **antibiotics,** a medicine that can destroy the growth of bacteria.

D. Tuberculosis is a lung disease which has been rare in America for some years. However, with many people with this disease coming to the United States from other countries, we are seeing a dramatic increase in cases in our country. The highest number of cases are in Texas, California, Nevada, and Florida.

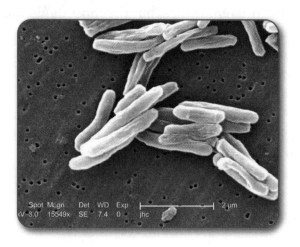

M. tuberculosis, a type of bacteria, usually affects the lungs, but can attack other parts of the body.
Credit: public domain

Tuberculosis is an infectious disease caused by bacteria that usually affects the lungs, but can attack other parts of the body. People sometimes have tuberculosis without showing any symptoms. Sometimes, however, tuberculosis becomes active. Today, tuberculosis can be treated with antibiotics, but if left untreated, it can be deadly.

E. Saints

Tuberculosis has claimed the lives of numerous saints throughout history, including St. Therese of Lisieux and St. Bernadette. St. Therese, the Little Flower, died of tuberculosis at the age of 24. She is a Doctor of the Church, known for her "little way" of becoming a saint by doing little things with great love. She has inspired many people, including heroes like St. Mother Teresa of Calcutta.

St. Bernadette died in 1879, but she continues to look as if merely sleeping.
Credit: public domain

St. Bernadette is best known for receiving the visions of Our Lady of Lourdes. Bernadette's body is miraculously incorrupt. Although she died in 1879, her body, which can be viewed in Nevers, France, appears to be peacefully sleeping. The miracle of the incorruptible saints is a great gift from God pointing to the resurrection of the body that all people will experience at the end of time.

Review Questions

1. Name three diseases of the airways.

2. What is tuberculosis?

_____

3. What usually causes pneumonia?

_____

VIII. Healthy Lungs

A. St. Blaise

If you have ever been to Mass on February 3, you may have had your throat blessed. Usually, crossed candles are placed over the throat of those who want the blessing. St. Blaise once healed a boy who had a fish bone stuck in his throat. Consequently, the Church has approved a special blessing asking the intercession of St. Blaise to heal those suffering diseases of the throat.

Remember to get your throat blessed on Saint Blaise's feast day (February 3).
Credit: Père Igor

B. Choking

One of the most serious problems which result in death is accidental choking. The third leading cause of death in the United States is choking or death by suffocation. In the United States, a child dies every 5 days due to death by choking on food.

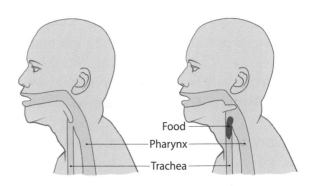

Chewing your food completely helps you to avoid choking.
Credit: shutterstock.com

As so many parents have told their children for hundreds of years: chew your food before you swallow. Be careful to avoid choking.

As so many parents and teachers have told older teenagers: To protect your respiratory system, be careful to avoid choking. By obstructing your airways, you do not allow the respiratory system to do its job. Chew your food completely when you eat. People who have problems with choking usually have not sufficiently chewed their food.

C. Heimlich Maneuver

It is good to know the **Heimlich** (HIME-lik) **Maneuver** (Ma-NEW-ver) which can dislodge items from a choking person's throat. By putting cupped fists under a person's abdomen from behind and giving or pulling sudden upward thrusts, you can save a person's life! With your parent's help, research the details of how to perform the maneuver and practice it. A person can even perform the Heimlich maneuver on himself by standing behind a chair and pushing his abdomen against the high back of a chair.

D. Smoking

An essential aspect of a healthy respiratory system is having healthy lungs. The most important thing to do to maintain healthy lungs is to avoid smoking. **Smoking** causes all sorts of health problems to many body systems, but because the smoke is inhaled directly into the lungs, it is the leading cause of lung cancer and emphysema, among other respiratory diseases. Also, try to avoid smoking areas. Tobacco smoke exhaled by smokers also can harm your lungs.

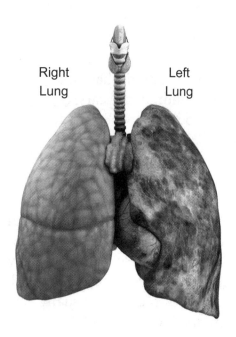

Right Lung

Left Lung

The right lung model is composed of healthy pink tissue. The left lung model shows damage caused by smoking.
Credit: shutterstock.com

E. Pollutants

Be aware of other dangers to your lungs, **pollutants**, such as chemicals from cleaning products, that you might accidentally breathe as well. The respiratory system works hard to stay clean and healthy, but we must avoid breathing pollutants for extended periods. If a person visits a particularly dirty or polluted area, or works with dangerous substances, he or she should wear a protective mask. Many people who work with pollutants for their jobs are required by law to wear specially-made protective masks.

Workers practice life-saving skills during this chemical spill exercise at a factory.
Credit: public domain

F. Diet and Exercise

Diet and exercise play important roles in maintaining a healthy respiratory system. **Regular exercise**, especially aerobic exercise such as running and swimming, increases the capacity of the lungs to provide oxygen to the blood. Eating foods that are high in **antioxidants** does the same, and helps protect the organs of the respiratory system.

Antioxidants, such as vitamin C, vitamin E, and beta-carotene, are most often found in <u>fruits and vegetables</u>. Usually, the stronger the color in the fruit or vegetable, the more powerful the antioxidant.

Kale.
Credit: public domain

Grapes.
Credit: public domain

Broccoli.
Credit: public domain

Blueberries.
Credit: public domain

Strawberries.
Credit: public domain

Five Top Sources of Antioxidants

Review Questions

1. On whose feast day do we have our throats blessed?

2. What is the purpose of the Heimlich maneuver?

3. What are some things we can do to maintain healthy lungs?

4. When is it wise to wear a protective mask?

Chapter Review Activity

Section A

Use the words and phrases in the word box to complete the sentences:

alveoli	bronchi	cilia	diaphragm
epiglottis	larynx	trachea	pharynx
positive pressure	negative pressure		

1. Air travels through a tube called the _____, which connects to the lungs.

2. The _____ is cartilage that covers the trachea when we eat so food does not go to the lungs.

3. The two tubes at the base of the trachea that lead to the lungs are called _____.

4. The _____, sometimes called the throat, directs air to the larynx and trachea and food to the esophagus.

5. The work of inhaling and exhaling is primarily done with the _____, a muscle located at the base of the lungs.

6. Oxygen passes through the thin walls of the _____ into the capillaries.

7. The _____ is sometimes called the voice box.

8. The iron lung is an example of a _____ _____ ventilator.

9. A _____ _____ ventilator pushes air into the lungs.

10. The tiny hairs in the trachea are called _____.

Chapter Review Activity

SECTION B

Fill in the table below with the parts of the respiratory system in the box below:

alveoli	bronchi	bronchioles	lungs
mouth	nose	pharynx	trachea

UPPER RESPIRATORY SYSTEM

11. _____

12. _____

13. _____

14. _____

LOWER RESPIRATORY SYSTEM

15. _____

16. _____

17. _____

18. _____

SECTION C

Write the letter of the correct answer on the line provided.

19. Which of these is associated with cardio-pulmonary resuscitation (CPR)? _____

    A. Rescue breaths

    B. Tracheostomy

    C. Intubation

    D. Iron lung

20. Which of these is a disease of the airways? Circle the correct answer. _____

    A. Lung cancer

    B. Tuberculosis

    C. Asthma

    D. Pneumonia

21. On whose feast day do we have our throats blessed? Circle the correct answer. _____

   A. St. Bernadette

   B. St. Teresa of Calcutta

   C. St. Bernardine of Siena

   D. St. Blaise

22. Tuberculosis took the life of which saint? Circle the correct answer. _____

   A. St. Bernadette

   B. St. Therese of Lisieux

   C. St. Blaise

   D. Both A and B

SECTION D

Complete the following exercises using the lines provided.

23. Compare and contrast the causes of coughing and sneezing.

_____

_____

_____

24. Describe three theories about why people yawn.

_____

_____

_____

25. What body parts protect the lungs?

_____

_____

_____

Brain and Nerves

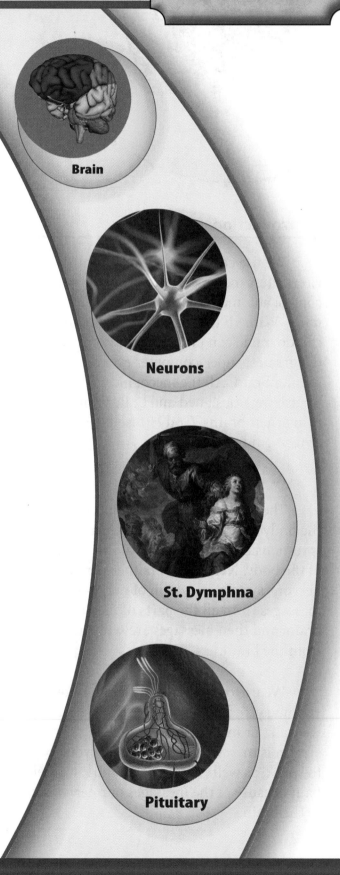

Brain

Neurons

St. Dymphna

Pituitary

Image credits (from top): shutterstock.com, shutterstock.com,
public domain, shutterstock.com

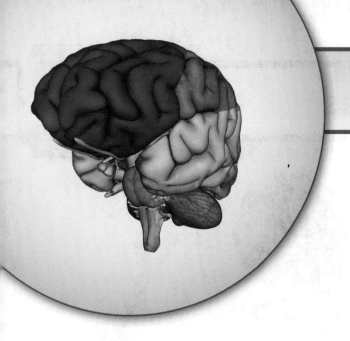

Brain and Nerves

Even our spiritual faculties make use of our nervous system. The intellect with which we think and the will with which we make decisions are both faculties of the invisible soul. Yet we use our bodies to exercise what we think with the intellect and what we decide with the will. Thinking and decision-making take place in the brain.

You may have heard someone say, "Use your brain." We use that amazing bodily organ, the brain, to perform functions that essentially come from the soul. For example, when you pray a Rosary, you are doing something very spiritual, and yet you need your brain to hear and remember the prayers and to speak the words. Your body and soul work together.

The nervous system is truly a mysterious and amazing display of God's loving and wonderful design of the human body. We study the nervous system in more detail in this chapter.

I. Introduction

We use computers for many things. Computers manage data, navigate airplanes, control automobile systems, and much, much more. With all the amazing things computers can do, none can even begin to compare with the greatest super-computer ever designed: the human brain. All the mechanical computers we use were designed and built by humans using their brains. God Himself designed the amazing human brain.

A. The Nervous System

The **brain** is the most important part of the body's nervous system. The nervous system is responsible for regulating all the other parts of the body. **Nerves** are another part of the nervous system. A system of nerves sends messages from all the parts of the body to the brain, and then messages are sent back again from the brain.

We use our nervous system for both voluntary and involuntary actions. Every time we walk, or move any body part, the nervous system is involved. We use our nervous system to speak, as well. When we get hurt, we feel pain because of the messages our nerves send to the brain.

B. Saint Dymphna

Saint Dymphna (DIMF-nuh) is the patron saint of those with nervous system diseases and mental disorders. Dymphna was born in Ireland in the seventh century to a pagan father and Catholic mother. She grew up as a pious and prayerful child, and consecrated herself to God. When her beloved mother died, however, her father became mentally ill. He decided he wanted to marry Dymphna, his own daughter! Dymphna fled to Belgium to escape her father. When her father tracked her down, Dymphna's refusal to go with him led him to an insane rage, and he killed her, his own daughter!

After Dymphna's death, miracles of healing began to be reported from those who prayed to her, especially for those with nervous system or mental disorders. People from many countries in Europe started to make pilgrimages, or long trips, to visit Dymphna's burial ground, and ask for her intercession for their illnesses. Because of her holiness and the miracles that were granted to those who prayed to her, the Catholic Church declared her a saint. St. Dymphna is a heroic witness of purity, courage, and devotion to God. Now she prays for us in His presence in Heaven.

Saint Dymphna is the patroness of those with nervous system diseases and mental disorders.
Credit: public domain

Review Questions

1. What is the nervous system?

_____

_____

2. Name two parts of the nervous system.

_____

_____

3. How does your brain help you to pray the Rosary?

_____

_____

II. Central Nervous System

The central nervous system is made up of the brain and the spinal cord. You can think of the central nervous system as "command central." The central nervous system receives information from all the parts of the body, then processes the information, and then sends information out to all the parts of the body.

This information is sent through nerves, which extend from the brain and spinal cord to the other parts of the body.

A. Brain

There are billions of very tiny nerves in the brain. As people learn information, the information is passed between nerve cells, called neurons. Eventually these neurons

JMJ

form connections called pathways. In this way, people learn information, develop various skills, and form memories.

Think of a skill you have learned, such as riding a bike. When you were acquiring that skill, it required a lot of concentration and you made a lot of mistakes at first. However, as you kept practicing, pathways were created between the nerve cells in your brain. Before long, you could ride a bike without even thinking about it. Riding a bike became "second nature."

When you were born, you had all the nerve cells you ever will have, but many connections between the nerve cells had not been made yet. Children's brains are very adaptable and ready to grow and develop. God has designed the brain so that, as it develops, one part can acquire the function that normally belongs to another part, especially if there has been damage done to the first part.

As we age, it is more difficult for one part of the brain to help another damaged part. It is important to continue reading, learning, and stimulating the brain as we grow in different ways so that the brain stays strong, alert, and able to continue to make new nerve brain pathways more easily.

Brain

Spinal cord

B. Spinal Cord

Another part of the central nervous system is the spinal cord. The spinal cord is a thick bundle of nerves that comes from the brain and runs down the spinal column. An adult's spinal cord is usually between 17 and 18 inches long and about three-fourths of an inch thick.

The thick bundle of nerves in the spinal cord is protected by the vertebrae, the 33 small bones in the spinal column. The spinal nerves run out from the spinal cord to the different parts of the body. The spinal cord is divided into 31 different segments, out of which nerves emerge to the right and the left of the body.

Besides the bones of the spinal column protecting it, the spinal cord is protected by three layers of tissues called meninges (meh-NIN-jeez). The meninges protect the brain as well as protecting the spinal cord.

The spinal cord is also cushioned by a fluid called cerebrospinal (suh-REE-bro-SPINE-uhl) fluid. Obviously, God's plan is to give great protection to the spinal cord through bones, tissues, and fluid.

If a person's spinal cord is damaged, as sometimes occurs in accidents, paralysis may result. The location of the damage done to the spinal cord may determine how much of the body becomes paralyzed. For example, if the damage happens very low in the spinal column, the person may lose the use of his legs. If the damage is higher up, more function is likely to be lost. You can see why it is so important to take extra care of the entire central nervous system—the brain and the spinal cord.

Image credit: shutterstock.com

Review Questions

1. What two main parts make up the central nervous system?

_____

2. What are "pathways" in the brain?

_____

3. What is the spinal cord?

_____

_____

4. What is one possible consequence of a damaged spinal cord?

_____

_____

III. Parts of the Brain

The body's super-computer, the "captain" of the central nervous system, is the brain. The brain is an organ in the head that <u>weighs about three pounds</u>. The brain contains more than 100 billion nerves, and trillions of **synapses** (sih-NAP-seez), which are the connections, or "pathways" between nerve cells. The brain is protected by the bones of the skull, and also a layer of tissue called **meninges** and cerebrospinal fluid.

A. Cerebrospinal Fluid is produced and circulated by four areas in the brain called **ventricles**. The cerebrospinal fluid is vital for good health because it provides nutrition and cushioning to the central nervous system. The cerebrospinal fluid reaches the spinal cord through a path called the central canal.

The brain contains billions of neurons, like this one.
Credit: shutterstock.com

B. Cerebrum

The cerebrum is the largest part of the brain. The cerebrum makes up approximately 85% of the brain's weight. The cerebrum is primarily responsible for our voluntary activity. This is the area in which thought occurs. The cerebrum also controls our sensory perception (sight, hearing, smell), and controls our speech and memory.

C. Cerebral Cortex

The cerebral cortex is the outer layer of the cerebrum, and it is the location where most of the thinking and perception is done. The cerebral cortex is made up of what is called **gray matter**, which is composed of nerve cell bodies. The gray matter is responsible for storing and processing information. The **white matter** underneath the gray matter is composed

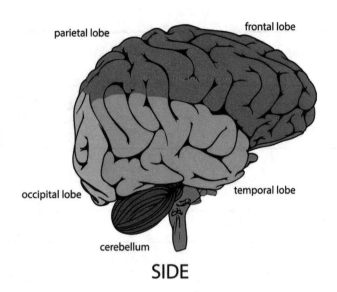

parietal lobe

frontal lobe

occipital lobe

temporal lobe

cerebellum

SIDE

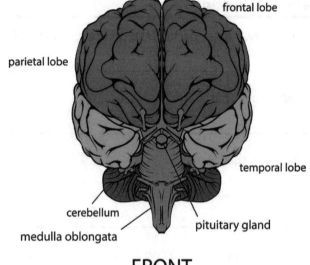

frontal lobe

parietal lobe

temporal lobe

cerebellum

pituitary gland

medulla oblongata

FRONT

of projections from the gray matter nerve cells called **axons**, which transmit information to different parts of the brain.

D. Hemispheres — The hemispheres are the two halves of the cerebrum. The hemispheres contain four lobes. A lobe is something that looks like the cartilage at the bottom of the ear. The left hemisphere controls the right side of the body, and the right hemisphere controls the left side of the body. Many scientists believe that the left half of the cerebrum is more helpful in analytical skills, for example, processing mathematical and logical thinking. These scientists also believe that the right half of the cerebrum is more creative, for example, more geared toward art or music. These scientists also believe that most people have one dominant or stronger side of the brain.

E. Cerebral Lobes — The four cerebral lobes of each hemisphere of the cerebrum are the frontal lobe, the temporal lobe, the parietal (puh-RIE-uh-tuhl) lobe, and the occipital (ok-SIP-uh-tuhl) lobe. Each lobe controls some different aspect of thought or perception.

The **frontal lobe** is responsible for decision-making, judgment, movement, and regulating a person's mood. The **temporal lobe** regulates memory, hearing, and language processing and usage. The **parietal lobe** controls sensory reception, such as pain, touch, and taste, and controls body position and movement. The **occipital lobe** is responsible for processing visual information; it helps people recognize what they see.

F. Cerebellum — Besides the cerebrum and cerebral cortex, another important part of the brain is the **cerebellum**. The cerebellum is located at the base and back of the brain. It is much smaller than the cerebrum, only about one-eighth of the size. The cerebellum is primarily responsible for balance and muscle coordination.

G. Brain Stem — Beneath the cerebrum and in front of the cerebellum, connecting the brain to the spinal cord, is the **brain stem**. The brain stem is a vital part of the brain because it regulates the bodily functions that keep us alive. The brain stem contains the **medulla oblongata** (muh-DULL-uh ob-long-GOT-uh). The medulla oblongata, only about one inch

Image credits: shutterstock.com

long, regulates breathing, blood circulation, digestion, and other vital involuntary functions.

H. Hypothalamus — Apart from these major parts of the brain, there are many other important areas as well. The **hypothalamus** regulates the body's temperature. For example, if you get overheated, your hypothalamus causes you to sweat.

I. Pituitary Gland — The **pituitary** (pih-TOO-ih-ter-ee) gland is a small gland, about the size of a pea, tucked inside the brain. This small gland plays a very important role. The pituitary gland regulates the body's hormones. These affect many aspects of life, including a person's growth. When a child grows or begins to go through changes during the teen years, the pituitary gland is doing its job.

You can see now why the brain can be called the world's greatest **super-computer**. It is truly a testament to what the psalmist says: "I praise You, for I am fearfully and wonderfully made" (Psalm 139:14a).

Review Questions

1. What is the largest part of the brain called?

2. What is the difference between gray matter and white matter?

3. What important functions does the brain stem perform?

4. Name the four lobes of the brain and one function each performs.

5. What are the functions of the hypothalamus and the pituitary gland?

_____

_____

_____

IV. Nerves

You've learned about the central nervous system and the anatomy of the brain, and you've learned that the nervous system transmits information through nerves. But what exactly are nerves and how do they work? In this section, we will take a look at these tiny wonders of God's creation, the nerves.

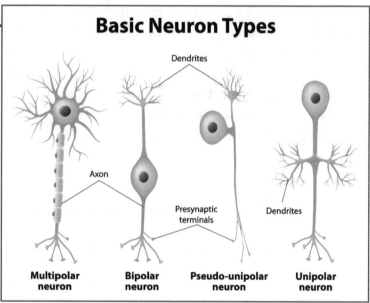

Basic Neuron Types

Dendrites

Axon

Presynaptic terminals

Dendrites

Multipolar neuron

Bipolar neuron

Pseudo-unipolar neuron

Unipolar neuron

A. Neurons — Nerves are bundles of special cells called **neurons**. Neurons are cells which <u>transmit information through electrical or chemical signals</u>. Neurons transmit these signals over **synapses**, which are special connections between neurons or connections from neurons to other cells.

Dendrites

Axon

Presynaptic terminals

Unipolar neuron

Each neuron has two types of projections, called dendrites and axons. Look at the illustration. **Dendrites** <u>receive</u> information and transmit it to the neuron's "body." The **axon** transmits information <u>away from</u> the neuron to be passed on to another neuron over a synapse.

B. Sensory Nerves and Motor Nerves — There are different types of nerves, which perform different functions. **Sensory nerves** transmit sensory information, such as temperature, pain, and smell. **Motor nerves** transmit information for movement. Moving your arm, for example, requires connections between multiple motor nerves, from your brain to your spinal cord, and then to your arm.

C. Autonomic Nerves — Both sensory and motor nerves can sometimes be classified as autonomic (aw-toe-NOM-ik) nerves. **Autonomic nerves** send information that control the body's performance of <u>automatic tasks</u>, such as breathing, digestion, and heartbeat.

Image credit: shutterstock.com

D. Cranial Nerves — Nerves can be classified based on where they are located. There are twelve nerves that come <u>directly from the brain to other tissues</u> without passing through the spinal cord. These are called **cranial nerves** because they emerge from the brain through the skull. Cranial nerves serve both sensory and motor functions for the head, face, neck, and heart.

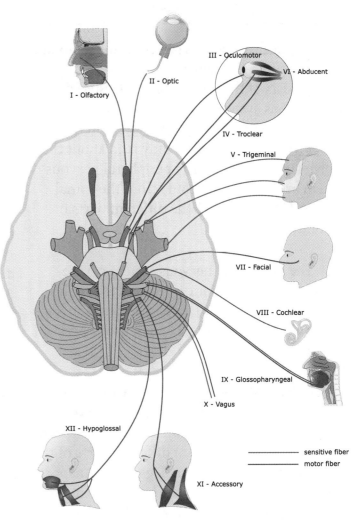

Each of the **twelve cranial nerves** serves different purposes. For example, cranial nerve I, the olfactory nerve, carries messages for our <u>sense of smell</u>. Cranial nerve IV, the trochlear (TROK-lee-er) nerve, regulates the movement of many of the <u>muscles of the eye</u>, controlling how the eyes move. Cranial nerve VII, the <u>facial nerve</u>, controls the use of our facial muscles so we can smile, frown, or make other facial expressions. And cranial nerve XII, the hypoglossal (HIE-puh-GLOS-uhl) nerve, regulates the movements of the tongue. Though they come directly from the brain, the cranial nerves are not technically considered part of the central nervous system.

Review Questions

1. What are neurons?

_____

_____

2. What are axons and dendrites?

_____

_____

3. What is the difference between sensory nerves, motor nerves, and autonomic nerves?

_____

_____

_____

Image credit: shutterstock.com

V. Peripheral Nervous System

The body's nervous system is made up of more than just the central nervous system. It also consists of the peripheral (puh-RIFF-er-uhl) nervous system, the system of <u>nerves that run from the central nervous system to the rest of the body</u>. You've already read about the twelve cranial nerves. The peripheral nervous system are nerves that come from the spinal cord and branch out to the different parts of the body.

The peripheral nervous system can be divided into the somatic nervous system and the autonomic nervous system, and it is made up of different types of nerves: sensory nerves and motor nerves.

A. Somatic Nervous System — The **somatic nervous system** consists of nerves that take in sensory information such as touch, pain, or temperature from different parts of the body, such as the arms and legs, and transport that information back to the brain. The nerves that perform this function are called <u>sensory nerves</u>.

The <u>motor nerves of the somatic nervous system</u> conduct messages between the brain and skeletal muscles. We use these nerves for movement. Sometimes sensory nerve fibers and motor nerve fibers can be bundled together in what is called a mixed nerve.

B. Autonomic Nervous System — The **autonomic nervous system** is a part of the peripheral nervous system that <u>regulates involuntary bodily functions</u>. For example, you learned that the medulla oblongata is the part of the brain that regulates breathing. How do these messages (to continue to breathe while we're asleep, for example) get to the respiratory system? They are carried by the peripheral nerves of the autonomic nervous system. Autonomic nerves control everything from your heartbeat to your body's digestion of food.

C. Reflexes — Have you ever been to the doctor and had your **reflexes** checked? Doctors check your reflexes to assess the health of your nervous system. Maybe you sat on the table and relaxed your leg. Then the doctor tapped you just below the knee with a little hammer, and your foot kicked forward. This is a reflex. It is an <u>involuntary response of the nervous system</u> to some stimulus.

Reflexes like the involuntary response mentioned above are <u>somatic</u>, while those <u>affecting inner organs</u> are <u>autonomic</u>. There are numerous reflexes a doctor can check to help determine the health of a patient's nervous system. Usually, a decreased reflex indicates a problem with the peripheral nervous system, while an exaggerated reflex may point to a problem with the central nervous system.

MOTOR NEURON

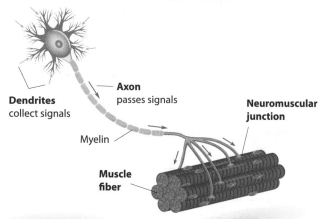

Dendrites collect signals

Axon passes signals

Myelin

Muscle fiber

Neuromuscular junction

Image credit: shutterstock.com

Review Questions

1. What is the peripheral nervous system?

_____

2. What is the difference between the somatic nervous system and the autonomic nervous system?

_____

_____

_____

_____

_____

_____

3. Why do doctors test reflexes?

_____

_____

_____

VI. Nervous System Disorders

The nervous system is such an essential part of the body, it is important to protect it and treat diseases or injuries carefully.

A. Brain Tumor — A **brain tumor** is an abnormal tissue growth in the brain. Some tumors may be cancerous, but even tumors that are benign (not cancer) can cause problems because of the pressure they can create on parts of the brain. Tumors must be removed through surgery, and surgeons must be very precise as they remove them, so as not to damage surrounding brain tissue.

B. Epilepsy — Another brain disorder is **epilepsy**. You may remember Matthew 17:14-21, when Jesus healed a boy with epilepsy. Epilepsy causes seizures. In extreme cases, people may experience uncontrollable body movements. Though in the Gospel an evil spirit was the cause of the boy's condition, epilepsy does have natural causes as well. It can be caused by head injury or infections.

C. Stroke — A stroke occurs when blood flow to part of the brain stops due to a blood clot or damaged artery. This part of the brain does not receive enough oxygen, which causes

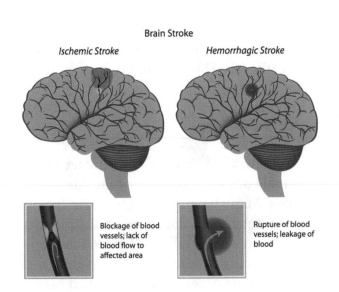

Brain Stroke
Ischemic Stroke / Hemorrhagic Stroke

Blockage of blood vessels; lack of blood flow to affected area

Rupture of blood vessels; leakage of blood

Image credit: shutterstock.com

serious damage. Symptoms include inability to move or feel one side of the body, headache, dizziness, slurred speech, and vision changes. Strokes can be fatal, and even when they are not, people who have suffered strokes often require a lot of physical therapy to regain some of the function they have lost.

D. Parkinson's Disease — Pope St. John Paul II died of a condition called **Parkinson's Disease**. Parkinson's Disease occurs when nerves in the central area of the brain begin to wear down. Usually people with Parkinson's Disease have trouble with <u>movement and coordination</u>. They often have little tremors, which are uncontrollable shaking of a body part. Other symptoms include soft speech and decreased ability to change facial expression.

Because this disease progresses over many years, people often live with it for a long time. The world was amazed as it watched the courage and joy of St. John Paul II as he approached the end of his life, and offered his sufferings with Christ for the Church he loved and served for so many years.

E. Meningitis — Another disease of the nervous system is **meningitis**, which can be caused by bacteria or a virus. Meningitis occurs when the meninges, the tissues surrounding the brain and spinal cord, become inflamed. Symptoms include fever, headache, and a stiff neck. This disease is treatable, but can be very dangerous.

VII. Nerve Damage

You already learned about damage to the spinal cord and how that can result in paralysis. Many people also suffer pain from **nerve damage**. A damaged nerve or a pinched nerve can be very painful. A pinched nerve is one that has pressure being put on it by a muscle or some other cause. A pinched nerve

often responds by sending pain signals back to the brain, and sometimes can cause the loss of motor function or some movement.

A. Concussion — While there are disorders that can affect the nervous system, it is also important to avoid injury to the head, especially a **concussion**. Blows to the head can cause damage to the brain. Doctors are becoming concerned about the number of children, and even adults, who are getting concussions playing games like football. Schools are now insisting that those playing football must wear protective helmets.

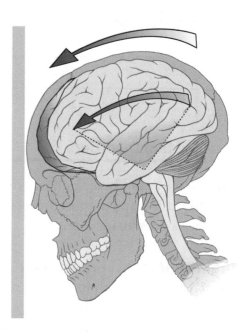

Blows to the head can cause damage to the brain.
Credit: Patrick J. Lynch, Medical Illustrator

The main sign of a concussion is a headache that won't go away. Other signs are weakness, numbness, sickness, vomiting, slurred speech, drowsiness, and unequal or enlarged eye pupils.

B. Pinched Nerves — Sometimes young people are careless in their determination while playing various sports. Being too aggressive or careless can result in a **pinched nerve**, which means a good deal of pain that can keep a young person from being active for some time. Most young people's bodies recover quickly, but they may need something to help reduce the pain while the nervous system is recovering.

It is important to show God gratitude for giving us a healthy body, and to treat the gift of our healthy nervous system with care. For those of us who suffer from sickness or poor heath, we should seek medical help, but we also need to trust God that He has allowed us this cross for a reason we may not understand now. Many saints are patrons of specific illnesses, so we can help ourselves and others by asking for their prayers.

Review Questions

1. What causes a stroke?

_____

_____

2. From what neurological condition did St. John Paul II die?

_____

_____

3. Which disease is caused by inflammation of the meninges surrounding the brain or spinal cord?

_____

_____

VIII. Mental Illness

A mental illness is a disorder that affects a person's mood, thinking, or ability to cope with certain situations. For example, a person may be depressed and not understand why. Another person may not always be able to distinguish reality from fantasy. Someone else may become terribly anxious around other people. Mental illnesses come in a wide range of mental disturbances, from very mild to very severe.

An important thing to remember is that a true mental illness is a mental condition, not a spiritual one. In other words, just as someone wouldn't consider himself "bad" if he had the flu, neither should he feel that way if he struggles with a mental illness. A strong spiritual life may help a person to deal with mental illnesses, but mental illnesses must be treated medically.

A. Chemical Imbalance — Mental illness can be the result of a biological problem. For example, a **chemical imbalance in the brain** can cause a person to suffer clinical depression. In this case, a doctor may prescribe medication to restore the proper chemical balance and allow that person's brain to function as it was created to function.

B. Traumatic Brain Injury — A traumatic brain injury can occur from a strong external force on the brain. Sometimes mental illness can result from such a **traumatic experience**, especially from a wartime experience. A psychologist may be able to help a person recognize these problems and then work and pray. A person may need to develop new thought patterns so he or she can heal and begin to respond to such trauma in a healthy way.

C. Dementia — Some mental illnesses are associated with advancing age. Dementia is a condition often caused by the **wearing down of the nerves** in the brain, making it difficult to think clearly or remember things. Scientists are continuing to study the causes of dementia because they are numerous and not always clear.

D. Avoid Mental Illness — To avoid mental illness, it is important to develop a healthy brain from a young age by **exercising** and doing challenging **mental activities**, such as crossword puzzles. Support from family and friends, as well as medical help and prayer, are essential for mental health.

E. Diet — Diet can be an important factor in mental health. People can respond differently to different foods. Many parents, for example, have found that a change in diet can be a key ingredient in successfully and safely treating a child with Attention Deficit Disorder.

F. Prayer — Seeking help in **prayer** is essential. Remember that Jesus said, "Behold, I make all things new" (Rev. 21:5). When someone is dealing with mental illnesses, we must include Jesus along with doctors in the healing process. We must spend time in prayer, attending Mass, and receiving Jesus in the most Blessed Sacrament.

Review Questions

1. What are some causes of mental illness?

_____

_____

2. What risk does advancing age pose to mental health?

_____

_____

3. How can we lessen those risks even when we are young?

_____

_____

IX. Keep a Healthy Nervous System

There are many things we can do to keep our nervous system healthy and functioning well.

A. Diet — Diet is a key component for a healthy nervous system. A **healthy diet** can help the way your brain functions. A healthy diet can help fight off diseases and help you continue to think well your whole life. Potassium and calcium are particularly important minerals for brain health. Also important are omega-3 fatty acids and vitamin E. Some of the best foods to add to your diet for brain health are blueberries, whole grain bread and cereal, nuts and fish. It is important to eat a diet rich in all vitamins and minerals.

B. Consistent Exercise — Consistent exercise is vital for a healthy nervous system. Good exercise keeps the brain well-oxygenated as you take deeper breaths. Exercise also helps maintain the body's flexibility, which is important because it can help prevent nerves from being pinched. Stretching is an important part of an exercise routine for this reason.

C. Avoid Injury to Spinal Cord — Another important aspect of nervous system health is to avoid injury. Protect your back and spinal cord by not lifting things that are too heavy. Always have an adult make sure you are lifting properly, with the proper support to protect your spinal cord and nerves.

D. Avoid Injury to Head — Avoid activities that are likely to result in blows to the head. The field of sports medicine is studying very carefully the dangerous effects of concussions. It is best not to get concussions in the first place. For this reason, you should always wear a helmet when riding a bike or skateboard, or doing any other activity in which your head may get injured. You should also wear a seat belt when riding in a car. This will limit blows to the head or violent shaking of your head from a crash or sudden stop, both of which are dangers to the nervous system.

E. Keep Brain Stimulated — Keep your brain stimulated. Learn new things, read, do crossword puzzles. Like any part of your body, the more you properly use your brain, the healthier it will be. Many doctors believe these activities are essential to allowing neurons to continue to make connections, and to fight diseases.

F. Daily Prayer — Prayer is about your relationship with God, which is far more important even than brain health. Pray every day, and often during the day. Our physical and spiritual health go hand-in-hand. Learn more about your patron saint or choose a saint whom you might like to ask to pray for you and help you in your studies and good health.

Review Questions

1. What are some foods important to brain health?

_____

_____

2. How does exercise promote a healthy nervous system?

_____

_____

3. What can you do to help protect your nervous system from injury?

_____

_____

4. What are some ways to continually stimulate the brain throughout life?

_____

_____

Our physical and spiritual health go hand-in-hand.
Credit: UPPER LEFT: public domain; UPPER RIGHT: public domain;
LOWER LEFT: shutterstock.com; LOWER RIGHT: Issagm

Chapter Review Activity

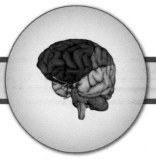

SECTION A

Use the words and phrases in the word box to complete the sentences:

axon	brain	dendrites	hemispheres
meningitis	neurons	spinal cord	
stroke	tumor	medulla oblongata	

1. The central nervous system is primarily made up of the _____ and the spinal cord.

2. The _____ _____ is a thick bundle of nerves that runs from the brain, down the spinal column.

3. Nerves are bundles of special cells called _____, which transmit information through electrical or chemical signals.

4. _____ receive information and transmit it to the neuron's body.

5. The _____ transmits information away from the neuron to be passed to another neuron over a synapse.

6. The cerebrum is divided into two halves called _____.

7. Breathing, blood circulation, digestion, and other vital involuntary functions are regulated by the _____ _____.

8. A _____ is an abnormal tissue growth in the brain.

9. A _____ occurs when blood flow to part of the brain stops.

10. _____ occurs when the tissue surrounding the brain and spinal cord becomes inflamed.

Chapter Review Activity

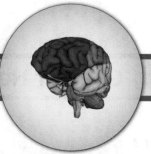

SECTION B

Fill in the table below with the parts of the brain indicated in the box below.

brain stem	cerebellum	cerebrum	cerebral cortex
hypothalamus	pituitary gland	frontal lobe	occipital lobe
parietal lobe	temporal lobe		

PART OF THE BRAIN

DESCRIPTION

11. _____   Location of the medulla oblongata

12. _____   Largest part of the brain

13. _____   Regulates memory, hearing, and language

14. _____   Responsible for judgment, decision-making, movement, and mood

15. _____   Outer layer of the cerebrum

16. _____   Responsible for processing visual information

17. _____   Regulates the body's temperature

18. _____   Responsible for balance and muscle coordination

19. _____   Controls sensory reception and body position

20. _____   Regulates the body's hormones

Chapter Review Activity

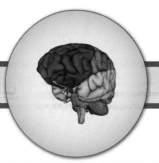

SECTION C

Write the letter of the correct answer on the line.

21. How many cranial nerves are there? _____
    A. Two
    B. Four
    C. Twelve
    D. Billions

22. At what point do people have all the nerve cells they will ever acquire? _____
    A. Birth
    B. Puberty
    C. Adulthood
    D. Death

23. What is the system of nerves that run from the central nervous system to the rest of the body called? _____
    A. The spinal cord
    B. The peripheral nervous system
    C. The somatic nervous system
    D. The reflexive nervous system

24. Who is the patron saint of nervous system disease and mental disorders? _____
    A. St. John Paul II
    B. St. Barbara
    C. St. Dymphna
    D. St. John XXIII

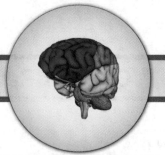

SECTION D

Complete the following exercise using the lines provided.

25. What are the different functions of sensory nerves, motor nerves, and autonomic nerves?

_____

_____

Skin and Hair

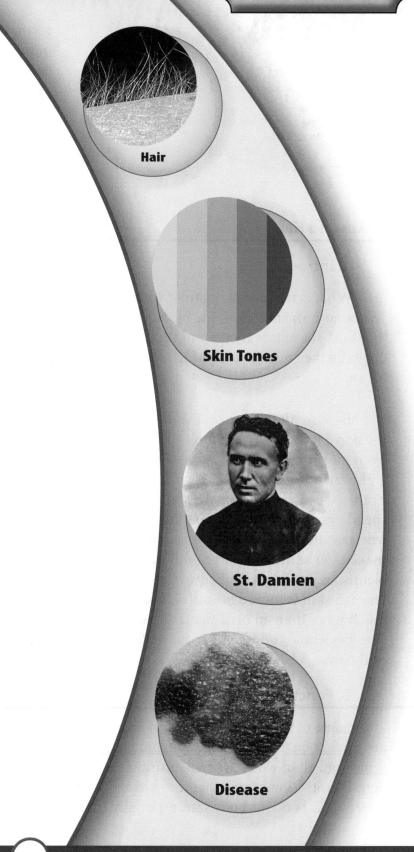

Hair

Skin Tones

St. Damien

Disease

Image credits (from top): EverJean, public domain, public domain, public domain

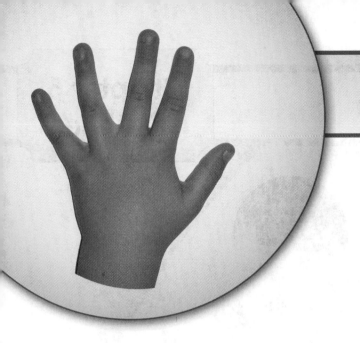

Skin and Hair

I. Skin and Hair

A. Introduction

What is the largest organ of your body? The bones? The muscles? The blood? Nope, it is the skin! The external organ of the skin covers virtually the entire body, and is your largest organ.

Because the skin is on the outside of the body, it is the part we look at every day, from morning to night. We cover our skin with warm clothes when it is cold, with pretty clothes when we go to a party. Some people spend lots of time beautifying their skin, whether they are trying to get rid of wrinkles, make their skin soft and smooth, remove blemishes, try to get a tan, grow a beard. Human skin is indeed beautiful, but skin is much more than an ornament! The skin has many essential functions for our health and well-being.

B. Functions of the Skin

Some of the main functions of skin are protection, temperature regulation, and sensation, all of which we will examine in detail. Protection means that the skin keeps the internal parts of our body safe, especially from germs and infection. Temperature regulation means that the skin can perform functions to both warm us up and cool us down so that we maintain a healthy body temperature. Sensation means that it is through our skin that we often feel pain, temperature, and pressure.

C. Covered with Hair

The skin is covered with hairs. When we are young, we don't notice them as much, but our skin is covered with very tiny hairs. Often when we think of hair, we think only of the hair on our heads. But there is hair all over our bodies. Take a closer look! Like skin, hair is not only ornamental. Hair contributes to warmth and even protection. For example, eyelashes and eyebrows are hairs that protect the eyes from dirt and other foreign substances. The little hairs in the nose even help filter the air we breathe before it reaches our lungs.

D. Skin Diseases

There are at least 50 skin diseases and maybe more. The sad thing about skin diseases is twofold: first, they often can be prevented with just a little care; and second, skin diseases can be a serious problem which leads to people being ashamed or embarrassed to be seen. People with skin diseases often stay away from other people, and sometimes won't go out or go to the store or church. Some people stay away from people with obvious skin diseases. Sadly, skin diseases often cause people to have mental problems, so skin diseases can be more serious than many people understand.

Top image credit: public domain

88

E. Jesus and Skin Diseases

Jesus gave a great example of compassion by welcoming people with skin diseases. He showed His love and concern for people with diseases whom other people shunned and avoided. In fact, people with certain diseases were forced to live in caves and were not allowed to walk in towns. The townspeople were afraid they would catch their skin diseases.

One of the skin conditions we read about in the Bible is leprosy. **Leprosy**, also called Hansen's Disease, is an infection that causes terrible sores on the skin. It can lead to permanent damage and deformation of fingers and hands. In the time when Jesus lived, there was no cure for leprosy, and those afflicted with the disease were required to live separately from everyone else, often being forced to leave their family.

Christ Cleansing the Leper
Credit: Jean-Marie Melchior Doze

F. Father Damien

One person who took the example of Jesus to heart was Father Damien. Damien was a Belgian priest who went to what is now known as Hawaii as a missionary. When sick people were dying in a leper colony on the Hawaiian island of Molokai, in 1873, Father Damien volunteered to live among them and take care of them. He knew he would probably catch the disease and be there for the rest of his life.

Saint Damien of Molokai
Credit: public domain

Father Damien spent his life trying to help the physical and spiritual needs of the lepers. Father Damien gave loving care to the sick people of Molokai for 15 years. Eventually, he himself was stricken with leprosy. Father Damien died in 1889, and was canonized (that is, declared a saint) by Pope Benedict XVI on October 11, 2009. St. Damien is the patron saint of people with skin diseases.

Review Questions

1. Name and describe three primary functions of skin.

_____

_____

_____

_____

_____

2. What is one important function of hair?

_____

3. Who is St. Damien of Molokai?

_____

_____

II. Layers of Skin

Let's learn more about the skin. Did you know that your skin contains three layers? The three layers are called the epidermis, the dermis, and the subcutaneous (sub-cue-TANE-ee-us), which means "under the skin" tissue, also known as the hypodermis.

People who became doctors long, long ago used words in their language which doctors continue to use to this day. The word "dermis" came from the Latin language, which was based on the Greek language. Doctors were studying skin diseases a long time ago, even before Jesus was born in Bethlehem!

A. The Epidermis

The outer layer of the skin is called the **epidermis**. The epidermis is the layer of the skin that people see. The thickness of the epidermis varies in different parts of the body. It is thinnest at the eyelids and thickest on the palms of the hands and bottom of the feet.

The epidermis performs many important functions. First, the epidermis is a barrier like a solid fence. The epidermis is the first layer of protection to keep germs out of the body. The epidermis also contains specialized cells called Langerhans' cells, which are part of the immune system and which fight infection and disease. Paul Langerhans was a scientist who discovered these special skin cells in 1869 while he was studying for his doctorate in Berlin, Germany.

The epidermis also gives the skin its color. The epidermis contains cells called melanocytes, which produce melanin, the pigment responsible for skin color.

The epidermis also makes new skin cells. The epidermis can be divided into five layers called **strata**. New skin cells are formed at the lowest layer and are pushed up to higher layers. The top cells eventually flatten and die. The top layer of the epidermis is made of flat, dead skin cells, which shed periodically.

B. The Dermis

Beneath the epidermis is the layer of skin called the **dermis.** The thickness of the dermis changes throughout the body. Like the epidermis, it is thinnest on the eyelids, but it is thickest on the back of the body.

The dermis performs many essential functions. The dermis contains sweat and oil glands. Sweat comes from glands in the dermis, then comes out through little holes called **pores** in the skin. Sweat helps keep people cool and is one of the most important ways the skin regulates the whole body temperature. Oil from glands in the dermis helps keep skin soft, smooth, and waterproof.

The dermis is also the part of the skin that contains nerve endings that allow us to feel sensations, such as pressure, temperature, and pain. The dermis contains blood vessels that provide oxygen for the skin. The dermis also contains hair follicles with the root of each of the hairs on the body.

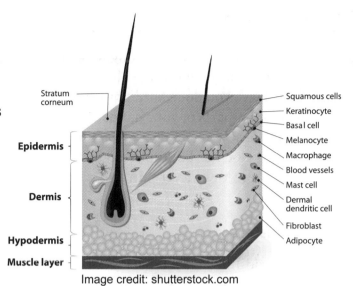

Image credit: shutterstock.com

C. The Hypodermis

Below the dermis is a layer often referred to as the **hypodermis.** This layer is made up primarily of fat and connective tissue. The hypodermis connects the skin to the muscles and bones of the body. The fat in the hypodermis, comprising about 50% of a person's body fat, serves as insulation to help regulate the body's temperature. The fat in the hypodermis serves also as padding to protect the body structures underneath.

Review Questions

1. Name two functions of the epidermis.

_____

_____

2. Which layer of the skin contains nerve endings and hair follicles?

_____

_____

3. Why is sweat important?

_____

4. What are two important functions of the fat of the hypodermis?

_____

_____

III. Skin Changes

Have you ever gone on a long hike and then found a painful, fluid-filled bump on your foot? Have you done hard physical labor and then found parts of your hands rough and hardened? These skin changes are actually helpful tools God has built into our skin to help protect the lower level skin and parts of the body.

A. Blister

The <u>fluid-filled bump</u> that can develop on the skin is called a **blister**. The type of blister on the foot from a long hike is called a friction blister. A friction blister occurs when fluid builds up between the epidermis and the lower layers of skin. It is caused by prolonged friction, or rubbing, such as that caused by shoes against an area of skin.

The fluid built up in the blister actually acts like a cushion <u>to protect the tissue underneath it from damage</u>. Blisters can be caused also by exposure to chemicals or extreme temperatures. A blood blister is caused when a blood vessel close to the skin breaks, due to a pinch or some other injury. In this case, the blister is filled with blood.

For a friction blister to heal, the affected area must be given time without the rubbing that caused the blister. A blister, especially if it has ruptured (broken open), should be kept clean and protected from germs to prevent infection.

B. Callus

A **callus** is <u>a thickened area of skin</u> that usually forms on the hands or bottom of the feet. A callus is caused by repeated friction or pressure. It is a protective skin change. The callus protects the skin and other structures beneath it.

People who repeatedly do hard physical work with their hands develop calluses. Sometimes musicians who repeatedly finger the strings of instruments develop calluses which protect their fingers. Often athletes such as gymnasts develop calluses. People who rarely wear shoes or people with structural problems in their feet also tend to develop calluses on their feet.

Poorly fitting shoes can cause thickened skin to develop on the top or side of a toe. This particular "blister" is called a **corn**. To prevent corns and calluses, people should wear properly fitting shoes and work gloves when doing work with their hands which causes constant pressure or repeated wear.

C. Wrinkles

Blisters and calluses are not the only changes the skin experiences. As they age, people develop **wrinkles** or <u>creases in the skin</u>. This is because, after time, skin begins to get thinner and lose elasticity. Older skin does not hold moisture as well, causing it to dry out more easily. All of these things cause wrinkles to form.

Other factors affect skin wrinkling, such as damage from too much <u>exposure to the sun</u>, repeated facial expressions like squinting, and smoking. All of these things increase wrinkling of the skin. A diet which includes fruits and vegetables is one way to help slow or prevent wrinkling. The antioxidants in fruits and vegetables help protect the skin from damage.

D. Sunburn

Many people have experienced a sunburn. A sunburn usually results in reddened, sensitive skin, and is caused by being out in the sun too long. The ultraviolet rays from the sun burn the skin. People don't realize the dangers of sunburn.

Although sunburns are common, they cause skin changes that should be avoided. The sun's ultraviolet rays not only burn the skin, but can even penetrate the skin and damage the cells underneath the skin. Too much exposure to sunlight has been linked to dangerous diseases, such as skin cancer. There are many different treatments for sunburns depending on their severity, and many products are available that promise to help protect the skin from the sun, but the best thing to do is to limit your exposure to the sun.

The sun, of course, is a great gift from God, whose energy provides for life on our planet Earth. Sunlight also provides vitamin D for good health. It is important, however, to be prudent and not let the sun become a source of danger to our skin and ultimately endanger our health.

Review Questions

1. Name three things that can cause blisters.

2. How is a callus a protective skin change?

3. What causes people's skin to wrinkle as they age?

4. Why can sunburns be dangerous?

IV. Hair Structure and Function

A. Gospel Passages

"Even the hairs of your head are all counted" (Mt. 10:30). In this passage from Matthew's Gospel, Jesus tells us that God knows us so well, He even knows each of the hairs on our head! We have approximately 100,000 hairs on our head. At least, most

young people do! They are all known by God, as St. Matthew writes, because God knows every single little thing about us. After all, He made each one of us, He planned for each one of us to exist, and He cares so much about us that His love cannot be expressed in human language!

Another Gospel writer, St. Luke, recounts to us in the seventh chapter of his Gospel how a sinful woman, after bathing Jesus' feet with her tears, dries them with her long beautiful hair. This was her way of showing repentance for her sins.

St. Mary Magdalen Bathing the Feet of Christ
Credit: Artus Wolffort

When we think of the marvels of God's creation, we may be tempted not to give much consideration to our hair, but as you will see, even our hair has been created with a purpose to keep us healthy.

B. Hair Parts

1. Follicles — Hairs are formed in tiny sacs or **follicles** (FALL-ih-kuls) in the layer of skin called the dermis. The follicle houses the very tiny bulb-like root of the hair, while the shaft comes out of the skin. It is the shaft of the hair that we see.

2. Sebaceous Glands — The hair follicle is surrounded by glands called **sebaceous** (se-BAY-shus) **glands**. These sebaceous glands secrete oil that protects the hair. Too much oil production causes a person to have oily hair, while too little results in dry hair.

3. Shaft of Hair — The shaft of the hair is made up of three layers. The **medulla** is the innermost layer. It is found only in thick hairs like those on the head, not on the skin. The medulla provides elasticity to the hair. This allows the hair to stretch a little and return to its normal state.

The middle layer, the **cortex**, gives the hair its strength, texture, and color. The third layer of the hair shaft is a thin protective layer called the **cuticle**.

The **natural curl** in a person's hair is determined by the shape of the cross-section of the hair shaft. For example, if the hair shaft is more circular, hair tends to be straight. A more elliptical hair shaft shape produces curly hair. Straight hair tends to be shiny because the oil produced by the sebaceous glands can travel down the hair more easily and quickly.

HAIR ANATOMY

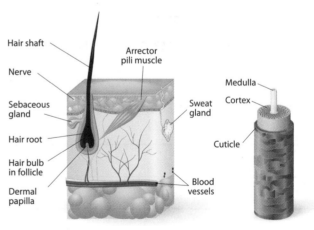

Think back to the last time you had a haircut. It didn't hurt, did it? As long as the shaft of the hair was being cut, you didn't feel pain. That is because the shaft of the hair is made of a non-living protein called **keratin**.

When someone pulls your hair, however, and the follicle in your skin, the dermis, is being disturbed, you are likely to feel pain. Ouch! This is because the **sensory nerve endings** are located in the dermis.

C. Functions of the Hair

1. Beauty — One of the functions of hair is aesthetics. This is a fancy word meaning **beauty**. It is a legitimate function of our hair that we fashion it in a way to make ourselves look nice. Human beings are the most beautiful of God's material creation; we cannot count angels, who are very beautiful, but angels are immaterial! It is appropriate to glorify God through helping ourselves look clean, neat, healthy, and beautiful. This, of course, must always be done with modesty and respect for the body God gave us.

2. Regulate Body Temperature — Hair also helps **regulate body temperature**. Of course, we use many means for protecting ourselves from extreme temperatures, including how we dress, but hair can help keep people from losing body heat through their heads, as well as protect the body from the strong rays of the sun.

3. Protecting the Eyes from Dust Hair can protect people from more than just the sun. The hairs around the eyes, such as the eyelashes and eyebrows, are vital in **protecting the eyes from dust**. The little hairs in the nostrils and the ears also help to keep unwanted dust or even flying bugs out of those areas.

Hair on the skin also has a **sensory function**. Hairs are connected to touch receptors in the skin, and help enhance our sense of touch. A current report on the Internet by Dr. David Ginty, a professor at Johns Hopkins, reports that the nerves in the skin which underlie the hairs send a message to

different parts of the brain, so that a person can "tell the difference between a raindrop, a light breeze, or a poke of a stick." The doctor said that there are more than 20 classes of nerve cells which receive a message from the tiny hairs on our skin!

4. "Goose bumps" with Hair on the skin: Have you ever thought about the "goose bumps" you get on your skin? Goose bumps refer to the tiny bumps that form on the skin, usually accompanied with the hair "standing on end," due to cold temperatures or intense emotion. Cold temperatures cause the tiny muscles around hair follicles to contract, causing the bunching of the skin (goose bumps), and the hair to stand on end. This reaction of "goose bumps" helps reduce heat loss. Goose bumps are obviously provided by God as an instant protection when we are in danger from the cold. Goose bumps can appear also in times of intense emotion as a protection to maintain the inner temperature of the body even in times of stress.

God provides goose bumps as an instant protection when we are in danger from the cold.
Credit: Everjean

Review Questions

1. What is the name for the sacs in the dermis where hair is formed?

_____

2. Name and describe the layers of a hair's shaft.

_____

_____

_____

_____

3. How does hair help regulate body temperature?

_____

_____

4. How does hair serve a protective function?

_____

5. Name one other function of hair.

_____

_____

V. Types of Hair

Usually, when we speak about someone's hair, we are talking about the hair on the top of the head. Perhaps sometimes we are talking about a man's facial hair, such as a beard. It is obvious we have different types of hair on our bodies. Medical people have classified hair as terminal, vellus, or lanugo hair.

A. Terminal Hair — What we normally think of as hair is **terminal hair**. This is the type of hair that people have on the tops of their heads, or men have on their faces. It is also the type of hair we grow more of in our teen years, in the arm pits, for example. It is also found on the arms, legs, chest, and back.

The amount of terminal hair a person develops varies among individuals, especially between men and women.

Terminal body hair also can be called androgenic (ann-dro-GEN-ik) hair, referring to the hormones responsible for its growth. Throughout most of the body, men generally develop more androgenic hair than women do. This is due to the different hormone production in men's and women's bodies.

B. Vellus Hair — Aside from terminal hair, people also have **vellus hair**. You may have noticed that children have a thin layer of body hair sometimes referred to as "peach fuzz." This hair is much thinner than terminal hair and is usually short and very light-colored. Unlike terminal hair, vellus hair is not connected to oil-producing sebaceous glands. Most of the vellus hair will be replaced with terminal hair as a child grows. However, people do retain some vellus hair. Women generally retain more vellus hair than men do.

C. Lanugo Hair — The other type of hair found on humans is **lanugo hair**. This hair is usually found only on unborn babies in the womb and newborn babies. Most of it is replaced by vellus hair shortly before or after birth. Lanugo hair helps keep the baby warm. You would think the doctors could just call it baby hair!

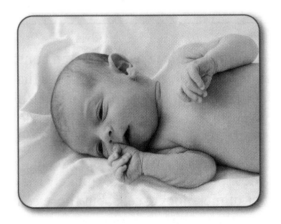

Look at the lanugo hair
on this beautiful newborn baby boy.
Credit: Evan-Amos of Vanamo Media

Surprisingly, an unborn baby will have all the hair follicles he or she will ever acquire by the 22nd week of life, in other words, about four months before the baby is even born! This amounts to approximately five million hair follicles! Amazingly, no new follicles will be added throughout the person's life. Many a teen girl or adult woman or balding man must wonder whatever happened to those hair follicles they had as a child!

D. Baldness — Why do some people, especially men, go **bald**? As they age, many men will begin to lose the hair on their heads. There are many causes, and this is an area that is always being researched. However, one major culprit for natural baldness seems to be a substance called dihydrotestosterone or DHT. **DHT** can cause hair follicles to die.

A certain enzyme, a chemical protein, can convert the hormone testosterone into DHT in men's bodies. The amount of this enzyme a man has in his body is genetic, or inherited, which is why baldness often occurs in families. The doctor who can cure baldness will be an instant millionaire!

Poor nutrition or disease, as well as extreme stress, can lead to loss of hair. Children usually have their hair grow back when they have lost it due to sickness.

Review Questions

1. Name some differences between terminal hair and vellus hair.

_____

_____

_____

_____

_____

2. What causes men to have more androgenic hair than women?

_____

_____

3. What is lanugo hair?

_____

4. At what age do people acquire all the hair follicles they will ever have?

_____

_____

5. What are some causes of baldness?

_____

_____

VI. Skin Pigmentation and Hair Color

A. Introduction

Each person is unique and unrepeatable, and this includes physical appearance. This is part of the beauty of God's creation! Some people are unhappy with their own appearance, but everyone is beautiful in different ways. It is best not to compare ourselves with other people because that can lead to vanity or jealousy, and does not make sense. God has His own special ideas for each one of us. We should thank God for making us the way He did.

B. Skin and Hair Color

Skin and hair color vary widely among different people. Although everyone has the same basic hair and skin structures, these structures can produce wide differences in the pigmentation, or color, of hair and skin.

The **epidermis layer** of the skin contains **melanocytes** (muh-LAN-o-sites), cells that produce a pigment called **melanin** (MEL-ah-nin). Melanin is the substance responsible for color for the skin, hair, and eyes.

Most people have approximately the same number of melanocyte cells, but those cells do not make the same amount of melanin in every person. The more melanin made by the body's cells, the darker the skin will be. The amount of melanin made in a person's body is primarily genetic, that is, it is determined by inheritance from parents.

C. Wrinkles and Freckles

The darker skin produced by melanin provides greater protection from the sun. To provide protection from the sun's rays, a person's skin naturally tans when it is out in the sun for long periods. However, by the time the skin tans, it has already suffered slight damage from the sun. People with darker skin have more protection from the sun, and tend to have fewer skin problems, fewer wrinkles, and fewer instances of skin cancer. Darker skin is no guarantee, however. All of us should be careful to protect ourselves from skin cancer risks.

Freckles, brownish spots on the skin, are also the result of melanin production. Freckles occur in small, concentrated areas of high melanin production. Freckles can be and often are inherited from parents. In some cases, freckles are inherited from a grandparent! Red hair and freckles come from the same gene, so you often see them both together. Surprisingly, it is not unusual for freckles to fade if the person spends less time in the sun!

D. Hair Color

Melanin is also responsible for hair color. You may remember when you studied blood that there are different blood types. These blood types are determined by the antigens that are found in the blood. Differences in hair color can be thought of in somewhat the same way.

There are two types of melanin pigments produced in hair follicles: eumelanin (you-MEL-uh-nin) and pheomelanin (fee-oh-MEL-uh-nin). Eumelanin pigment is dominant in darker hair, such as black or brown hair. Pheomelanin pigment is dominant in red hair. Blond hair generally results when there are low levels of both eumelanin and pheomelanin. The different concentrations of these two pigments account for all the different shades of hair color.

As we get older, the <u>pigment cells in our hair follicles gradually die</u>. When there are fewer pigment cells in a hair follicle, that strand of hair will no longer contain as much melanin and will become a more transparent color — like gray, silver, or white — as it grows.

As people continue to get older, fewer pigment cells will be around to produce melanin. Eventually, some people's hair follicles stop producing melanin altogether, and their hair becomes completely gray or white. However, some people begin to have gray hair early, even in their twenties, some even in high school or college. Hair turning gray because of a decrease in melanin, at whatever age, is basically an inherited trait, usually going back to parents and to grandparents.

Review Questions

1. What pigment is responsible for both skin and hair color?

_____

2. Which cells in the skin produce melanin?

_____

3. What accounts for the different hair colors people have?

_____

_____

_____

JMJ

VII. Skin Diseases and Hair Problems

Like other parts of the body, the skin and hair can get diseased or injured. There are many ways the skin can be injured or affected by disease. The following are just a sample.

A. Skin Injuries and Diseases

1. Cuts — Probably the most common skin injury is a **cut**. When the skin is cut, **platelets** in the blood immediately begin forming a clot to prevent too much blood from being lost. This clot is what you call a scab, although it may take a day or two before your cut has a noticeable scab.

2. Larger Wounds have a more complicated healing process. Wounds need to be kept moist in order to provide an appropriate environment in which new skin cells can grow. Keeping a wound clean, keeping it covered, and ensuring good nutrition are the best ways to heal any wounds.

3. Diabetes or Poor Circulation — Conditions like **diabetes or poor circulation** can slow down proper wound healing. Infected, chronic (repeated), or frequent wounds, or non-healing wounds, may require more complicated wound care by a healthcare professional, such as a doctor or nurse.

4. Skin Cancer — Probably the most serious skin disease is **skin cancer**. There are different types of skin cancer, the most dangerous being **melanoma** (mel-uh-NOH-muh). Though it is not as common as other types of skin cancer, melanoma is the most common cause of death from skin disease. It is caused when the melanocytes, the cells that produce melanin, are affected. Sometimes melanoma produces visual abnormalities on the skin, such as a mole that changes its appearance.

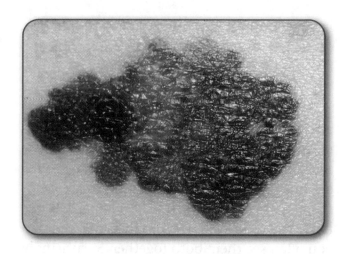

One of the most serious skin diseases is skin cancer.
Credit: public domain

5. Eczema, or Dermatitis — Some people experience **eczema**, or **dermatitis**. These terms are used to express similar conditions: dry or itchy skin, or skin with a rash. Eczema is more common in infants than in adults. The exact cause of eczema is unclear, but many doctors believe it is a body's overreaction to an irritant, something irritating the skin. It is important to find out what is irritating the skin and avoid it, as well as to avoid scratching the rash. Some creams are available to help treat eczema.

6. Psoriasis — Sometimes skin rashes are caused by a disease called **psoriasis** (so-RIE-a-sis). This disease is believed to be genetic, that is, inherited. Psoriasis can range from causing small rashes to large severe rashes. There is no cure for psoriasis, so people with this skin disease must control it with calming medication.

7. Acne — A very common skin condition, especially among teenagers, is **acne**, often referred to as pimples. Acne occurs when hair follicles become plugged with oil or with dead skin cells. Overproduction of oil from the sebaceous glands can be a factor in acne. Hormones play a role in this, and since teens are experiencing new hormones, they often struggle with acne. However, hormones can be the cause of adult acne as well.

8. Contagious Infections — Some diseases cause red spots on the skin. Two examples are **measles** and **chicken pox**. Both measles and chicken pox are <u>contagious infections caused by a virus</u>. They are usually treated at home and are not dangerous for healthy children (although chicken pox is dangerous to adults who have not had it before). Babies, elderly people, those with weakened immune systems, and pregnant women are more at risk for complications resulting from these diseases. Strangely, the chicken pox virus can become active again in elderly people; the virus can cause a painful rash called **shingles** in older people.

There are <u>vaccines for both chicken pox and measles, as well as shingles</u>. Some parents have concerns about the safety of over-vaccinating their children. This is a decision that parents need to make with prayer and good information.

There are also some ethical concerns among some parents about some vaccinations. It is up to parents to keep informed about issues relating to specific vaccinations.

B. Hair Problems

1. Hair Loss — You have already read about hair loss. Children sometimes experience hair loss through a disease. This occurs when the hairs become loose in the hair follicles, probably caused by unhealthy hair roots. With this condition, the hair does not grow much and comes out easily. This condition usually occurs in young children but goes away during the teenage years.

2. Hair Disease or Disorder — Some hair disorders or problem conditions occur when the hair shaft is missing the outer cuticle layer, leaving the cortex underneath vulnerable to damage. These disorders can be genetic or can be caused by excessive manipulation of the hair. In other words, too much brushing, dying, or "perming" can lead to problems. If those behaviors are the cause, treating the hair more gently is an effective treatment.

3. Head Lice — Many children have had experience with **head lice**, and the condition has been growing dramatically in the schools, especially in the elementary grades. Lice are tiny wingless insects that often live on the human scalp and lay eggs among human hair. The lice bite the scalp which can be very itchy for the child. Head lice suck blood, like mosquitoes. Although lice are not dangerous, they are very easily spread to other children. Schools insist that children with lice must stay home, but many often do not stay home, and the lice often becomes an epidemic. Head lice can be treated, however, by using a medicated shampoo that kills the little pests.

Hopefully, you will never experience a blood sucking head louse, like this one!
Credit: Gilles San Martin

Review Questions

1. What is the most dangerous type of skin cancer called?

_____

2. What causes acne?

_____

_____

_____

3. What is the treatment for head lice?

_____

_____

VIII. Keeping Skin Healthy

As you have been learning, your skin is a bodily organ with important functions. It can also be vulnerable to disease. Therefore, maintaining healthy skin is important.

A. Do not Smoke — One extremely important thing to do to maintain healthy skin is to **avoid smoking**. Smoking has numerous dangerous health consequences, and some of them can be deadly. Smoking is a major contributor to unhealthy and blotchy skin.

B. Avoid Too Much Sunshine — Be careful about too much exposure to the sun. Though the sun does provide vitamin D, which is good, too much sunshine can be dangerous to the skin. Too much sunshine or lying in the sun for a tan is a major contributor to the development of skin cancer. Sometimes the skin cancer does not show up for years! It is important to be aware of how much time you are spending in the sun. Find shade and wear enough clothing to protect your skin from the sun.

Sunscreen must be an important part of sun protection. It is worth the time to examine the chemical content of your sunscreen and possibly even seek natural products. The content of the natural products should be checked as well. A doctor or nurse can help find a product that is safe and effective for you.

C. Diet — is a key component to healthy skin. Eat foods like berries, which have antioxidants. Antioxidants provide numerous health benefits, including benefits for the skin. Omega-3 fatty acids are also healthful for the skin. Perhaps most important to maintaining your skin, hair, and body's health is to drink plenty of water to keep your bodily fluids moving.

D. Daily Exercise — As with all bodily systems, daily healthy exercise is a great benefit. Exercise can help lower stress, which is important to maintaining healthy skin.

E. Manage Stress — Another activity to keep healthy and manage stress is prayer. Besides the spiritual benefits, nurturing our relationship with God helps our physical being as well. God has created us as integrated beings, of matter and spirit. Neglecting the spirit affects us as a whole person, including our physical bodies.

F. Care for Skin — It is important to <u>care for skin properly</u>. Be careful not to use harsh skin care products, including strong soaps. After bathing, do not rub hard with a rough towel. And, of course, treat all injuries and skin conditions with care.

G. Proper Grooming — The last thing to remember about the skin is that we must guard against vanity, but it is good to <u>present ourselves in a well-groomed manner</u>. It is also important to dress and behave modestly. Modesty is a virtue that respects our body by presenting it in a respectful and dignified way. It includes dressing appropriately as a Christian.

H. Modesty — <u>Modesty is a virtue that shows respect to God, preserves chastity, and honors the dignity of our God-given bodies</u>. One of the key ways we can respect ourselves and have modesty is by being cautious about how much of our skin we display. Your parents are your best guides in choosing clothing that

presents you in a manner which respects your dignity as a child of God and which honors God and His Blessed Mother. Pope Pius XII was very concerned with modesty in dress, as well as modesty in speech and activities. He taught:

"The good of our soul is more important than the good of our body; and we have to prefer the spiritual welfare of our neighbor to our bodily comforts . . . If a certain kind of dress constitutes a grave and proximate occasion of sin, and endangers the salvation of your soul and others, it is your duty to give it up . . . O Christian mothers, if you know what a future of anxieties and perils, of illguarded shame you prepare for your sons and daughters, imprudently getting them accustomed to live scantily dressed and making them lose their sense of modesty, you would be ashamed of yourselves and you would dread the harm you are making for yourselves, the harm which you are causing to these children, whom Heaven has entrusted to you to be brought up as Christians."

Families should pray for guidance and study the Church's position on this, and all important issues.

Review Questions

1. Name two ways to protect yourself from the sun.

_____

2. How can you manage stress well?

_____

3. What is modesty and why is it important?

_____

_____

_____

Chapter Review Activity

SECTION A

Use the words and phrases in the word box to complete the sentences:

callus	dermis	epidermis	follicle
hair	hypodermis	lanugo	sebaceous
shaft	skin	terminal	vellus

1. The largest organ of the body is the _____.

2. The _____ is the outermost layer of the skin.

3. Each hair is formed in a sac called a _____.

4. The _____ is made up primarily of fat and connective tissue.

5. The type of hair seen on the top of the head is called _____ hair.

6. The type of hair commonly referred to as "peach fuzz" on children is called _____ hair.

7. The type of hair that keeps unborn babies warm is called _____ hair.

8. The part of the hair that comes out of the skin is the _____.

9. A _____ is a thickened area of the skin often found on the hands or bottom of the feet.

10. The _____ is the layer of skin that contains sweat glands.

11. The _____ glands surround hair follicles and secrete oil.

12. In the Gospel, after the sinful woman washed Jesus' feet with her tears, she dried them with her _____.

Chapter Review Activity

SECTION B

Fill in the table below with the three layers of the skin:

LAYER OF SKIN	DESCRIPTION
13. _____	Contains melanin
14. _____	Contains nerve endings, blood vessels, and hair follicles
15. _____	Connects the skin to bone and muscle
16. _____	Serves as insulation for the body
17. _____	Where new skin cells are formed

SECTION C

Fill in the table below with the skin and hair conditions listed in the box:

acne	blisters	chicken pox
lice	melanoma	wrinkles

CONDITION	DESCRIPTION
18. _____	Insect that often lives among human hair
19. _____	Cause of the most deaths from skin disease
20. _____	Contagious disease that causes red spots
21. _____	Can occur when hair follicles get clogged with oil and dead skin cells
22. _____	Occurs when people age; increased by smoking and sun damage
23. _____	Can occur from repeated rubbing of some area of skin

SECTION D

Complete the following exercises using the lines provided.

24. Explain where on the body the epidermis and dermis are the thinnest and thickest.

_____

25. Explain the cause of brown, red, blond, and gray hair.

_____

Digestion & Nutrition

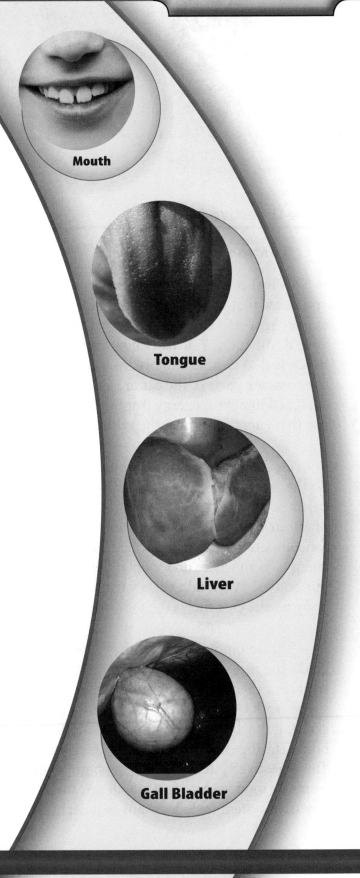

Mouth

Tongue

Liver

Gall Bladder

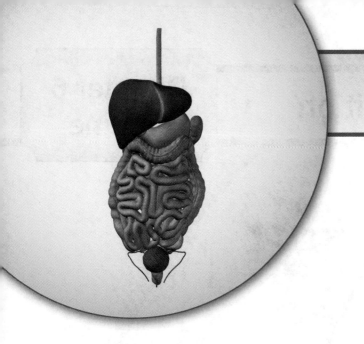

Digestion & Nutrition

I. The Digestive System

A. Introduction

When you travel somewhere in a car, you know that there are many complex parts in the car which work together to get you to your destination. You also know that the car needs fuel to be able to move. In fact, many of the complex parts of the car are specifically designed to obtain energy from the fuel, and to use that energy to power the vehicle.

God has designed the human body to do the same thing. Every function our bodies perform requires <u>energy</u>. From the beating of our hearts to all the movements necessary for competing in sports, our bodies require energy. From where do we obtain energy for our bodies? We obtain energy from the fuel our body needs. <u>Our fuel is the food we eat</u>.

The automobile makers that design and create the fuel systems of cars do impressive work, but their work is nothing compared to the work God has done in designing and creating the digestive system of the human body. The digestive system is our "fuel" system. The **digestive system** <u>helps us to obtain energy from the food</u> we eat. As you will see, the digestive system includes many wonderfully

designed parts, each with specific functions, but they all work together to provide us energy and keep us healthy.

So how does that apple you had for lunch turn into the energy you need in the afternoon to play baseball outside with your friends? In this chapter, you will study all the details of that remarkable digestive process. Put simply, the apple moves through the parts of your digestive tract, where it will undergo numerous physical changes and chemical changes, and ultimately give you the energy and health you need to play an active game of baseball!

B. How It Works

The human body's digestive tract is basically one long tube that begins at the **mouth**. Along with your teeth, certain <u>chemicals</u> in your mouth begin the digestive process of breaking down the food into smaller particles. Food travels from the mouth, down through a tube called the esophagus (eh-SOF-a-gus), down to the stomach. The process of digestion continues the breaking down of food into smaller and smaller parts that can be used by the body for various activities. <u>Digestion continues for some hours</u> in the stomach, which is why sometimes when we jump and play hard right after eating, we might get a stomach ache!

When food becomes small enough to leave the stomach, it travels down through the small intestine, where even more digestion continues from various acids. However, this is also where various <u>nutrients from the food are absorbed into the bloodstream</u>. This process is aided by secretions by different parts of the body, especially the pancreas, the liver, and the gallbladder.

Top image credit: shutterstock.com

From the small intestine, the basically now-liquid food travels to the large intestine, where water and nutrients are absorbed, and waste is compacted so it can exit the body.

C. Thank God

As you learn more of the details of this process over the next few lessons, take some time to thank God for the care He has shown in developing the digestive system. Most of us like to eat, especially pizza and chocolate cake and ice cream, so we should be careful to take care of our bodies so we can enjoy eating and feel well afterward.

You have already learned in the Bible that "the hairs of your head are all counted" (Mt. 10:30). This means that God loves us so much that every little thing about us, even like the hairs on our heads, is of concern to Him. When you learn about the different systems of the human body, remember that they are a testament to our <u>Divine Father in Heaven Who has shown much loving care</u> in every aspect of the creation and health of His children.

D. St. Timothy

The patron saint of digestive problems is St. Timothy. It is believed he had some sort of stomach problem which, back then, doctors did not understand. He was the son of a Greek father and a Jewish mother, who had converted to Christianity as did Timothy.

Timothy became a good friend of St. Paul and accompanied St. Paul on his second missionary journey. Timothy became an important leader in the early Church. He was appointed the first bishop of Ephesus, a city located in modern-day Turkey. It is estimated that Ephesus had 200,000 residents at the time of St. Timothy.

Ephesus was on the coast of the Aegean Sea. Visitors and merchants would come every day to visit and do business in the large city. St. Paul wrote two letters to Timothy to encourage him as he taught the crowds of people in the city. St. Paul's letters to Timothy are now two of the books of the New Testament.

Bishop Timothy eventually, at the age of 80, was stoned to death by a group of evil men. St. Timothy's feast day is January 26.

Review Questions

1. What is the main function of the digestive system?

_____

2. Where does digestion begin?

_____

3. What is the digestive tract?

_____

4. Who is St. Timothy?

_____

_____

_____

II. The Mouth

You may be familiar with the Scripture passage in the seventh chapter of St. Mark's Gospel, in which Jesus says, "Nothing that goes into a person from outside can defile … But what comes out of a person, that is what defiles." In this passage, Jesus was emphasizing that food cannot make one spiritually unclean, but rather sin makes one unclean. Sin, which we commit with our bad thoughts, words, and actions, reveals what is in our minds and hearts. We must be careful to use our mouth to say kind things, to say Thank You, and to say our prayers.

A. Purpose of Digestion

God has designed our digestive system so that food, which is meant to support life and health, can keep us healthy and active. The rather complicated digestive system breaks food down so that all the different parts of the body can benefit from the components of food, and the body can also rid itself of waste, that is, unusable parts of food.

1. Mechanical Breakdown

Digestion actually begins in the mouth. Two types of food breakdown take place in the mouth. The first is mechanical breakdown. **Mechanical breakdown** is the physical breaking down of food into smaller pieces. In the mouth, this is primarily done by the teeth. When the teeth chew food, the food pieces are broken down into smaller chunks that are more easily swallowed and able to be chemically digested.

By breaking food down into many small pieces, the breakdown increases the surface area of the food, allowing digestion to work more effectively. If you don't chew your food well, the digestive process takes longer as the stomach must work harder. People can get a stomach ache if their stomach needs to work too hard because food was not chewed long enough and swallowed too quickly! Have you ever felt kind of sick after eating too fast?

2. Chemical Breakdown

The other type of breakdown that occurs in the mouth is a **chemical breakdown**. Chemical breakdown occurs when substances naturally produced in the mouth called enzymes (EN-zimes) create a chemical change in the food that we chew. Enzymes in the mouth react with the food to break the food down into simpler and smaller chemical substances. Adequate chewing of food is the necessary beginning of a breakdown in the food which is necessary for the nutrients or nutrition in food to be absorbed eventually into the bloodstream.

a. The Mouth

In the mouth, chemical breakdown of food is accomplished by the **saliva**. Saliva glands are located on the inside of the cheeks and on the floor of the mouth. These glands secrete saliva which helps us to swallow the food. However, the saliva contains a chemical called an enzyme. Therefore, besides helping us swallow, the enzyme helps in digestion by chemically breaking down the food in our mouth. Once the food is chewed and broken down chemically, we can swallow it. It is important to chew the food and let the saliva work to allow the stomach to properly digest the food.

b. The Tongue

An important organ of the mouth is the tongue. The tongue helps direct food in the mouth to the teeth so it can be chewed, and then pushed to the back of the mouth so it can be swallowed. The tongue contains a few thousand taste buds. The taste buds are very tiny sensory organs that allow us to taste different kinds of food, such as sweet or salty or sour. Different areas of the tongue contain the different kinds of taste buds.

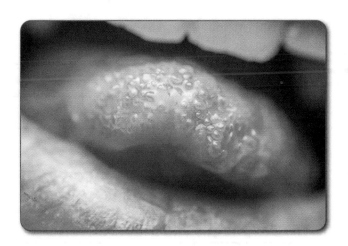

Taste buds help us to eat well, so that we can remain healthy.
Credit: shutterstock.com

The taste buds allow us to enjoy the tastes of food that we like, which makes us happy! It is important, however, that our eating habits not become unhealthy to the point that they undermine or undo the primary purpose of food, which is to maintain good health. This is why moderation in eating is important when it comes to food, and why we must be on guard against temptations to gluttony. **Gluttony** is one of the seven deadly sins, and it refers to misuse of the great gift of food by eating or drinking too much. God intended food and drink to support a healthy life, but gluttony can actually harm life and health.

B. Conclusion

Remember that food has two purposes. The primary purpose is to promote good health. The secondary purpose is to be enjoyable. The goods we experience in this life, such as delicious desserts, are just a very small hint of the unimaginable goods of Heaven. Also, enjoying good meals with family and friends has always been a way that people build relationships. Of course, our relationships will extend beyond this life and into Heaven if we remain united to one another through Christ's Mystical Body.

Review Questions

1. What is mechanical breakdown of food?

_____

_____

2. What substance in the mouth contains an enzyme that causes the chemical breakdown of some food?

_____

3. What is gluttony?

_____

_____

_____

III. The Esophagus and Stomach

A. The Esophagus

You have already learned that food is mechanically broken down in the mouth with chewing. Food is then chemically broken down by enzymes in the saliva. Enzymes are substances which promote chemical reactions, in this case, to break down food in the digestive process. Then the food is swallowed and begins its travel down the **esophagus**, the tube that connects the mouth to the stomach.

The muscles of the esophagus contract in a wave-like motion called peristalsis (pear-uh-STALL-sis) to push the food down and into the stomach. The esophagus is coated in mucus, a thick substance that allows the food to slide down more easily into the stomach.

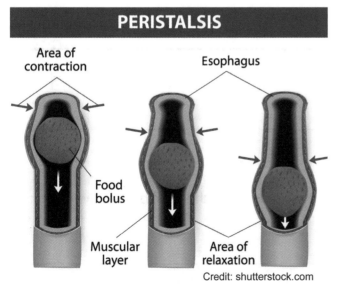

PERISTALSIS

Area of contraction

Esophagus

Food bolus

Muscular layer

Area of relaxation

Credit: shutterstock.com

Do you remember how we can both eat and breathe through the mouth? Food travels down the esophagus to the stomach, while air travels down the trachea to the lungs. There is a flap of tissue called the **epiglottis** that covers the opening of the trachea when we eat, keeping food out and ensuring that food will travel through the esophagus. If food does get stuck in the trachea, we must cough it out. If air gets into the stomach, by swallowing, or through a carbonated beverage, the air is usually released through a burp. Don't forget to say "Excuse me!" if you burp!

B. The Stomach

Both mechanical and chemical digestion of food continues in the stomach. The stomach is like a muscular bag. When food enters the stomach, the stomach muscles contract, thus crushing the food and continuing the process of mechanical breakdown.

1. Chemical Digestion

The stomach is an important organ for chemical digestion of food. The stomach produces a liquid called gastric juice. Gastric juice contains two enzymes, that is, two substances that promote chemical reactions: pepsin and rennin. The gastric juice also contains hydrochloric (hi-dro-KLOR-ik) acid and water.

The enzymes pepsin and rennin, along with the hydrochloric acid, chemically break down **proteins** in the stomach. Hydrochloric acid also kills harmful

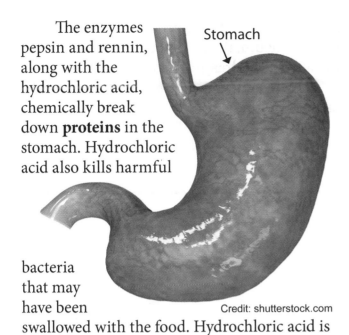

Stomach

Credit: shutterstock.com

bacteria that may have been swallowed with the food. Hydrochloric acid is extremely strong and powerful. To protect the stomach lining from being affected by the acid, the stomach is coated with mucus.

2. Mechanical Digestion

The stomach provides the last step of mechanical breakdown of food. Chemical breakdown is not complete, however. Different enzymes (which protect chemical breakdown) break down different types of foods. Enzymes in saliva break down starches in the food, and enzymes in the stomach break down proteins in the food. However, not all foods are broken down in the stomach. Most notably, fats and

Digestion

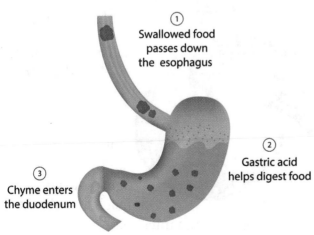

① Swallowed food passes down the esophagus

② Gastric acid helps digest food

③ Chyme enters the duodenum

Credit: shutterstock.com

oils still need to be digested. The next location for the fats and oils type of food is the small intestine.

By the time food is ready to pass from the stomach to the small intestine, the food has been softened and turned into a thick, creamy mixture, called **chyme** (KIME). The chyme moves into the small intestine. Before digestion can be completed and nutrients absorbed into the blood, a few other organs need to get involved.

C. The Heimlich Maneuver

Before we continue, we need to discuss the Heimlich Maneuver. The Heimlich Maneuver is a method which children and adults should know how to use, in case someone is choking because of food that is stuck in the throat. All doctors, nurses, policemen, and emergency persons, as well as some restaurant workers, are taught how to help someone who is choking. It is estimated that four to five thousand Americans a year have a serious choking problem. The Heimlich Maneuver has saved thousands of lives every year.

Learn the directions of the Heimlich Maneuver: Stand behind the person who is choking. Place one hand on top of the pelvis line, in the middle of the abdomen. Put your other hand on top of your first hand. Pull upward, suddenly, forcefully, toward the person's nose, in a series of five quick jerks or thrusts. The purpose is to make the person cough up whatever is obstructing the breathing.

For a small child, place the child face down across your lap. Put one fist below the point where the ribs meet the breastbone. Give a solid whack to the back, between the lower shoulder blades, with your other hand.

All members of the family should practice the Heimlich Maneuver.

Important: Children should be reminded to chew their food well, not to talk with food in their mouths, and be careful to swallow before trying to talk. If people talk with food in their mouth, the food might slip down into the lungs! Children should be encouraged not to talk while sucking on a cough drop or hard piece of candy.

Review Questions

1. What tube connects the mouth to the stomach?

____

2. What important role does the epiglottis play?

____

____

3. How does the stomach continue mechanical digestion?

____

____

4. What foods are chemically digested in the stomach?

____

5. What is chyme?

____

____

IV. The Liver, Gall Bladder, and Pancreas

A. Introduction

You may remember that at His Crucifixion, Our Lord was given gall to drink. but did not take it. This meaning of the word "gall" is simply a bitter substance, most likely made from herbs. However, the type of gall that is produced by the human body for digestion is different. The gall in the human body plays an important role in digestion. A more common name for gall is bile. **Bile** is a fluid produced by the liver that aids in the digestion of fats and oils.

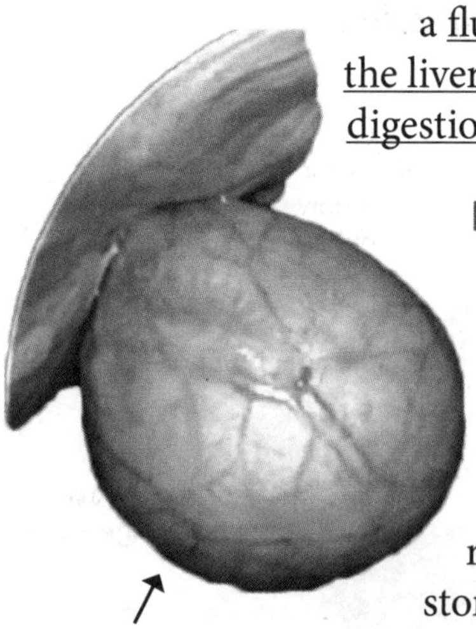

Gall bladder

Credit: public domain

B. The Liver and Gall Bladder

The **liver** is the largest of the internal organs and sits to the right side of the stomach and above the intestines. An important function of the liver is to produce the green liquid called bile. Bile is stored in a small sac under the liver called the **gall bladder**. When bile is needed for digestion, it is released from the gall bladder, through a duct, to the small intestine, where it mixes with the chyme that comes from the stomach.

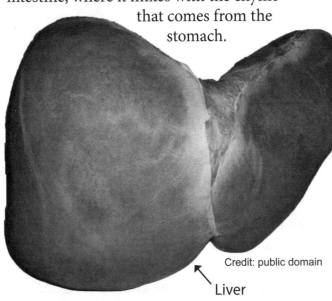

Credit: public domain

Liver

The bile breaks down large droplets of fats and oils and turns them into small droplets through a process called emulsification (ih-MUHL-suh-fuh-KAY-shun). This is important because it makes the fats and oils easier to digest in the small intestine. The bile does not chemically break down the fats and oils; it only separates them into smaller parts so chemical digestion can occur later.

Pancreas

Credit: shutterstock.com

C. The Pancreas

The **pancreas** (PAN-kree-us) plays an important role in digestion at this stage. The pancreas is located between the liver and the small intestine. The pancreas releases pancreatic fluid through a duct into the small intestine. Pancreatic fluid is made up of different enzymes or chemicals that <u>assist with the digestion of multiple types of food, such as fats and proteins</u>, as they enter the small intestine.

The bile and the pancreatic fluid mix with the food at the beginning or entrance of the small intestine, called the **duodenum** (doo-uh-DEE-num).

D. Summary

To sum up the path of the food since it was eaten, it has gone from the mouth, where it was both mechanically and chemically broken down; through the esophagus to the stomach, where it was both mechanically and chemically broken down even more, and turned into chyme; then the chyme flowed to the beginning of the small intestine (the duodenum). In the small intestine, the food encountered bile, which broke larger fat and oil droplets into smaller ones through a process called emulsification. In the small intestine, the food also encountered pancreatic fluid, which contained enzymes to help with chemical digestion.

Thus far, while the food has been broken down both mechanically and chemically, the body still has not received any nutritional benefit from the food. You will study how that happens in the next lesson.

Review Questions

1. How do the gall bladder and liver work together to aid in the digestion of oils and fats?

_____

2. What role does the pancreas play in digestion?

_____

_____

3. What is the duodenum?

_____

_____

V. The Intestines

A. Introduction

By this time, you may be feeling like you are on an interesting journey, exploring an unknown frontier. You've "traveled" through many different parts of the digestive tract. Since the digestive tract is one continuous path, it is easy to trace the food you eat all the way through. Now you are at the small intestine. Here, the different components of the food will begin to take different journeys.

B. Small Intestine

Recall that at the end of the last lesson, we had reached the duodenum, the beginning of the small intestine, where the food interacts with bile from the liver and interacts with enzymes from the pancreas. Now the food will begin a winding trip through a thin muscular tube, which is the small intestine. This muscular tube, located in the abdomen, is about 23 feet in length on average! The length can vary significantly between individuals.

The small intestine contains many enzymes or chemicals that complete the chemical digestion of food. One of these enzymes is **lipase** (LIE-pase), which breaks down the fats and oils that were prepared for digestion by the bile.

Besides finishing the chemical breakdown of food, the small intestine moves nutrients from the food to the bloodstream. Nutrients from food pass through the "wall" of the small intestine and enter into the bloodstream

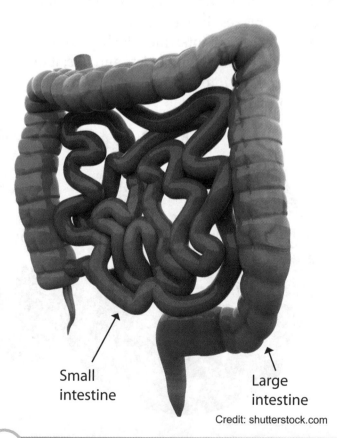

Small intestine

Large intestine

Credit: shutterstock.com

through tiny, finger-like projections called **villi** (VILL-eye). This is the whole purpose of eating, to provide nutrients or nutrition into the body through the bloodstream.

Millions of very tiny villi projections line the walls of the small intestine. The villi contain capillaries and tiny lymph vessels. The villi absorb nutrients from the food, finally <u>transferring the nutrients from the small intestine into the bloodstream.</u> The nutrients "feed" the different parts of the body.

C. The Liver

The nutrient-rich blood goes first to the liver. The liver performs other essential functions besides making bile. **First**, the <u>liver processes the nutrient-rich blood</u>. The process of the liver converts sugary carbohydrates into glycogen, an important source of energy. **Second**, the <u>liver also converts certain proteins to new proteins</u> more useful throughout the body. A **third** important function of the liver is that <u>the liver breaks down unwanted chemicals</u> so they can be filtered out and then exit the body as waste through the urinary system.

D. Large Intestine

The villi do not absorb all of the food. Some parts of food remain <u>undigested</u> and become waste. This waste passes into the **large intestine**. Though the large intestine is not as long as the small intestine, its <u>diameter</u> is approximately twice as big as the small intestine. In other words, it is about twice as wide inside. The first part of the large intestine is called the cecum (SEE-come), followed by the colon. The colon makes up most of the large intestine. The colon can be as large as two inches in diameter and five feet long!

As food passes through the large intestine, water is absorbed, thus turning the <u>waste into solid</u> waste. Helpful bacteria in the large intestine feed off some of this waste, producing vitamins that then are absorbed by the large intestine.

The last part of the large intestine is called the rectum. This is where solid wastes are stored until they are ready to be expelled from the body.

Review Questions

1. From which organ do the nutrients from food enter the bloodstream?

_____

_____

2. What are villi?

_____

_____

3. Which organ processes the nutrient-rich blood?

_____

4. What important roles does the large intestine play?

_____

_____

_____

VI. Breathing, Sweating, and the Urinary System

So far you have learned how food is digested and how nutrients from food are absorbed into the bloodstream to provide fuel and nutrition for the body. You have learned that some of the food we eat is not digested and absorbed, but turned into waste. You followed the journey of solid waste through the large intestine to the rectum, from which it can be expelled from the body.

A. Breathing

There are other ways the body gives off waste as well. Breathing, for example, brings more than oxygen into the body. When people exhale, carbon dioxide and other wastes are released. Every time you breathe out, useless things in the air are expelled. Sometimes a cough is necessary to clear waste that has managed to enter the respiratory system, your throat, or your lungs.

B. Sweating

Sweating is another way in which the body gives off waste. Salt is water soluble, which means it dissolves in water. Salt can be absorbed into the bloodstream from the skin; salt does not need to be digested to be absorbed into the bloodstream. Excess salt is given off through sweat.

C. Urinary System

Some other wastes from food pass into the bloodstream but need to be expelled from the body in a different way. Remember that after nutrients from food pass through the wall of the small intestine, and into the blood, the nutrient-rich blood goes to the liver, which breaks down chemical waste. Cells dispose of waste, too, and these cellular wastes get into the blood. The job of purifying the blood of all these wastes belongs to the urinary system. The main organs of the urinary system are the kidneys and the bladder.

1. Kidneys — The **kidneys** are a pair of organs that filter waste out of the blood. Unfiltered blood enters each kidney through an artery. You may recall that an artery is a blood

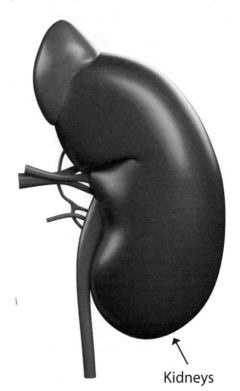

Kidneys

Image credit: shutterstock.com

vessel that carries blood from the heart to the rest of the body. As the blood travels through the kidneys, the blood is filtered by millions of tiny, microscopic structures called nephrons. Tubes in the kidneys collect the waste filtered by the nephrons.

2. Nephrons — The **nephrons** actually filter more than just wastes out of the blood. Materials necessary for the body are filtered by the nephrons, including water and important salts, which are then reabsorbed by the blood. The waste, however, mixed with water, forms the waste product we call urine. Healthy kidneys are very important because they keep toxic or poisonous substances out of the bloodstream. By controlling the amount of water that is reabsorbed by the blood, the kidneys play an essential role in regulating the amount of water in the body.

3. Ureter — The filtered blood leaves each kidney through a vein to circulate again through the body, while the urine leaves each kidney through a tube called a **ureter** (you-REE-ter). The two ureters empty into the bladder.

4. Bladder — The **bladder** is the organ that stores the urine. When enough urine is in the bladder, and the urine is ready to be released, the muscles of the bladder contract, and the urine exits the body through a tube called the **urethra** (you-REE-thruh).

Review Questions

1. What are nephrons?

_____

2. Why are the kidneys so important?

_____

_____

3. What does the bladder do?

_____

4. What is the difference between the ureters and the urethra?

_____

_____

VII. Digestive Diseases and Disorders

Because there are so many different parts that make up the digestive system, there are many diseases or disorders that can affect the digestive system. This lesson will cover only a few of the more common ones.

A. Acid-Reflux Disease

One of the most common disorders of the digestive system is gastroesophageal (GAS-tro- ih-SOF-uh-jee-uhl) reflux disease (GERD). This is often simply called **acid-reflux disease**. Acid-reflux disease is a condition in which the acid from the stomach backs up through the esophagus. This occurs when the muscle at the base of the esophagus, the esophageal sphincter (SFINK-ter), which snaps shut to seal it from the stomach, doesn't close properly. GERD can be dangerous because the stomach acid is unhealthy for the esophagus.

B. Heartburn

A common disorder <u>resulting from acid-reflux disease</u> is "**heartburn**." Heartburn is a painful burning in the esophagus caused by the backed-up acid. GERD can also cause vomiting. Often children with acid-reflux disease will outgrow it. Sometimes this is a chronic condition, however, meaning it keeps occurring again and again. Acid-reflux disease can be treated with medication, but if it continues, usually it needs to be cured with surgery.

C. Irritable Bowel Syndrome

Irritable bowel syndrome is a common condition of the intestines that causes cramps and bloating in the stomach. Although it is not life threatening, irritable bowel syndrome can be quite painful. Treatment can include medication, but often what is really needed is a change in diet and better stress management.

D. Lactose Intolerance and Celiac Disease

Sometimes a person's body has difficulty digesting certain foods. **Lactose intolerance** refers to a difficulty in digesting <u>dairy products</u>. A person with **celiac disease** cannot properly digest <u>gluten</u>, which is found in many foods, including wheat products. People with these conditions must adjust their diets to avoid the foods they cannot digest while still obtaining the necessary nutrients.

E. Diverticulitis

Diverticulitis (DIE-ver-tik-yuh-LIE-tis) is a condition in which <u>pouches form on the</u>

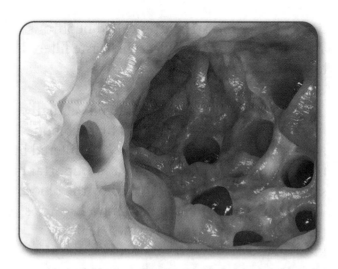

Diverticulitis is a condition in which pouches form on the wall of the large intestine.
Credit: shutterstock.com

<u>wall of the large intestine</u>, and then they get inflamed or infected. It can be very painful. Although the causes of diverticulitis are not fully understood, it is believed that a diet too low in fiber can play a role. Fiber is a complex carbohydrate that can not be digested and turns into solid waste. It plays an important role, however, in the composition of waste by making it easier to pass through the large intestine. Fiber thus helps to keep the large intestine healthy. Doctors use a variety of treatments for diverticulitis.

F. Ulcers

You learned that the stomach lining is protected from the harsh acid in gastric juice by protective mucus. If there is a break in this protective mucus lining, an ulcer may occur. **Ulcers** usually happen in the stomach or the duodenum. In either case, the <u>lining of the organs is not adequately protected from acid</u>, and a burning pain results. Ulcers are usually easy to treat, but can become dangerous, especially if left unattended. Overuse of some pain medications has been linked to the development of ulcers.

G. Hernia

Anytime an internal body part squeezes into an area it doesn't belong, it is called a **hernia**. A person can be born susceptible to a hernia, or it can be caused by intense pressure and low muscle tone, causing the organ to slip where it does not belong. A hiatal hernia occurs when the upper part of the stomach squeezes through an opening in the diaphragm, the muscle just above the stomach.

Sometimes a hernia causes no symptoms and requires no treatment, and sometimes surgery is necded to put an organ back where it belongs.

H. Lifestyle Affects Health

Many digestive problems are related to a person's lifestyle. For example, being overweight or smoking makes someone far more at risk for many physical problems. Excessive drinking of alcoholic beverages can damage the liver and other important organs. Of course, moderating alcohol intake is a moral requirement as well as a health requirement. Drinking too much alcohol has bad consequences for a person's body and mind. It can cause a person to lose balance and hinder the ability to think clearly and make good, intelligent decisions. In fact, the Church has declared it is a mortal sin to deliberately drink alcohol to the point where clear thinking is impossible.

Often, adjustments in diet can help many digestive conditions. A visit to the doctor may help determine specific dietary strategies for relief. For a healthy digestive system, a healthy lifestyle, daily exercise, and nutritious food are vital.

Review Questions

1. What is acid-reflux disease?

2. What are lactose intolerance and celiac disease?

3. What is the difference between a hernia and an ulcer?

VIII. Nutrition

Imagine you are sitting down to Thanksgiving dinner. The table is filled with all sorts of different foods. There is turkey filled with stuffing, cranberries, rolls, peas and carrots, mashed potatoes with gravy, and pumpkin pie in the oven. Before you sit down, you see a feast consisting of carbohydrates (starches, fiber, sugars), protein, fats, vitamins, and minerals. At least some of all that wonderful food is going to make its way through your digestive system. Most of it will be used as fuel for your body. You will take in a wide array of valuable nutrients before the holiday is over.

A. Nutrients

So what exactly are nutrients? **Nutrients** are the materials in food that your body uses for energy, growth, and tissue repair. Nutrients are usually classified into one of six categories: carbohydrates, proteins, fats, vitamins, minerals, and water. Your body uses each of these types of nutrients differently.

B. Carbohydrates

Carbohydrates are a main source of energy. Have you ever been buzzing with energy and had someone ask you how much sugar you've had? The reason is because sugar is a carbohydrate. Since sugar is a simple carbohydrate, it doesn't need to be broken down. Simple carbohydrates can be absorbed quickly into the bloodstream, so they give quick, though often short, bursts of energy. Starches are complex carbohydrates, which need time to be digested, as you have learned. Complex carbohydrates generally provide more sustained, longer-lasting energy.

C. Fiber

Fiber is another type of complex carbohydrate, but fiber cannot be digested. It comes out of the body as waste but, because of its composition, it plays an important role in keeping the colon clean and free of infection.

D. Proteins

Proteins are sources of energy as well. However, the main role of protein is to support growth and tissue repair. This is why athletes are often careful to make sure they get plenty of protein. Protein supports muscle growth.

E. Fats

Fats are the most energy-dense of the nutrients. Fats provide twice as much energy as carbohydrates. A small chocolate bar provides instant energy because it is mostly sugar and fat. Too much sugar and fat, though, is bad for our teeth and can make us sick. Fats that are not immediately used for energy can be stored in the body. Some fats are stored around major organs to provide protection. However, adipose (AD-uh-pohs) tissue, or fat tissue, can be stored in many locations in the body. Storing too much fat can be unhealthy. In our country, many people eat too much, causing extra fat deposits, which leads to obesity, or being overweight. Excess fat can cause health problems.

F. Vitamins

Vitamins are substances that assist important chemical reactions in the body. Different vitamins support different functions, so eating a variety of foods with the proper vitamins is important to good overall health.

G. Minerals

Minerals are important nutrients. Minerals are found in rocks and soil, but we can obtain minerals from certain plants and animals. Vegetables and other plants absorb minerals from the soil, so when we eat vegetables, we also take in those minerals. In a similar way, we obtain minerals when we eat meat from animals that ate mineral-rich plants.

H. Water

It is important to eat a well-balanced diet. Over-emphasizing some nutrients or under-emphasizing others does not promote good health. One nutrient that most people are not getting enough of is water, just plain ordinary water, God's greatest gift for a healthy body.

Drinking water promotes health in many different ways. Most of the body's essential functions require water. <u>Water in the blood carries nutrients</u> to the different parts of the body. In fact, water is a necessary part of most of our bodily fluids. A person can live for many days, sometimes weeks, without food, but would last only a few days without water. Some signs that a person is dehydrated, or not getting enough water, are dry lips and sometimes headaches.

Since water is the substance on Earth most necessary to life, is it a surprise that it is a fundamental part of the Sacrament of Baptism?

A person's soul is washed clean through the waters of Baptism, and he or she is born into a new life in Christ.

It was through the waters of the Red Sea that Moses led the Hebrews out of slavery in Egypt, to freedom in the Promised Land. It is through the waters of Baptism that Christians are led out of slavery in sin, to freedom in Christ. In many ways, it is through water that our physical life is sustained.

Review Questions

1. What are the six categories of nutrients?

_____

_____

2. What is the difference between simple carbohydrates and complex carbohydrates?

_____

_____

_____

_____

3. What is the most energy-dense nutrient?

_____

4. What are vitamins and minerals?

_____

_____

_____

Chapter Review Activity

SECTION A

Use the words and phrases in the word box to complete the sentences:

digestive tract	duodenum	fats	fiber
gluttony	hernia	liver	pancreas
proteins	ulcer		

1. The _____ _____ is the long, continuous tube beginning at the mouth through which food travels.

2. The _____ is the beginning of the small intestine.

3. The _____ processes blood that has just received nutrients from digested food.

4. The _____ secretes digestive enzymes into the duodenum to aid with the digestion of foods such as fats and proteins.

5. _____ are the most energy-dense nutrient.

6. The main role of _____ is to support growth and tissue repair.

7. _____ is a complex carbohydrate that cannot be digested.

8. An _____ occurs when there is a break in the protective lining of the stomach or the duodenum.

9. A _____ occurs when an internal body part squeezes into an area it doesn't belong.

10. _____ is the vice that refers to the misuse of the gift of food by eating or drinking too much.

Chapter Review Activity

SECTION B

Fill in the table with the parts of the digestive system in the word box below:

bladder	esophagus	gall bladder	kidneys
large intestine	liver	mouth	pancreas
small intestine	stomach		

PART OF THE DIGESTIVE SYSTEM

DESCRIPTION

11. _____ — Contains teeth for mechanical breakdown and saliva for chemical breakdown

12. _____ — Tube that connects the mouth to the stomach

13. _____ — Turns food into chyme through both mechanical and chemical digestion

14. _____ — Produces bile

15. _____ — Stores bile until it is released into the duodenum

16. _____ — Releases digestive enzymes into the duodenum

17. _____ — Nutrients from food enter the bloodstream through the walls of this organ

18. _____ — Where undigested food is turned into solid waste

19. _____ — Filter the blood to remove wastes

20. _____ — Stores urine until it exits the body

Chapter Review Activity

SECTION C

Write the letter of the correct answer on the line.

21. What substance in the stomach helps kill harmful bacteria that may have been swallowed? _____
    A. Pancreatic Fluid
    B. Hydrochloric Acid
    C. Bile
    D. All of the above

22. Which is a simple carbohydrate? _____
    A. Starch
    B. Sugar
    C. Fiber
    D. None of the above

23. Which is/are part of the urinary system? _____
    A. Small intestine
    B. Stomach
    C. Kidneys
    D. Gall bladder

SECTION D

Complete the following exercises using the lines provided.

24. Name the six categories of nutrients.

_____

_____

25. What is the difference between mechanical digestion and chemical digestion?

_____

_____

Glands

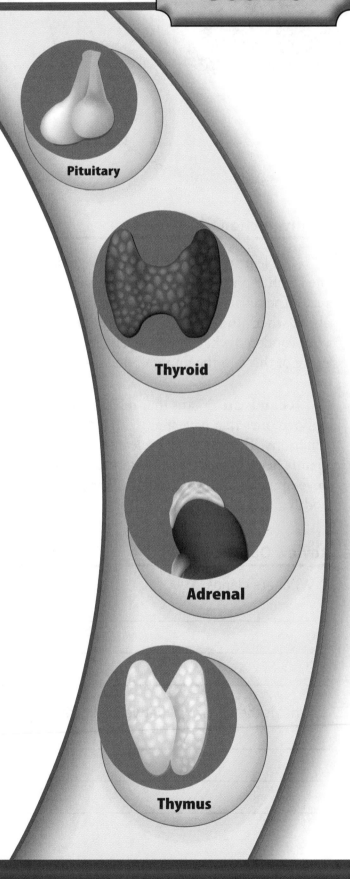

Pituitary

Thyroid

Adrenal

Thymus

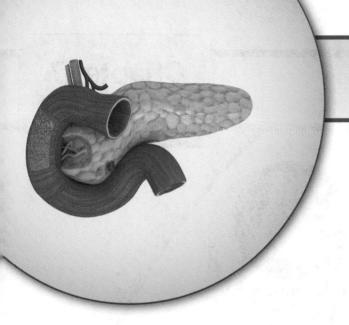

Glands

I. Introduction

We learned about the pituitary gland in the chapter on the nervous system. Perhaps you recall the sebaceous glands, which you read about when studying skin and hair. Perhaps you wondered what glands are, or if there are more of them in the human body.

Glands are organs that release fluids or hormones that have many different functions. The substances released from glands help maintain health, guide growth and development, and work together for proper bodily functioning.

A. Glands: Two Systems: Exocrine & Endocrine

The glands of the human body are divided into two systems: the **exocrine** system and the **endocrine** system. The glands of the <u>exocrine system release fluids</u>, such as sweat and tears, through ducts, or tubes, often outside the body. The glands of the <u>endocrine system</u>, however, <u>release fluids inside the body</u>, directly into the bloodstream.

B. Glands: Tubular Glands & Alveolar Glands

Glands can be <u>classified by their shape</u>. There are two main types of glands according to shape: tubular glands and alveolar (al-VEE-o-ler) glands. **Tubular glands** maintain the shape of a tube. **Alveolar glands** have a sac-like cavity from which fluids are secreted, which is why these glands are also called saccular (SACK-yuh-ler) glands.

Review Questions

1. What are glands?

_____

_____

_____

2. What is the difference between exocrine glands and endocrine glands?

_____

_____

_____

_____

Top image credit: shutterstock.com

3. What are the two main classifications of glands by shape?

_____

_____

II. The Exocrine Glands: 6 Types

The glands of the exocrine system secrete substances through tubes called ducts. Often, these secretions are released outside of the human body. Some of the glands you've already learned about, such as sebaceous glands and sweat glands, are exocrine glands. The exocrine system is not considered a separate bodily system. These glands are simply referred to as the exocrine glands.

A. Sebaceous (Se-BAY-shus) glands are found in the skin, and they produce an oil called sebum. Some teens believe they have too much sebum on their face because their skin feels too oily. Sebum protects the hair located all over the body and forms a water-repellant layer on the skin.

B. Sweat glands, located beneath the skin, release sweat when a person experiences excessive heat. The sweat travels from the gland, through the duct, where it comes out through pores in the skin. This helps maintain the body's temperature and keeps the person from overheating.

C. Lachrymal (LACK-ruh-mal) glands are also part of the exocrine system. Lachrymal glands are located in the eye cavity and are responsible for producing tears. Tears are not merely signs of grief. In fact, there is a constant film of tears covering our eyes. Tears lubricate the eyes and keep them clean and free of germs.

D. Mammary glands are stimulated by a woman's hormones to produce milk after having a baby. This is important for the proper nourishment of a new baby.

E. Salivary (SAL-uh-ver-ee) glands are located in the mouth and throat. These salivary glands produce saliva, which is important for eating. Saliva keeps the mouth moist and helps prevent tooth decay.

F. Pancreas Gland

The **pancreas** (PAN-cree-us) is a part of the digestive system that has exocrine functions. In other words, the pancreas secretes fluids, such as digestive enzymes, through ducts. However, the pancreas has both exocrine and endocrine functions.

The exocrine function of the pancreas includes the secretion of digestive enzymes through ducts (not directly into the bloodstream). These enzymes are important because they help break down the food that we eat so our bodies can absorb nutrients from the food.

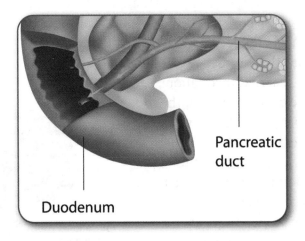

Pancreatic duct

Duodenum

The pancreatic duct allows enzymes and other fluids to flow into the duodenum.
Image credit: shutterstock

The stomach and the liver, though not glands, also perform exocrine functions that help with digestion.

Review Questions

1. What makes exocrine glands different from endocrine glands?

_____

_____

2. What is the exocrine function of the pancreas?

_____

_____

3. Name two other exocrine glands and their functions.

_____

_____

III. Endocrine Glands of the Brain

A. The Endocrine Glands

The **endocrine glands** of the human body primarily release hormones. Hormones are chemical messengers that affect the activities of other parts of the body. Endocrine glands release hormones directly into the bloodstream, so they are carried throughout the body. However, the hormones affect only the particular cells that have specific receptors, allowing them to react with the particular hormone. There are different hormones produced by the different endocrine glands, each with unique functions in the human body.

Thalamus

Pineal gland

Hypothalamus

Pituitary gland

The functions of the endocrine system are controlled by two parts of the body you have already learned about: the pituitary gland and the hypothalamus, both located in the brain.

B. The Pituitary Gland

The pituitary gland stimulates the release of hormones by other glands. In other words, many of the hormones released by the pituitary gland trigger other glands of the system to release their hormones.

The pituitary gland produces human growth hormone. As its name suggests, human growth hormone regulates people's growth. Differences in people's sizes are often attributable to the work of the pituitary gland and how much of the human growth hormone it releases.

Image credit: shutterstock.com

C. The Hypothalamus

Although the pituitary gland does so much work in regulating other glands, it itself is regulated by something else: the hypothalamus. The **hypothalamus** is a part of the brain that contains special cells called neurosecretory (noor-oh-see-KREE-tuh-ree) cells. If you examine that long word, you can break it up into two words: <u>neuro</u> and <u>secrete</u>. So the hypothalamus contains neurons that secrete or send out hormones. The hormones secreted by the neurons in the hypothalamus <u>regulate the function of the pituitary gland</u>.

The hypothalamus also controls many **automatic bodily functions** and keeps the human body in a state of homeostasis (hoe-mee-uh-STAY-sis). <u>Homeostasis means a state of internal stability</u>. For example, you have already learned that the hypothalamus regulates the body's temperature to keep it stable.

D. The Pineal Gland

Another endocrine gland found in the brain is the **pineal** (PIN-ee-uhl) **gland**. This small pinecone-shaped gland is located in the center of the brain. The pineal gland is responsible for the release of the hormone melatonin (mel-uh-TOE-nin), which regulates a person's sleep-wake cycle.

Light receptors in the eye inhibit this activity of the pineal gland, which means the gland releases more melatonin in darker conditions. The <u>pineal gland is essential for normal sleep patterns</u> and for recovering from jet lag after a long flight across time zones. The pineal gland also plays a role in a person's development during puberty.

The endocrine glands in the brain play important roles in regulating the endocrine system and maintaining some of our most vital functions. There are other endocrine glands with other important roles in the body as well. Because the endocrine system is created in such a way as to moderate or regulate our growth and maturity, it gives us a glimpse into the loving foresight of God, who cares so deeply for us and our development, provided for from the very first moment of our conception.

Review Questions

1. Name two functions of the pituitary gland.

_____

_____

2. In what way does the hypothalamus affect the function of the pituitary gland?

_____

_____

_____

3. The pineal gland regulates our sleep-wake cycle through the release of what hormone?

_____

IV. Thyroid and Parathyroid Glands, and the Pancreas

A. The Thyroid Gland

1. Controls the Body's Metabolism — The **thyroid** (THIGH-royd) **gland** is located in the neck, just below the larynx or "voice box." The thyroid gland is a butterfly-shaped gland. The thyroid gland generally weighs less than an ounce, which is very, very light, but the thyroid gland is one of the larger endocrine glands. The thyroid gland plays important roles in the body; the major role is <u>controlling the body's metabolism</u> (muh-TAB-uh-liz-um).

a. Metabolism refers to the rate at which a person obtains energy from the food he or she eats. Therefore, the thyroid influences our energy level.

b. Gain or Lose Weight — The **thyroid** is a key component in how we <u>gain or lose weight</u>.

c. Secretes Numerous Hormones — The **thyroid gland** <u>secretes numerous hormones</u>.

The three major hormones secreted by the thyroid gland are Calcitonin, Triiodothyronine (T3), and Thyroxine (T4). Though we don't need to remember the names of these hormones, we should remember some of the things they do.

Calcitonin (kal-si-TOE-nin) <u>helps regulate calcium levels</u> in the body and is involved in the process of bone-building. T3 and T4 work together to <u>regulate the body's metabolism</u>. Thyroid hormones are crucial to brain development in children, especially before birth.

<u>Excessive production</u> of thyroid hormones can result in weight loss and nervousness. <u>Insufficient production</u> of thyroid hormones can result in weight gain and a slowing of bodily functions, including a lack of energy. Thyroid problems can cause other symptoms as well. The mineral **iodine** plays an important role in the production of T3 and T4. If a person does not have enough iodine, the result can be <u>a swollen thyroid gland, known as a goiter.</u> Doctors have medication for goiters.

B. Parathyroid Glands

At the back of the thyroid gland are four tiny **parathyroid** (pair-uh-THIGH-royd) **glands**. The parathyroid glands are as small as grains of rice. These glands produce a hormone that is primarily responsible for <u>controlling the level of calcium in the blood</u>.

Calcium is essential for healthy bones and teeth, and also for proper nerve functioning, muscle contraction, blood clotting, and more. If the blood lacks enough calcium, the blood may take some calcium from the

THYROID HORMONES

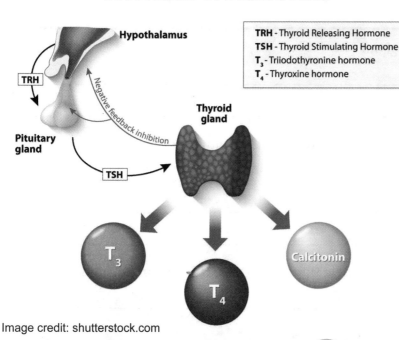

TRH - Thyroid Releasing Hormone
TSH - Thyroid Stimulating Hormone
T₃ - Triiodothyronine hormone
T₄ - Thyroxine hormone

Image credit: shutterstock.com

Image credit: shutterstock.com

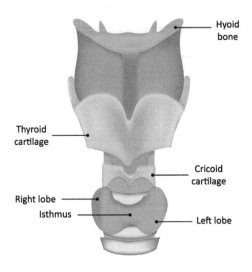

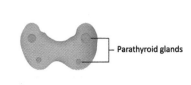

ANTERIOR   **POSTERIOR**

endocrine functions [the release of hormones directly into the bloodstream].

The pancreas releases two hormones: **glucagon** (GLUE-kuh-gon) and **insulin.** Glucagon is responsible for raising blood sugar levels, while insulin lowers blood sugar levels. Therefore, the pancreas is essential for maintaining healthy blood sugar levels.

Glucose, the sugar found in the blood, is the primary source of energy for most of the body's cells. There are serious long-term health risks associated with high blood sugar levels, such as heart disease, kidney disease, and eye and nerve damage. A person with **diabetes** has consistently high blood sugar levels and needs to regulate them with a strict diet or injections of **insulin**, depending on the type of diabetes he or she has.

bones, causing the bones to weaken. Calcium deficiency can lead to other problems, some serious. At the other extreme, too much calcium can lead to weakening of muscle tone and even kidney stones, which are very painful.

C. The Pancreas

You have already learned about some of the functions of the pancreas, another important gland involved with proper digestion of food. Besides the exocrine functions of the pancreas about which you've already studied, the pancreas also has

Low blood sugar levels can lead to a severe lack of energy, trouble thinking clearly, or in extreme circumstances, loss of consciousness or fainting.

Review Questions

1. Why is a healthy thyroid especially important for babies and children?

_____

_____

_____

2. How can thyroid problems affect a person's weight?

_____

_____

_____

3. What is the main function of the parathyroid glands?

_____

_____

_____

4. What is diabetes, and how is it related to the functions of the pancreas?

_____

_____

_____

_____

_____

V. Adrenal Glands, the Thymus, and Other Glands

A. Adrenal Glands

The adrenal glands are **two glands,** one located on top of each of the kidneys. The adrenal glands are small and triangular in shape. These two small glands produce an amazing three dozen hormones that perform many important functions in the body. Each of the adrenal glands are divided into two distinct layers. The outer layer is called the adrenal cortex, and the inner layer is called the adrenal medulla.

1. Adrenal Cortex

The outer layer, the adrenal cortex, releases hormones that are vital to life. Some of these hormones relate to a person's metabolism. In other words, these hormones regulate the way a person converts food into energy. Other hormones regulate mineral levels in the body, notably, salt and potassium. Still other hormones released by the cortex layer of the adrenal glands assist the immune system by acting as a natural anti-inflammatory. This means these glands keep inflammation down when the immune system is busy responding to a disease or injury. Finally, the adrenal cortex helps regulate blood pressure.

ADRENAL GLAND

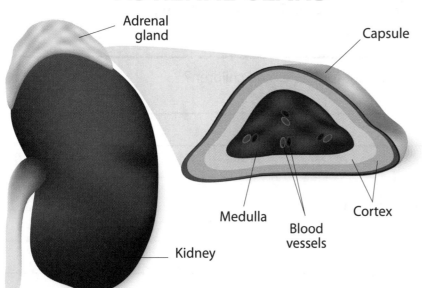

Adrenal gland

Capsule

Medulla

Blood vessels

Cortex

Kidney

Image credit: shutterstock.com

2. Adrenal Medulla

The inner layer of the adrenal gland is the adrenal medulla. The <u>adrenal medulla produces hormones that are not vital to life</u>. This does not mean they are not important, though. The most well-known hormone produced by the adrenal medulla is adrenaline. Adrenaline, along with other adrenal medulla hormones, is important to a person's response to stress. These adrenal medulla hormones <u>work to increase the heart rate and rush blood to the muscles and brain</u>. They help a person's reaction to stress in numerous ways, and lead to the "fight or flight" response.

If you've ever been particularly excited, scared, or under pressure, you may have experienced an "adrenaline rush." This is usually accompanied by increased energy. This response to stress or danger may not technically be a vital function, but is important to survival and successful functioning.

B. The Thymus

Another important endocrine gland is the thymus, located in the chest. The **thymus** is unique because it grows throughout childhood and then begins to shrink during adulthood, as it functions less. The thymus is a key ingredient in the development of the immune system, which fights diseases.

The thymus can be seen as a "training center" for important immune cells known as T-lymphocytes, or T cells. The hormones produced by the thymus <u>aid in the maturing of T cells</u> so they can develop the ability to fight disease. Because new T cells are produced mostly during childhood, the role of the thymus diminishes as a person ages.

C. Other Glands of the Endocrine System

There are other glands of the endocrine system, namely the **gonads** and **prostate**, which are important for a person's ability to have a baby. We hear a lot about the prostate—a gland that only men have—because <u>prostate cancer</u> is so common among men. As men age, it is important that they and their doctors pay close attention to the health of the prostate, since treatment of prostate cancer is very successful when it is identified early.

Review Questions

1. What is the difference in the functions of the adrenal cortex and the adrenal medulla?

_____

_____

2. What role do the adrenal glands play in the body's immune functions?

_____

_____

_____

3. What role does the thymus play in the body's immune functions?

_____

_____

4. Why does the thymus begin to shrink during adulthood?

_____

_____

5. For what common disease of the prostate should men regularly be checked?

_____

VI. Hormones and Feedback

Introduction

You have learned about the different glands in your body and what they do. In studying the endocrine glands, you have read about hormones being released into the bloodstream, and influencing many things, such as how you grow and develop, how your body can metabolize food, and how you react to stress. In this section on hormones, you will learn some of the specifics about how hormones work and how our bodies keep the hormones in proper balance.

A. Hypothalamus and Pituitary Gland

You've already learned that the **hypothalamus and pituitary gland** (in the brain) are the main regulators of the endocrine system, releasing hormones that stimulate other glands to release their hormones. **Hormones** are chemical messengers that affect the activities of other parts of the body.

B. Endocrine Glands

Unlike exocrine glands that use ducts to release their secretions to specific locations in the body, endocrine glands release hormones directly into the blood. So a question might arise: why does the adrenaline released by the adrenal glands (in times of stress) increase only the heart rate, while leaving other parts of the body unaffected? The reason is that hormones interact only with their target cells, not with the whole body or even sections of the body.

Have you ever put together a model airplane? When you construct a model airplane, you can't just cram any two pieces together any way you like. Usually there is a structure that causes one piece to fit properly with another piece. When God created the human body, He constructed possibly the greatest "model" of material creation of all. God has designed each hormone with a certain chemical structure. Target cells of the hormones are designed with specific receptors that allow the target cells to interact properly with the hormone they receive. Cells that are not the target of a particular hormone will not interact with the hormone.

The endocrine system ensures the body has the proper amount of a hormone through a feedback mechanism to stop the release of a hormone when the proper amount has been reached. In a feedback mechanism, the response to some action influences the continued exercise of that action, or sends the message to discontinue (stop) the action.

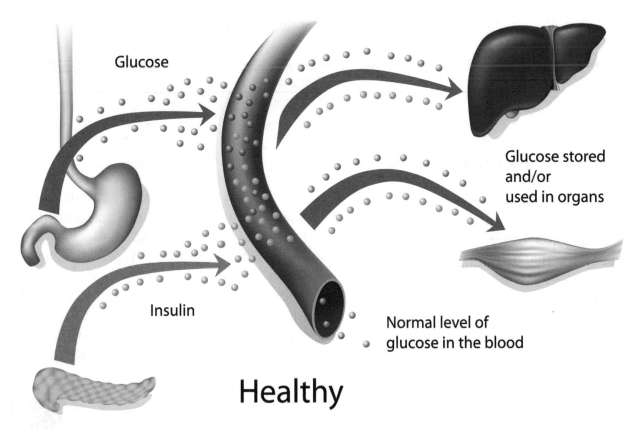

Glucose

Glucose stored and/or used in organs

Insulin

Normal level of glucose in the blood

Healthy

For example, after eating certain foods, a person's blood sugar level may suddenly rise. High blood sugar levels will likely trigger the pancreas to release insulin, which is the hormone to lower the blood sugar level. As the insulin does its job, blood sugar levels will come back down to normal. The lower blood sugar level is "feedback" for the pancreas, telling the pancreas to stop producing insulin. The initial action (the release of insulin) caused a response (the lowering of blood sugar levels). The response in turn caused the pancreas to stop releasing insulin.

The endocrine system consistently uses this type of feedback mechanism to keep hormones in the bloodstream at their proper levels after being increased to solve a particular situation.

Review Questions

1. What are hormones?

_____

_____

2. Why do hormones affect only some cells?

_____

_____

_____

Image credit: shutterstock.com

3. How does the body's feedback mechanism keep hormones at their proper levels?

_____

_____

_____

VII. Gland Diseases and Disorders

You have learned that your glands play very important roles in your body. The endocrine glands release hormones into your bloodstream that help you grow, metabolize food, and perform many other functions important for your development. When this system isn't functioning properly, numerous diseases or disorders can result.

A. Endocrine Gland Disorders
1. Diabetes

One of the most common endocrine disorders is diabetes. There are two types of diabetes: Type 1 and Type 2. With both types of diabetes, high blood sugar is the result. **Type 1** is less common and usually begins at a younger age, often in childhood. Type 1 diabetes occurs when <u>the pancreas does not produce enough insulin when it is needed</u>.

Insulin, remember, is the hormone that lowers blood sugar levels. People with Type 1 diabetes must consistently check their blood sugar levels and take insulin to make up for what the pancreas is not producing.

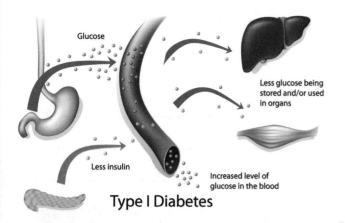

Type I Diabetes

2. Type 2 Diabetes

Type 2 diabetes usually results when a person's <u>body doesn't respond to insulin properly</u>. Genetic factors can affect a person's likelihood of developing Type 2 diabetes, but lifestyle choices also can be important. For example, a poor diet and lack of exercise can make a person more susceptible to Type 2 diabetes. For this reason, Type 2 diabetes often can be treated with healthy lifestyle changes.

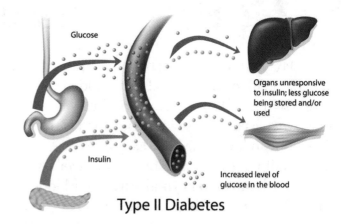

Type II Diabetes

3. Hyperthyroidism and Hypothyroidism

Other disorders of the endocrine system include those affecting the thyroid and parathyroid glands. <u>Hyperthyroidism</u> occurs when the thyroid gland produces too much hormone. The most common cause of hyperthyroidism is Graves' Disease, named for the doctor who first described it. <u>Hypothyroidism</u> refers to an underactive thyroid gland, one that does not produce enough hormone. These conditions can affect a person's weight gain, among other symptoms.

Image credits: shutterstock.com

The parathyroid glands can be overactive or underactive. When either occurs, it leads to calcium levels in the blood that are either too high or too low.

4. Growth Hormone

Remember that the pituitary gland produces growth hormone. Growth Hormone Deficiency results when the pituitary gland does not produce enough growth hormone. This is often the cause of a condition that is commonly called dwarfism, which simply means that a person is short in stature due to a medical condition.

The opposite, commonly called **gigantism**, can be the result of too much growth hormone produced by the pituitary gland. This leads to extremely tall height.

B. Exocrine Gland Disorders

One of the more common exocrine gland disorders is salivary gland disease. The salivary glands produce saliva. Problems with these glands can cause symptoms, such as pain or dry mouth. The salivary glands often get swollen due to infection. For example, people with the flu may experience swelling of the salivary glands.

Review Questions

1. What is the difference between Type 1 and Type 2 diabetes?

_____

_____

_____

_____

2. How can disorders of the thyroid gland or the pituitary gland affect a person's size?

_____

_____

_____

_____

3. Name a disorder of an exocrine gland.

_____

_____

VIII. Recipe for Healthy Glands

With all the important roles that glands play in the human body, it is important to do what we can to keep them healthy. Besides maintaining overall health, it is important to have a healthy diet and manage stress to have healthy glands.

You have already read some of the benefits of eating healthy Omega-3 fatty acids. They support the endocrine system by helping the transportation of hormones through the bloodstream.

A. Fruits and vegetables are healthy foods. Vegetables especially support the endocrine system because of the minerals they contain without the sugar that many fruits provide. It is important to control the amount of sugar in one's diet to maintain healthy glands.

B. Nutrients — Studies have suggested that certain **nutrients** are particularly effective in protecting against pancreatic cancer, which is one of the deadliest cancers. Some of the foods containing these nutrients are onions, kale, spinach, apples, blueberries, and white beans.

C. Garlic, Seeds, and Nuts — Garlic is a food that supports immune function as well as the function of the pancreas and adrenal glands. Seeds and nuts also support healthy glands.

D. Do not Smoke — As always, it is important not to smoke. Smoking seriously undermines the health of the glands, especially by raising the risk of pancreatic cancer, among other cancers.

E. Manage Stress — It is important to manage stress properly because many of the glands produce hormones to deal with stress. These glands can be overworked and produce too much of these hormones if a person is too often under stress.

Do your best not to have stress in your life. Talk to your mom or dad about what might be causing your stress. Keep up your daily prayers, such as the daily Rosary. Attend Mass with your family. The time you spend with God in prayer can help lower your stress levels. God will give you the strength to endure difficult situations.

Manage stress by getting regular exercise, playing basketball or baseball, for instance. Fly a kite or build a model. Spend time in recreation, reading a good book. Help your family with making meals or cleaning the house, or taking care of the youngest children in the family.

Take time to study, and do your best with your school work. If your studies cause you stress, ask your parents for help, and maybe an older brother or sister. You can also ask your guardian angel, who is always there to help you with everything.

Studies show that onions and white beans are effective in protecting against pancreatic cancer.
Image credits: public domain

Garlic helps support the immune system. Seeds and nuts are healthy foods that help support proper functioning of glands.
Image credits: public domain

JMJ

Review Questions

1. Name some foods that may protect against pancreatic cancer.

_____

_____

2. Why are vegetables important for healthy glands?

_____

_____

3. How does prayer support a healthy endocrine system?

_____

_____

Take time to pray every day. The Rosary is an especially important way to pray.
Image credit: shutterstock.com

Attend the Holy Sacrifice of the Mass with your family as often as possible.
Image credit: FSSP

You can manage stress by participating in active games, such as baseball.
Image credit: public domain

Take time to study, and do your best with your school work.
Image credit: shutterstock.com

Chapter Review Activity

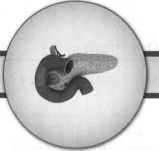

SECTION A

Use the words and phrases in the word box to complete the sentences:

brain	endocrine	exocrine	glands
hormones	hypothalamus	metabolism	pancreas
target cells	thymus		

1. _____ are organs that release fluids or hormones.

2. An _____ gland releases its substance through a duct.

3. An _____ gland releases hormones directly into the bloodstream.

4. Chemical messengers that affect the activities of other parts of the body are called
_____.

5. Hormones only interact with their _____ _____.

6. _____ refers to the rate at which a person obtains energy from the food he or she eats.

7. The hormones secreted by the _____ regulate the function of the pituitary gland.

8. The _____ has both exocrine and endocrine functions.

9. The _____ shrinks as a person ages.

10. The pineal gland is located in the _____.

Chapter Review Activity

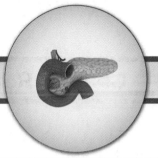

Fill in the following two tables with the correct gland from the box:

adrenal	lachrymal	mammary	pancreas
parathyroid	pineal	pituitary	prostate
salivary	sebaceous	sweat	thymus
thyroid			

EXOCRINE GLAND	DESCRIPTION
11. _____	Responsible for producing tears
12. _____	Produces saliva
13. _____	Produces an oil that protects the hair and forms a water-repellant layer on the skin
14. _____	Produces a fluid that helps keep people from overheating
15. _____	Produces milk for the nourishment of babies

ENDOCRINE GLAND	DESCRIPTION
16. _____	Releases human growth hormone
17. _____	Regulates a person's sleep-wake cycle
18. _____	Releases hormones that regulate the body's metabolism
19. _____	Releases a hormone primarily responsible for controlling the amount of calcium in the blood
20. _____	Aids in the maturing of T cells
21. _____	Responsible for the production of adrenaline
22. _____	Helps maintain healthy blood sugar levels
23. _____	Men have to monitor their risk for cancer of this gland

SECTION C

Fill in the following two tables with the correct gland from the box:

24. List five foods doctors think may help protect against pancreatic cancer.

_____

_____

25. Compare and contrast Type 1 and Type 2 diabetes.

_____

_____

Immune System

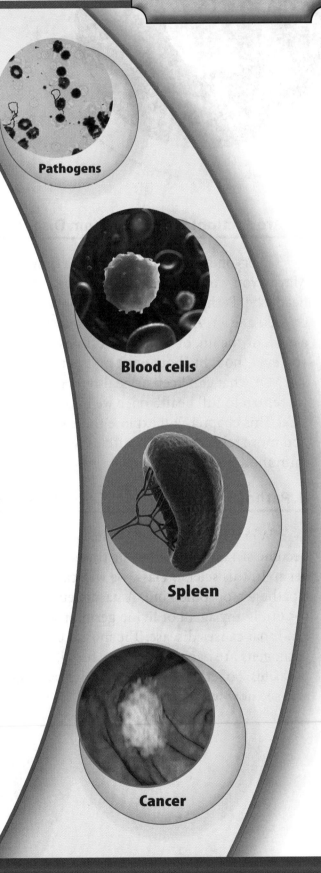

Pathogens

Blood cells

Spleen

Cancer

Image credits (from top): public domain, shutterstock.com, shutterstock.com, Bluce Blausen

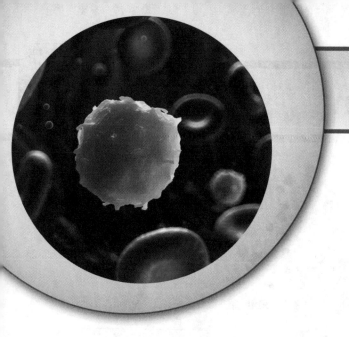

Immune System

Immune System

I. Introduction: Protection from Disease

Everyone has been sick at some time. Maybe you woke up with a sore throat or a headache. Perhaps you have had stomach pains or even a fever. At some time you may have had a cold, or the flu, or some other illness. Have you ever thought about what makes people sick? Or what can keep us healthy? How do we return to full health once we have been sick? This chapter will explore these questions and more related to our health as we study the immune system.

II. Pathogens: Agents That Cause Diseases

What makes us sick? When people become sick, it can usually be traced to a germ. In this science class, we will call a germ a pathogen of some kind. A **pathogen** (PATH-o-gen) is any agent or living germ of some kind that causes disease. The most common pathogens are bacteria, viruses, fungi, and parasites. So let's take a look at these pathogens and see how we can avoid them!

A. Bacteria

Bacteria are a group of microorganisms (very small living things) that can not be seen by the naked eye. While we cannot see them because they are so small, they can cause big trouble!

Bacteria exist in a variety of habitats or locations. There are many different types of bacteria and, surprisingly, some can even be beneficial to human health. For example, you have already learned that the bacteria in the large intestine in your stomach feed on undigested food and even produce vitamins for the body.

Some bacteria, however, are not good for people and can cause sickness and disease. Some bacteria can make us sick and miserable for days or even a very long time, or for a lifetime. Tuberculosis is a disease caused by bacteria, which can make people sick for a very long time. Tuberculosis attacks the lungs. Over

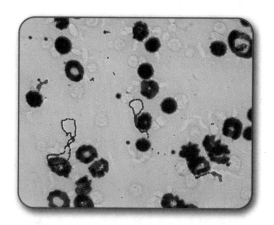

This type of bacteria causes disease, including strep throat.
Image credit: viridans streptococci CDC

Top image credit: shutterstock.com

9000 people in the United States suffer with tuberculosis! We should keep tuberculosis victims and other sick people in our prayers.

B. Viruses

A **virus** is a very strange type of pathogen. Although a virus is technically not alive as a bacteria is, a virus does contain genetic material which can move inside cells. Cells are the building blocks of our bodies. Consequently, when the cells reproduce, the virus spreads with the cells. A common virus disease is the flu. While just about everyone has experienced flu at one time or another, we need to pray for the good health of everyone in our family since the flu is so contagious. Nowadays, doctors recommend some people, especially elderly people, get a flu shot to protect them from the disease.

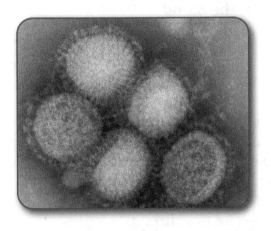

An electron microscope can take pictures of super tiny objects, including viruses. This one is a picture of the swine flu virus.
Image credit: H1N1 influenza virus CDC

C. Fungus

A **fungus** is a living thing that is generally beneficial in nature. Fungi are decomposers, meaning that they break down dead materials in the soil and turn them into nutrients that go into the soil. However, some fungi (plural of *fungus*) can cause disease in humans. A common disease caused by a fungus is *athlete's*

foot, which is an itchy, red rash that usually occurs on the feet. Be sure you wear clean and dry socks; don't wear socks that are wet with sweat! Careless children and athletes get this fungus which can be miserable!

A common disease caused by a fungus is athlete's foot, which is an itchy, red rash that usually occurs on the feet.
Image credit: Ecorahul

D. Parasites

A **parasite** is an organism that feeds off a host organism, though the "host" does not appreciate the unwelcome guest! For example, a mosquito is a parasite because it feeds off the blood of animals or people. Some parasites can cause people to get very sick. For example,

The head louse is a parasite that you never want to experience in person.
Image credit: Gilles San Martin

"roundworm" refers to an infection caused by a species or kind of a parasitic worm. Parasites that occur in children are lice, white worms, ticks, and fleas.

III. Defenses of the Human Body

With all these pathogens, you may wonder why people are not constantly sick or diseased. Well, don't worry; there is no reason to be in fear of getting sick. Although it is true that most people will get the occasional cold or flu, God has designed many defenses into our bodies that help keep us well, or make us well when we do get sick. Basic but daily health and hygiene practices are the keys to good health.

A. The Skin

Before studying the immune system, which is the body system given to us by God that fights pathogens or germs, let's review some of the external defenses of our bodies. Do you know that most pathogens never make it inside the human body? The first and most powerful external "wall of <u>defense</u>" of the human body is our skin. Have you ever thought about the fact that our **skin** provides a waterproof covering for our bodies? Our skin not only keeps the internal parts inside, it keeps dangerous pathogens outside! The **sweat and oil glands** in the skin aid in that process, and so does the **hair** in the skin. Of course, it is our responsibility to wash our skin

several times every day. How often do you wash your hands each day? It's important to keep our hands clean, especially before we eat or touch our nose or mouth.

B. Gastric Juice

If a pathogen <u>does</u> get inside the body, due to a cut or something we have eaten, for example, there are a few first lines of defense. The hydrochloric acid in the gastric juice of the **stomach** is very powerful and destroys most pathogens we consume.

C. The Respiratory System

The **respiratory system** is also a first line of defense against disease. Tiny hairs in the nostrils filter the air we breathe and help to push harmful particles in the air out of the nose.

D. The Blood

If a pathogen enters through a wound or cut in the body, immediately blood flow will increase to the location. Blood flow causes swelling and redness, referred to as inflammation. **Platelets** in the blood begin closing the wound by clotting, or forming a scab over the wound. Then the body's defense system begins attacking the pathogen at the point of entry. We will study this further throughout this chapter.

Review Questions

1. What is a pathogen?

_____

_____

2. What is the difference between bacteria and viruses?

_____

_____

_____

3. What is a parasite?

_____

_____

4. What are some of the body's external defenses?

_____

_____

5. How do the stomach, respiratory system, and platelets in the blood act as first-line defenders against disease?

_____

_____

_____

_____

_____

IV. Non-Infectious and Infectious Diseases

Diseases can be classified as either non-infectious or infectious. Infectious diseases are diseases caused by outside organisms, such as bacteria, viruses, a fungus, or a parasite. These organisms live either in or on the human body.

A. Non-infectious Diseases

Non-infectious diseases are not caused by pathogens or outside organisms, and they cannot be spread from one person to another. A non-infectious disease can be <u>a condition</u> that one is born with, or can be the <u>result of a condition</u> that one is born with. A non-infectious disease also can be caused by outside environmental factors, such as breathing in smoke or a gas.

You have already studied some non-infectious diseases that people can be born with. <u>Diabetes</u>, for example, is a non-infectious disease that can result when the pancreas does not produce enough insulin to keep blood sugar at a healthy level. <u>Hemophilia</u> is a non-infectious disease in which the blood does not clot properly in order to stop cuts from bleeding. You cannot catch these diseases from someone who has them because they are a result of internal conditions.

Sometimes environmental factors can cause non-infectious diseases. Exposure to carcinogens (car-SIN-o-jens) can cause cancer. A carcinogen is any cancer-causing substance. Cigarette smoke and nuclear radiation are carcinogens, for example. So a person who smokes or a person exposed to a nuclear accident would be at risk for cancer, but you cannot catch cancer from a person who has cancer. People can catch cancer by being daily exposed to the smoke of a person who smokes. Some families protect their children by asking family members or visitors to smoke outside the house. Even the clothing of smokers carries smoke.

B. Infectious Diseases

An **infectious disease** is a disease that is caused by a pathogen or an agent or germ that causes disease. Infectious diseases generally are contagious, so you could catch an infectious disease from someone or something. For example, the flu is caused by a <u>virus</u>. If you picked up germs from someone who has the flu, even by touching something that was touched by the sick person, you likely will catch it.

Mosquitos can spread disease, such as malaria.
Image credit: public domain

People are not the only agents that can spread infectious disease. Sometimes **bacteria** can get in food. For example, meat needs to be properly (usually thoroughly) cooked in order to kill any harmful bacteria (or parasites) that could be in it. If you shared a glass with a sick person, the person's **germs** may be on the glass, and then you could get the germs and the disease. Wise children never use the same glass or utensils recently used by another person. Wise children don't "share" the same cookies or food items.

Animals also can spread infectious disease. The pathogen that causes malaria, for example, is spread by mosquitoes.

It is important to stress again, however, that God has given the human body **powerful defenses** to keep pathogens out. God has given us powerful defenses to fight pathogens if they get in our body. Common sense is what is necessary. For example, washing your hands before you eat is an effective way to keep pathogens out of your body.

In the Old Testament, we learn that the Jewish people had many dietary and purification of food laws. They had laws about purifying their hands, their plates, their cups, and so on. These dietary laws, given by God, well protected the ancient Jews from pathogens and diseases in a way that most ancient tribes were not protected. These laws of cleanliness for our food, our hands, and our eating utensils are still effective today.

Review Questions

1. What is the difference between an infectious and a non-infectious disease?

_____

_____

_____

2. Name two non-infectious diseases.

_____

_____

3. Name three things that can spread infectious diseases.

_____

_____

4. How did God help the ancient Jewish people protect themselves from disease?

_____

_____

V. The Immune System

You have learned about different types of pathogens, and the difference between infectious and non-infectious diseases. You have learned about the body's first-line defenses against pathogens, including the external defenses that keep pathogens out of the body. But what if pathogens **do** get inside your body? That's when the immune system goes to work.

A. Primary Function of the Immune System

The immune system is truly a wonder of God's creation. The primary function of the immune system is to **fight pathogens** in order to keep us from getting sick or to help us to get well again. You can think of it as your body's own internal army against the invasion of enemy pathogens. Different types of soldiers perform different functions. Certain cells of the body identify the enemy, other cells mark the enemy for destruction, and still other cells launch the attack against the enemy. Truly, the coordinated response of the immune system would make any military general proud!

B. How the Immune System Works

To understand how this incredible army works, let's follow the path of a pathogen in the human body.

1. Fever

Imagine that your friend, who has the flu, accidentally sneezes on you, exposing you to the influenza virus. If any of the viruses penetrates your body's external defenses, one thing your body might do is raise its temperature. A rise in body temperature, called a **fever**, slows the growth and activity of some pathogens. A fever can enhance or give more power to the immune response. You can see that a fever can actually help in the fight to destroy an invader.

2. White Blood Cells

You may remember that **white blood cells** (also known as leukocytes (LU-ko-sites)) fight disease in the body. The white blood cells are carried through the body by a fluid called lymph (limf), through lymphatic (lim-FAT-ik) vessels, and then through blood vessels. Once a pathogen enemy enters the body, it will be recognized as a foreign substance by your body's defense system. The cells of your body all have the same surface proteins that mark them as part of your unique body. The immune system recognizes your own distinctive unique markers and will not attack the cells of your body. A foreign invader, a pathogen, however, is not so marked, and can be recognized by your body's defense system as not being part of your body.

There are two major kinds of white blood cells. They are called phagocytes and lymphocytes.

3. Phagocytes

At this point, our terminology (the words we are using) will change a little. Once a pathogen triggers an immune response from the human body, the enemy pathogen is then called an **antigen**. (Think of antigen as anti-genuine; it does not belong in your body. It is a foreign substance and an enemy.) The first thing the enemy antigen may encounter is a white blood cell known as a **phagocyte** (FAG-oh-site). The type of the body's phagocyte depends on the type of enemy antigen the phagocyte must fight. Like an army attack, the phagocytes engulf or surround some of the enemy antigens and "digest" them or eat them up!

4. Lymphocytes

Lymphocytes come in several kinds, which we divide by their different jobs.

Helper T cells may be the most important cells of the adaptive immune system. They act as scout cells to determine nearly all adaptive immune responses. Helper T cells help to activate B cells to destroy ingested microbes. Helper T cells also help to activate killer T cells to kill infected target cells. Helper T cells must first be activated by antigens on target cells.

Killer T cells are different from Natural Killer cells. Killer T cells share properties of both Helper T cells and Natural Killer cells. Killer T cells are important in recognizing and eliminating certain lipids from bacteria, such as those that cause tuberculosis.

Natural Killer cells act independently, and are not as specific as the adaptive Killer T cells. The Killer T cells only attack certain foreign cells that have been marked with antigens, and identified by the Helper T cells. Natural Killer cells can attack any cell that they don't recognize as from the body.

Going back to the military analogy, the phagocyte cells were the first to engage the enemy. In destroying some of the antigens, this phagocyte cell acquired "knowledge" of the structure of the enemy cells, which it is able to pass on to the Helper T cells. The Helper T cells take that information and carry it to the B cells and Natural Killer cells. The B cells will "mark" the enemy for destruction, and the Natural Killer and Killer T cells will finish the job.

B cells are something like army scouts. After they have been activated by Helper T cells, they can mark and identify the pathogen, or enemy cells.

Like in an army in which different soldiers have different jobs, God has arranged for a variety of human cells to attack and destroy enemy cells.

Phagocytosis

Leukocyte absorbs bacteria

Leukocyte ingests bacteria

Leukocyte expands from ingesting large numbers of bacteria

and lyses

White blood cells lyse releasing cytokines (chemical signals) which cause local inflammatory reaction (cascading) including swelling, redness and fever

The pus (dead leukocytes)
Cytokines attract new leukocytes to fight bacteria

5. Antibodies

Once the B cells are activated by Helper T cells, the B cells make and release **antibodies**. The antibodies are shaped to bind to the exact structure of the enemy antigen. These antibodies mark the infected cells for destruction. Killer T cells target the cells that are marked with the antibodies that were

Image credit: shutterstock.com

released by the B cells, and then Killer T cells destroy the infected cells.

One thing is certain: the wonderful workings of the human body give evidence for the incredible power and love of God Who made us!

Review Questions

1. What is the primary function of the immune system?

_____

_____

2. How does a fever assist the work of the immune system?

_____

_____

3. What important roles do phagocytes play?

_____

_____

4. Explain the function of Helper T cells, B cells, and Killer T cells.

_____

_____

5. What are antibodies?

_____

_____

VI. Parts of the Immune System

In the last lesson, you learned the names and roles of many different cells that make up the immune system. The classification of these cells can be very confusing, so it is worth reviewing.

A. White Blood Cells

White blood cells can be divided into two groups: phagocytes and lymphocytes. There are different types of phagocytes, which engulf some of an enemy antigen when it enters the body. The rest of the antigen will be dealt with by the lymphocytes. There are both B-lymphocytes and T-lymphocytes. The B-lymphocytes can be divided into B-cells and

natural killer cells. The T-lymphocytes can be divided further into Helper T cells and Killer T cells.

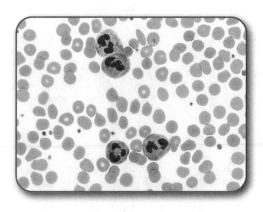

The larger cells are called neutrophils, which are one of several types of white blood cells.
Image credit: Dr. Graham Beards

B. Lymph Nodes

White blood cells are not the only parts of the immune system. The white blood cells are aided in their work to destroy enemy cells by other parts of the body. In chapter two, you learned that white blood cells are formed in the bone marrow. In the previous lesson, you learned that the white blood cells are carried throughout the body by a fluid called lymph.

Lymph Fluid circulates throughout the body, collecting waste to get rid of it, and carrying important vitamins to help different parts of the body. **Lymph nodes** are small <u>glands</u> situated in different parts of the body, such as in the neck, the chest, and the abdomen. When the human body is fighting disease or infection, the <u>lymph nodes filter enemy antigens</u> out of the lymph, and lymphocytes destroy antigens in the lymph nodes.

Lymph nodes are important to the white blood cells' communication. For example, B cells are activated and produce antibodies in the lymph nodes. Because of all this activity, the lymph nodes may swell during illness. When you visit the doctor, he often can see the swelling of the lymph nodes in your neck, telling him your body is fighting off infection.

C. The Spleen

The spleen is an organ seven to fourteen centimeters long (or about 2.75 to 5.5 inches) that sits on the left side of the human body near the stomach. The spleen plays an important role in immune function. The spleen <u>filters enemy antigens out from the blood</u>. The spleen is also an important storage location for white blood cells.

D. The Thymus

In Chapter Seven, you learned about the thymus. The thymus is an important gland located in the chest that <u>helps T cells mature</u>. Because new T cells are formed in childhood, the thymus becomes less active and shrinks as a person ages.

E. The Appendix and Peyer's Patches

The **appendix** is a small organ in the abdomen that puzzled scientists for years. The function of the appendix was unknown for a long time. Now medical scientists believe that the appendix plays an important function in the immune system. One function of the appendix seems to be to help B cells mature.

Additional tiny structures known as **Peyer's Patches**, located in the digestive tract, seem also to help B cells mature.

F. Tonsils and Adenoids

The tonsils and adenoids also play a function in the immune system. The tonsils, located in the throat, and the adenoids, located

The Lymphatic System

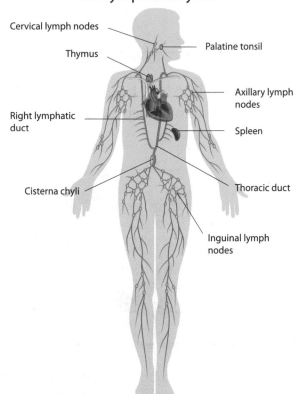

Cervical lymph nodes
Thymus
Palatine tonsil
Axillary lymph nodes
Right lymphatic duct
Spleen
Cisterna chyli
Thoracic duct
Inguinal lymph nodes

Image credit: shutterstock.com

in a cavity just in front of the ear, play a similar role to that of the lymph nodes; they <u>filter enemy antigens</u>. Years ago, doctors took out the tonsils of many sick children, but now doctors leave them if at all possible since they help fight off enemies of the body.

VII. Removing Parts of the Immune System

You may know someone who has had some of these parts removed. For example, if the appendix becomes inflamed, it may need to be removed to prevent it from bursting. If the appendix bursts, it can be deadly. It used to be very common to remove inflamed tonsils and adenoids. Some people even need to have their spleen removed. God has designed the immune system so well, with so many levels of defense by different organs, that <u>people can be very healthy even if some of the immune system parts need to be removed</u>.

Review Questions

1. Why are lymph nodes important?

_____

_____

_____

2. What role do scientists now think the appendix plays?

_____

_____

_____

3. Why can people be healthy even if some parts of their immune system have been removed?

_____

_____

_____

_____

VIII. Kinds of Immunity

You may have heard it said about some diseases that once you have had them, you cannot get them again. This is because your body has built up immunity to the enemy pathogen or the disease. The same principle is at work with **vaccines** that people get from the doctor, usually by a shot, that protect people from certain diseases.

A. Antibodies

How does immunity work? Remember that when your immune system attacks an antigen, your B cells produce antibodies that attach to the enemy antigen. The structure of the antibody is very precise, to fit with the structure of the antigen, like a key and a lock. Then the infected cell, and only the infected cell, can be destroyed by T Killer cells.

B. Memory Cells

After you have recovered from being sick, your body has "memory cells." These lymphocytes "remember" the pathogen that made you sick. The antibody has been produced automatically in your body and remains in your body. So if you encounter that same antigen or disease again, your immune system is already prepared to destroy it before it can make you sick. You then have immunity to that antigen or disease.

C. Active Immunity: Antibodies and Vaccination

People can have active immunity or passive immunity to an enemy pathogen. **Active immunity** is the type mentioned above. The body contains antibodies and memory cells that do not allow a pathogen to harm it.

People can obtain active immunity to a disease also by being vaccinated. A **vaccine** is a medication that is created from a weak or dead pathogen. This weak or dead pathogen is not potent enough to make you sick, but it does stimulate the immune cells to recognize the pathogen and to produce antibodies against the disease or pathogen.

The decision of whether someone should get a vaccine is one to be made with a parent and doctor. As discussed in Chapter 5, many people have concerns over the health of taking some vaccines, and there are ethical concerns with some vaccines (that is, concerns about whether they are right to do).

D. Passive Immunity

Passive immunity refers to immunity received from someone else, and it generally lasts for only a fairly short period of time. A perfect example is a newborn baby who has

inherited some of his mother's immunity by receiving nourishment from her body for so long. This protects the baby while his own immune system is strengthening. Breast milk gives passive immunity to nursing babies.

E. Immune Systems Vary

People's immune systems vary. Some people are more susceptible to becoming ill from a pathogen, and some people can be exposed to a pathogen and never get sick! You learned earlier about Saint Damien of Molokai, who, for many years, took care of people with leprosy in Hawaii. Saint Damien did not contract leprosy for many years. Many people's immune systems are very successful at fighting the bacteria that causes leprosy, but the native people of the Hawaiian Islands were particularly susceptible to contracting leprosy.

F. Innate Immunity

Some people have something called **innate immunity** to certain pathogens. Innate immunity is present at birth and the body's immune system does not need to be trained by exposure to a pathogen. For example, some of the pathogens that make our pets sick are not able to harm us. Humans do not have innate immunity to all pathogens that affect animals, however. Consider the avian (bird) flu and the swine (pig) flu. God is very good and protects us from many diseases. Many saints are patron saints of those suffering with specific diseases.

Review Questions

1. What is the difference between active and passive immunity?

_____

_____

_____

_____

_____

2. What are two ways a person can have active immunity to a pathogen?

_____

_____

_____

_____

3. What is innate immunity?

_____

_____

_____

_____

IX. Immune Challenges: Allergies and Cancer

A. Allergies

Have you ever seen a friend who looked sick? Perhaps she had watery eyes, a stuffy nose, and a sore throat. When you asked her, she said that she was not sick; it was just allergies. What is the difference?

1. Allergies

Allergies refer to a person's exaggerated immune system response to a foreign substance that would not trigger a response in most people. These foreign substances are called **allergens**. For example, if someone is allergic to peanuts, coming in contact with a peanut can trigger a major response of the immune system, whereas to most people a peanut would not cause a problem. Note that a person with allergies is not contagious.

2. Antibodies

An allergic person's immune system produces **antibodies** identifying the allergen as something harmful for his body. Continued exposure to the allergen means a continued immune response. Inflammation and swelling in the mouth, nose, and throat often occur. Some allergic reactions can be severe.

3. Inherited Traits (Genetics)

Some childhood allergies are eventually outgrown, while other allergies develop at a later age. Genetics or inherited traits play a big role in how likely someone is to have allergies. If a parent has an allergy, it is likely that some of the children will have the same allergy. Sometimes even a grandchild will inherit an allergy from a grandparent. There are environmental factors, as well, which trigger an allergy, such as exposure to tobacco smoke. Doctors are continuing to study the causes of various allergies.

Another major kind of allergen is wind blown pollen from trees and plants. Pollen can be viewed close up using a scanning electron microscope.
Image credit: William Crochot

Hay fever is the most common allergy. Hay fever refers to symptoms occurring around the nasal passages and eyes, such as a runny nose and/or watery eyes that are caused by airborne allergens like pollen. Pollen is a powder, sometimes so fine it cannot be seen. Pollen comes from plants and is spread by breezes through the air. People who live in a mountain area, or in a valley, are often affected by the amount of pollen in the air, especially in the spring, and sometimes in the fall.

B. Cancer

1. Tumors

Cancer is a condition that refers to out-of-control cell growth. Abnormal growths of cells are called tumors. Benign, or harmless, tumors do not spread. The opposite kind of tumors are called malignant tumors, from a Latin word *malus*, meaning bad. A malignant or cancerous tumor grows and can spread quickly throughout the body, disrupting the function of one or more of the bodily systems.

2. Genetic (inherited)

There are over 100 types of cancer! Some cancers are genetic or inherited.

3. Cancer-Causing Factors

Most cancers are the result of exposure to carcinogens (kar-SIN-o-jins), or cancer-causing factors. Lifestyle factors can affect a person's risk of cancer.

a. Smoking is the biggest risk factor for cancer. The ten top diseases which cause death result from smoking. Heart diseases and lung cancer are the most common among Americans.

b. Poor Diet — Another risk factor for cancer is **poor diet**. A diet high in fruits, vegetables, and whole grains, and low in junk foods, lowers the risk of cancer. So does maintaining fitness through daily exercise.

c. Exposure to Radiation, including overexposure to sunlight radiation, is another risk factor for cancer. **Melanoma** is a common skin cancer among people who get sunburned too often, such as more than six or seven times in their lifetime. Some young people, especially some teenagers, get sunburned every summer. These people are likely to develop skin cancer at some point in their lives. The Skin Cancer Foundation can help young people learn about limiting exposure to the sun, especially on a beach.

Scientists are constantly studying the causes of cancer.

4. Treatment

Treatment for cancer includes ridding the body of the cancerous tumors and keeping them from spreading. For this reason, the earlier cancer is identified, the more successfully it can be cured. Some common treatments include **surgery** to remove cancerous cells, as well as **chemotherapy** and **radiation** to kill the cells. Doctors are continually developing new treatments for cancer.

5. Patron Saint for Cancer Patients: St. Peregrine

St. Peregrine is the patron saint of cancer patients. Peregrine was born in Italy in 1260. He had a powerful conversion as a young man. St. Peregrine joined the Servites and became a priest. He was known for his personal penitential habits, and for being a powerful preacher and a good confessor. St. Peregrine developed cancer on his leg, and was scheduled for an amputation. He spent the night before the operation in prayer before an image of our crucified Lord. The next morning, his leg was miraculously healed. St. Peregrine lived another 20 years, and died in 1345, at the age of 85.

Review Questions

1. What are allergies?

_____

_____

2. What is cancer?

_____

_____

3. Name three risk factors of cancer.

_____

_____

_____

X. Immune System Diseases

The immune system is the incredible system of defense that God has designed to combat disease in our bodies. But we live in a fallen world, and we have a fallen nature. Our Lord has purchased our salvation if we follow Him, but until we receive our glorified bodies, we have to deal with the reality of illness and disease.

A. Immune Disorders

So what happens when the immune system itself becomes diseased? In the last lesson, you learned about allergies and

SCIENCE 5 FOR YOUNG CATHOLICS — 159 — CHAPTER 8 IMMUNE SYSTEM cancer. In this lesson, you will explore two specific types of immune system disorders: immunodeficiency disorders (immune deficiency disorders) and autoimmune disorders (auto immune disorders).

1. Immunodeficiency: weakened immune system

Immunodeficiency disorders refer to conditions in which part of the immune system is not working well. This leaves a person with a weakened immune system, making him more susceptible to serious diseases. A deficiency that a person is born with is called a primary immunodeficiency. There are also acquired immunodeficiencies, which can be the result of a **disease, a medication, malnutrition, or other health problems.**

Some medical treatments can actually cause immunodeficiency. For example, chemotherapy is a medical treatment that attacks cancer cells, but it also leaves a person with a weakened immune system. A person who has received an organ transplant may need to take drugs intended to suppress the immune system. This is so the person's body will not attack the transplanted organ as a foreign invader. But that can cause problems and may lead to a person not being able to fight off a disease.

2. Immunodeficiency Disease: AIDS

Probably the best known immunodeficiency disorder caused by a disease is AIDS (Acquired Immune Deficiency Syndrome), which is caused by a virus called HIV (human immunodeficiency virus). The HIV virus attacks T Helper cells. With a low T Helper cell count, B cells and T Killer cells cannot be activated, leaving the person dangerously vulnerable to becoming very ill.

There is currently no cure for this deadly disease, but treatments attack the virus's ability to reproduce, keeping T Helper cell counts high. Several religious orders of priests and of nuns offer hospital care for patients suffering from AIDS.

This is a scanning electron micrograph of HIV (yellow) particles infecting a human T cell.
Image credit: National Institute of Health

B. Autoimmune Disorders
1. Rheumatoid Arthritis

In **autoimmune disorders**, a person's immune system mistakenly attacks healthy tissues as if they were foreign invaders. **Rheumatoid (ROO-muh-toyd) arthritis** is an autoimmune disorder in which the immune system attacks the joints, causing pain and making it difficult to move.

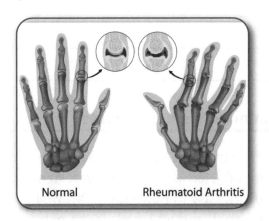

Normal   Rheumatoid Arthritis

Rheumatoid arthritis can bend joints out of alignment as in this example.
Image credit: shutterstock.com

2. Lupus & Scleroderma

Lupus (LOO-pus) is an autoimmune disorder that causes muscle and joint pain. Lupus can attack organs like the kidneys. A person with **scleroderma** (skleer-o-DUR-muh) has an immune system that attacks the skin, joints, and organs.

Many autoimmune disorders have no cure, but can be treated with medications that keep the immune system under control so the condition does not get worse.

Review Questions

1. What is the difference between immunodeficiency disorders and autoimmune disorders?

_____

_____

2. Name three ways someone might acquire an immunodeficiency disorder.

_____

_____

_____

3. Describe two autoimmune disorders.

_____

_____

_____

_____

XI. A Healthy Immune System

As you have learned, the immune system is an essential part of the body. By defending us from sickness and disease, the immune system plays a vital role in our health and well-being, and in keeping us alive. It is important, therefore, to do what we can to keep our immune system strong and functioning properly.

There are many products that claim to promote an enhanced immune system. However, scientists are still learning about the immune system and how the different parts

of it work together. So far, there has been no definitive evidence behind a "magic bullet" for maintaining a supercharged immunity, although the results of some studies have been hopeful. Products that claim to "boost" certain immune cells have caused doubt among doctors, especially since the coordinated response of the immune system means that boosting the level of some cells may not be a healthy way to treat the whole immune system.

The first thing most doctors would recommend for a powerful immune system is basic healthy living. First and foremost, don't smoke, don't take drugs, and don't drink excessive amounts of alcohol. Maintain a healthy weight, exercise every day, and consume a diet with plenty of fruits, vegetables, and whole grains. Scientists have noticed a connection between certain vitamin deficiencies and increased vulnerability to infectious disease, so it is wise to eat a balanced diet for the best immune response. Garlic is helpful for maintaining a healthy immune system. It is a good idea to limit sugar intake because some studies show high amounts of sugar may promote inflammation, which can lead to a variety of problems.

Be sure to wash your hands frequently with soap and water.
Image credit: Arlington County

A 2004 study suggested that certain vegetables, called cruciferous (kroo-SIF-er-us) vegetables, may have anti-cancer properties. "Cruciferous" means *cross-bearing*, and the four petals of these vegetable's flowers resemble a cross. Some common cruciferous vegetables include kale, broccoli, cabbage, cauliflower, Brussels sprouts, turnips, and many more.

Studies have shown a weakened immune system can be a result of increased stress, too little sleep, and isolation. Scientists are currently studying the effects of aging on the immune system.

There are some other commonsense things people can do to protect themselves from getting sick. One is washing their hands. Simple hand-washing before eating can keep

numerous germs from entering the body. There is nothing promoted more among health workers than washing the hands.

Whenever you go anywhere, such as the library, the grocery store, or a friend's house, you pick up many germs. So, it is a good idea to wash your hands as soon as you come back home. Wash your hands before eating anything, which means meals, a piece of candy, a piece of fruit, an ice cream cone. It should go without saying that you should wash your hands after using the bathroom. Wash your hands before cooking or handling food, and make sure silverware and cooking utensils are cleaned after each use. Also, make sure that foods, especially meats, are cooked long enough to kill bacteria on them. Don't eat meats that haven't been cooked.

Broccoli, cauliflower, and cabbage are three examples of cruciferous vegetables.
Image credit: public domain

Don't share silverware, cups, or glasses with others.

It is important that we treat others with concern and respect. When we cough or sneeze, we should cover our mouths with our arm to reduce the spread of germs. If we are sick, we should stay home.

Of course, sickness will still happen on occasion. It is a part of life. Nonetheless, maintaining a healthy immune system is important. Simple, commonsense steps make a big difference. They protect our own health and show respect for other people.

Review Questions

1. Name three simple things you can do to prevent the spread of disease.

_____

_____

_____

2. How can you use your diet to promote a healthy immune system?

_____

_____

3. Name some times when you should wash your hands.

_____

_____

Fruits and whole grains are also important foods for a healthy lifestyle.
Image credit: public domain

Chapter Review Activity

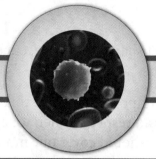

SECTION A

Use the words in the word box to complete the sentences:

allergy	antigen	autoimmune	B cells
cancer	immunodeficiency	infectious	Killer T cells
lymph	pathogen	phagocytes	virus

1. Any agent that causes disease is a _____.

2. A _____ is not alive, but contains genetic material that can get inside cells.

3. _____ destroy infected cells that are marked with antibodies.

4. _____ make and release antibodies shaped to bind to the exact structure of the antigen.

5. An _____ disease, such as the flu, can be passed from one person to another.

6. Once a pathogen triggers an immune response, the pathogen is then called an

   _____.

7. _____ disorders refer to conditions in which part of the immune system is not working well.

8. In an _____ disorder, a person's immune system mistakenly attacks healthy tissues.

9. _____ is out-of-control cell growth.

10. White blood cells are carried throughout the body by a fluid called _____.

11. _____ engulf and "devour" some antigens and activate T Helper cells.

12. A person's exaggerated immune response to a foreign substance that would not trigger a

    response in most people is an _____.

Chapter Review Activity

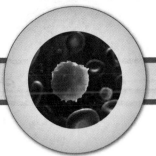

SECTION B

Mark the following statements (#13-20) "true" or "false." If false, tell why.

13. Skin is an external defense against pathogens.

_____

14. T cells, B cells, and phagocytes are all white blood cells.

_____

15. T cells, B cells, and phagocytes are all lymphocytes.

_____

16. The only way infectious diseases can be spread is from contact with an infected person.

_____

17. Bacteria, viruses, fungi, and parasites can all be pathogens.

_____

18. Memory cells are easily infected by the same pathogens multiple times.

_____

19. The appendix, the spleen, the lymph nodes, and the adenoids are all parts of the immune system.

_____

20. Immunodeficiency disorders, like lupus, cause the immune system to mistakenly attack healthy tissue.

_____

SECTION C

Circle the correct answer.

21. Which of the following is non-infectious?

    A. Influenza (the flu)

    B. Malaria

    C. Diabetes

    D. None of the above

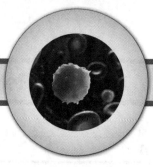

22. _____ are produced by B cells and mark infected cells for destruction.

    A. Pathogens

    B. Antibodies

    C. Antigens

    D. Allergens

SECTION D

Answer the following questions.

23. Give one example each of how a person can acquire active immunity and passive immunity.

_____

_____

_____

_____

24. How can a person's diet support a healthy immune system?

_____

_____

_____

_____

25. What is the primary function of the immune system?

_____

_____

_____

_____

Mammals

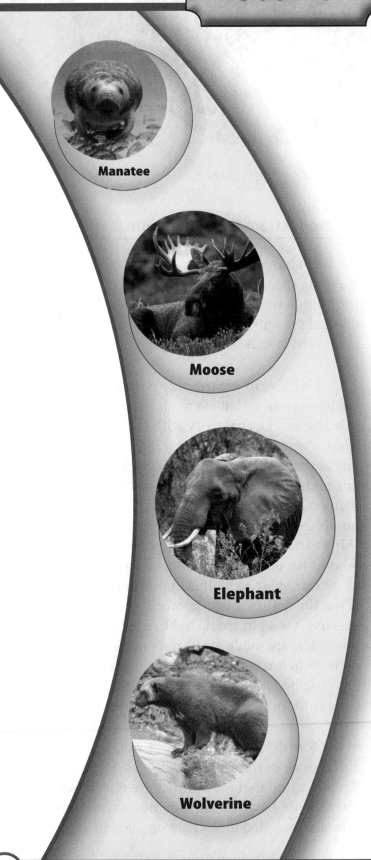

Manatee

Moose

Elephant

Wolverine

Image credits: all unknown

Mammals

I. Introduction: God's Creation

You have spent much of this course studying the wonder of God's creation that is the human body. You have learned of the many distinct systems in the human body and God's great care in making the human body.

We humans are the only part of God's Earthly creation that He made for our own sake, for our eternal glory with Him in heaven. We are surrounded, of course, by all the physical creations of God, which He made for our pleasure and well-being. God has created many plants, animals, and other living and nonliving things on Earth. These material things on Earth are made for people, for our food or for our transportation, for our shelter or for our enjoyment. It is important to learn about the natural material world around us because it is a gift from God to us. The things around us are made for us not only to enjoy, but perhaps to learn more about God and what He has provided for us that can be helpful for us, such as for our food and for our clothing.

Over the next few chapters, you will learn about some of the animals God has created. Keep in mind that the animals are gifts to us. They do not have the same dignity as humans; they are provided for us here on planet Earth.

We humans have been created in the Image and Likeness of God; each human being has a spiritual, rational, immortal soul. It is God's plan that we spend eternity in the great everlasting joys of Heaven. We do, however, have a duty to show gratitude to God by respecting His gift of animals and other gifts He has provided us on the Earth. Humans are meant to be good stewards, or caretakers, of the Earth and its living and non-living creatures.

II. Classification System of Carl Linnaeus

Scientists currently classify living things into five Kingdoms. This is known as the Linnaean (Le-NEE-un) classification system, named after Carl Linnaeus, the scientist who devised the system, though he only recognized two kingdoms. Animals make up one of the five Kingdoms. This system is for scientific classification of only living, material organisms. Thus, even though humans are distinct from the rest of material creation because we have a spiritual nature, humans are included in the Linnaean system since humans are also material

Carl Linnaeus developed
a system for classifying living things.
Image credit: unknown

beings. Of course, we all know that God created us with a spiritual soul. We are nothing like animals which are only material beings.

The Animal Kingdom is divided into many smaller designations, until each species has its own unique place. After the large Kingdoms category comes the Phyla category. We will be studying the phylum Chordata, which refers to vertebrates. **Vertebrates** are animals that have a backbone. The next designation in the Kingdoms is "Class." This chapter will focus on the class Mammalia or mammals. Humans are mammals. Just what classifies humans as mammals? Let's look at the "signs" for humans being classified in the mammals class.

III. Characteristics of Mammals

A. Mothers Produce Milk

The basic reason why scientists include humans in the Mammal Class is that human mothers produce milk to feed their young. Many animals are in this category, such as dogs and cats! Of course, mother dogs and cats may produce milk to feed their young, but never can be the kind of mother that a human mother is who loves her children so much that she "feeds" them truths about Jesus and Heaven, and prays for them daily.

B. Warm-Blooded

Scientists group animals with certain characteristics into class Mammalia. Besides being vertebrates, meaning with a backbone, mammals in this class are **warm-blooded**. This means that the bodies of mammals maintain a constant temperature. The normal body temperature for most people is approximately 98.6 degrees Fahrenheit. Of course, not all animals are warm-blooded. Cold-blooded animals must depend on their surroundings to control their internal body temperature. All mammals, however, are warm-blooded.

C. Hair or Fur

Two other characteristics of mammals are that they have **either hair or fur**. The amount of hair or fur on different types of mammals can vary greatly. Some animals, like bears and dogs, can have thick coats of fur. In fact, sea otters have the thickest fur of all mammals. Other mammals can have very little fur. Marine mammals like whales and dolphins have very few hairs on their bodies. Hair or fur is important, however, because it helps regulate a mammal's body temperature.

Sea otters have the thickest fur among mammals.
Image credit: unknown

D. Lungs for Breathing Oxygen

Another characteristic of mammals is that they have **lungs** for breathing oxygen in the air. Even mammals that live in the water must obtain oxygen for breathing.

E. Give Birth to Live Young

Finally, almost all mammals give birth to live young. There are only a couple of exceptions to this rule. Two kinds of mammals, the duck-billed platypus and the spiny anteater, actually lay eggs. These egg-laying mammals are called **monotremes**.

Remember that the Linnaean classification system is an attempt by scientists to group God's creation of living things into categories. Because God has created the universe according to His intelligent design, the classification system is quite effective.

However, since scientists can only generalize and since they cannot always "fit" an animal into a specific classification, occasionally we find an animal in the classification system that does not seem to fit anywhere perfectly.

Review Questions

1. Name four characteristics of mammals.

_____

_____

2. What is a monotreme?

_____

_____

3. Name the two egg-laying mammals.

_____

_____

4. What does it mean to be warm-blooded?

_____

_____

5. What is the most important way humans are different from all other mammals?

_____

_____

IV. Basic Needs of Mammals

All animals have certain needs that must be met in order to stay alive. Some of the basic needs of animals are oxygen, water, food, and shelter. Because mammals have many things in common, they have some similarities in the ways they meet these needs. However, there are many variations even among mammals, so animals that live in different environments often have unique ways of meeting these needs.

A. Need for Oxygen

Mammals meet their need for oxygen by obtaining it from the air. Mammals have lungs and breathe air. Different mammals have different lung capacities, but all mammals have been designed by God with lungs suitable for meeting their oxygen needs.

Some mammals live high in the mountains where the air is thinner, with less oxygen. God has designed these animals with special adaptations that help them survive with less oxygen. God has given some of these mammals, with adjusted blood composition, a reduced heart rate and slower metabolism to help them survive with less oxygen.

Some mammals, such as whales, live exclusively in the water. Unlike the fish that are their neighbors, whales must obtain their oxygen from the air. They must come to the surface to breathe through their blowholes. Whales have been given huge lung capacities. God has given them the ability to hold their breath for long periods of time, even when they sleep, so they can live comfortably under water! If you've ever been whale-watching, you can be grateful that God designed these majestic creatures with blowholes so we have more opportunity to see them! Travelers in ships sometimes have the opportunity to enjoy seeing whales and dolphins as they come up for air.

these mammals to meet their need for water by eating plants which contain water. Plants store water in their stems and roots. By eating the plants that store water, some mammals can obtain enough water for their needs.

Besides the moisture in their food, some mammals are actually able to obtain water as a byproduct of metabolizing food in their digestion process. What an amazing way to obtain water! God has designed some salt water mammals to obtain water from their digestion process, since they drink very little of the salt water around them. The kangaroo rat that lives in the desert can actually produce the water it needs in the process of digesting dry seeds! In fact, when you or any animal digests carbohydrates, water is a byproduct, but only a very small amount of water. However, it is enough water to sustain kangaroo rats! God has a plan for all animals to obtain the water they need for life.

Dolphins meet their need for oxygen by coming to the water's surface to breathe.

Image credit: unknown

Kangaroo rats obtain water from the process of digesting food.

Image credit: unknown

B. Need for Water

Mammals need water as well as air. Most mammals drink water from rivers, streams, ponds, even puddles. Some mammals, however, live in environments where there is very little rainwater. God has arranged for

C. Need for Food

Mammals, including humans, eat many different types of food. God has given different kinds of teeth for the different kinds of food that animals must eat. In fact, unlike other kinds of animals, which often have similar teeth, mammals have many different types of teeth. Teeth called **incisors** have flat edges for biting off parts of food. **Canines**, dogs and dog-like animals such as foxes, have sharp teeth, which are even called canine teeth, that can stab and tear into food. **Premolars and molars** can chew up and grind the food so it can be swallowed easily.

Looking inside their mouths and studying the teeth of different mammals gives clues as to the kinds of food they eat. **Carnivores**, such as lions, are meat-eaters. Carnivores have sharp teeth and powerful jaws that can be used to catch prey, and specific teeth to chew and specific teeth to eat the prey. **Herbivores**,

Red foxes have sharp teeth that can stab and tear into food.

Photo by Peter G Trimming

such as cows, eat plants. Their teeth are more flat, but have more surface area to chew the plants. **Omnivores** eat both plants and meat. A bear, which eats fish as well as berries, among other things, is an omnivore. Bears, other omnivores, and even humans have different kinds of teeth for different kinds of food.

D. Need for Shelter

Do you remember when Jesus said, "Foxes have dens and birds of the sky have nests, but the Son of Man has nowhere to rest his Head" (Mt. 8:20)? Jesus was telling a man, who had said that he would follow Jesus wherever He went, that His disciples need to be willing to make sacrifices to follow Him. Looking at that quote, we can see Jesus acknowledging one of the basic needs of all animals and people: shelter.

Animals need shelter to protect themselves <u>from the weather</u>, as well as <u>from predators</u>, other animals that try to eat them!

Animals use shelter to give birth to their young and to keep their young protected from enemies. Different animals have very different types of shelters. Some mammals have dens, like the foxes Jesus referenced. These dens may be holes dug into a hill. Sometimes an animal may use a cave or even a hollow log for shelter.

Some animals live in burrows underground. Prairie dogs, for example, dig extensive tunnels underground. They use them for shelter from the sun as well as from predators. Even marine mammals may seek out specific places for shelter. There are many caves underwater, for example, in which sea lions like to shelter.

Prairie dogs find shelter by burrowing underground.

Image credit: unknown

Mammals may make their shelter in trees! Howler monkeys in the rain forest live in trees. It is safer for them in a tree than finding shelter on the forest floor, where many predators live and seek them for meals!

Besides the need for oxygen, water, food, and shelter, animals may have other needs. Some animals need more space than others. Some animals need a specific kind of climate. Animals are usually best suited to a particular climate. Polar bears, for example, can survive the freezing arctic temperatures, while jack rabbits can handle the harshness of the desert. Many animals wouldn't stand a chance in either of those environments.

Over the next few chapters, we will explore some of the environments in which mammals live and see how animals are well-designed by God to meet their needs in those particular environments. As we explore the complexities of these different environments, you might be amazed by the wonder of nature and the great design of nature given to it by God.

Remember that before the creation of the planet Earth, God knew everything about the planet, even to our present time. As the planet has gone through changes, such as disasters of nature, some species of animals have become extinct; they ceased to exist. However, God designed in His creation incredible adaptability so that amazing numbers of living things, from different times and different parts of the world, could survive and continue to testify to His everlasting glory.

Review Questions

1. Name some ways animals who live in very dry environments meet their need for water.

_____

_____

2. Why is shelter important?

_____

_____

3. What is the difference between a carnivore, an herbivore, and an omnivore?

_____

_____

4. What different types of teeth do mammals have?

_____

_____

_____

V. Mammals of the Forests

An **ecosystem** consists of <u>all the living and the nonliving parts</u> of a particular area or environment. So in a forest ecosystem, for example, all the plants and animals in the forest are part of the ecosystem. The ecosystem of the forest also includes, however, the rocks, the sources of water, and even the climate.

There are many different types of ecosystems. Different types of animals are interdependent, meaning that they interact with and even rely on each other for survival. We will be studying some of the mammals that can be found throughout some of the different ecosystems of the world.

In this chapter, we will study the mammals of <u>forest ecosystems</u>. There are different types of forests or forest ecosystems. In fact, three of the six land biomes are labeled as forests. A biome (BY-ome) is a <u>large-scale ecosystem</u> that can be found throughout the world. So, for example, though there are numerous rain forests in the world, and though they are not all identical, they all share enough similarities around the world so that they can be <u>classified</u> as "rain forests." Thus, rain forests are an example of a biome.

Before exploring the rain forests, however, we will be looking at the two other forest biomes: the deciduous (dih-SIJ-oo-us) forest and the taiga (TIE-guh).

A. The Deciduous Forest

The **deciduous forest** is known for its "change of seasons." This means that the spring is usually temperate, and the summer can get very warm; in the autumn you will find orange, yellow, and brown leaves falling from the trees, and in winter there often will be snow. Deciduous forests generally have broad-leaf trees, such as birch and oak. Deciduous forests are found all throughout the world, and make up most of the Unites States' east coast.

There are a wide variety of animals that live in deciduous forests, including many mammals. Some of the predatory mammals that live in deciduous forests are black bears, foxes, and coyotes.

Although black bears eat grasses, roots, and berries, they also will eat insects, fish, and occasionally mammals like mice and even small deer. Red foxes, found in deciduous forests, eat mice, rabbits, and birds, as well as plants. Coyotes will eat small mammals, fish, birds, and even larger prey like deer.

Many mammals in the deciduous forest are not predators; they are prey animals, that is, animals that are sought, killed, and eaten by other animals. Squirrels are prey animals. They make their shelter in deciduous trees, although they often can be found on the ground looking for food. Deer are another prey animal that live in deciduous forests. Squirrels and deer rely on their coloring to blend in among trees

The deciduous forest is known
for its change of seasons.

Image credit: unknown

The red fox is a deciduous
forest omnivore.

Image credit: unknown

or tall brush to try to avoid predators anxious to eat them. **Camouflage** is coloring that helps an animal blend in with its surroundings and avoid being seen.

Moose can often be found in the taiga.

Image credit: unknown

Deer are prey animals found in the deciduous forest.

Image credit: unknown

such as moose and elk. Lynxes hunt at night and eat mice, squirrels, birds, and especially snowshoe hares. Wolverines are very solitary omnivores whose meat diet includes small animals like rabbits, and even large prey like elk.

B. The Taiga

The **taiga** (TIE-guh) is a forest biome that is usually found farther north than the deciduous forest. Taigas are known for their evergreen needle-leaf trees, such as pine, fir, and spruce. The winters are harsher in the taiga, and survival can be difficult. However, many animals, including numerous mammals, make the taiga their home.

In the taiga, there are often moose and elk. Moose and elk are larger than the deer normally found in the deciduous forest. Squirrels and chipmunks make up some of the prey animals found in the taiga. So do snowshoe hares. These hares have a white coloring which blends in with the snowy background, making it harder for hungry predators to spot them.

Some of the predators found in the taiga are wolves, lynxes, and wolverines. Gray wolves hunt in groups called packs. They will eat small animals or, often as a group, attack larger prey

Wolverines can kill prey many times larger than themselves.

Image credit: unknown

There are bears in the taiga as well. Besides black bears, grizzly bears also make their home in the taiga. Grizzly bears, on average, are larger than black bears, and they are more aggressive. They are also distinguished by the hump on their shoulders.

C. Behavior for Survival

As you study different ecosystems, you may be amazed at the way so many different types of animals can survive and even can thrive in a particular area. <u>God has given each animal certain traits to help it</u> survive. Predators have certain strengths that help them catch food, while prey animals have characteristics that help to keep them from becoming a meal for the predators.

As this plays out in the wild, the strengths of each species provide a balance. Different types of predators compete with each other for food, each winning some of the time. Often, the prey avoids being caught. In this way, God has ensured that the species of both predator and prey animals will be able to survive.

God has given some of the animals in the deciduous forest and the taiga amazing behaviors that help them survive. Two of these are hibernation and migration. These behaviors are instincts. An **instinct** is a behavior that an animal is born with; it does not need to be learned.

D. Hibernation

Hibernation is a way that many mammals survive the extremely cold winters of the deciduous forests and especially the taiga. When an animal hibernates, it goes into <u>a long period of inactivity for the winter</u>. The hibernating animal seems to be asleep, and wakes up again in the spring, when the weather has changed and food or prey is more easily found. Hibernation is not actually sleep.

Before an animal hibernates, it eats extra food so as to store up fat in its body. The animal can then live off of that fat during its hibernation. During hibernation, the animal's body temperature cools way down (even in warm-blooded mammals), and its heart rate and

breathing slow down as well. God has arranged this so the animal can conserve energy over the long winter. Two animals from these biomes that hibernate are squirrels and bears.

Some mammals hibernate during the long winter, like these grizzly bears.
Image credit:unknown

E. Migration

Another way an animal may avoid the difficult winter is to spend it somewhere else, that is, move to a warmer area. This is called **migration**. When an animal migrates, it moves from one area to another for a period of time and then comes back. The elk are an example of taiga animals that migrate.

Studying these two forest biomes, we can see many similarities in the animals. God has used patterns of design to create these wondrous ecosystems. Yet He has also designed His creation so that <u>species could display different adaptations in different environments</u>, making for beautiful variation in the natural world.

Review Questions

1. Compare and contrast the deciduous forest and the taiga.

_____

_____

_____

2. What is an instinct?

_____

_____

3. Name two prey animals that live in deciduous forests.

_____

4. What is camouflage?

_____

5. Name two predators from the taiga.

_____

6. Compare and contrast hibernation and migration.

_____

_____

_____

_____

VI. Mammals of the Tropical Rain Forest (The Jungle)

A. Description of the Tropical Rain Forest

One very interesting biome or ecosystem that teems with mammals is the tropical rain forest. The tropical rain forest, often referred to as the jungle, is the ecosystem on Earth with the most diversity of life. In other words, there are more different species in the rain forest than in any other ecosystem.

Tropical rain forests receive an abundance of life-giving rain.
Image Amazon Rain Forest by Neil Palmer

Tropical rain forests, found mostly around the center of the Earth, by the equator, are known for their warm temperatures and huge amounts of rainfall. This has led to an abundance of plant life, which can support lots of animal life. Rain forests are found primarily in <u>South America, Southeast Asia, and parts of Africa.</u>

Animals have many different habitats in the rain forest. A **habitat** is the part of an ecosystem in which a species lives. So in the rain forest, some species have river habitats, while others live on the forest floor, and still others live in the many trees. Mammals can be found in all of these places.

B. Mammals of the Tropical Rain Forest or Jungle

1. Tigers and Jaguars — In the jungle or tropical rain forest, the top predators are **tigers and jaguars**. The tiger, with its orange fur and beautiful stripes, prowls the jungles of Southeast Asia. The tiger is the largest of the big cats.

The tiger prowls the jungles of Southeast Asia.
Image credit:unknown

2. Jaguars are usually orange-brown, with black spots, but they can also be entirely black. Jaguars roam the rain forest in South America as the top predator, also known as the apex predator, meaning that the jaguar has no natural predators and is therefore at the top of

the food chain. Jaguars are the largest cat in the Americas and prefer to attack larger prey like deer, foxes, and wild dogs, or even caiman, a South American creature similar to a crocodile.

Jaguars are apex predators in the South American rain forest.
Image credit:unknown

3. African Forest Elephant — One interesting mammal of the African rain forest is the African forest elephant, sometimes called the <u>pygmy elephant</u> because it is so much smaller than the larger African elephant. The African forest elephant lives in dense forests and is rarely seen.

4. Chimpanzees, Gorillas, and Monkeys — Many primates live in the rain forest. Primates, such as **chimpanzees, gorillas,**

Gorillas are primates found in the rain forest.
Image credit:unknown

and monkeys, are omnivorous animals. Most primates make their homes in the trees, but one that can be found on the forest floor in Africa is the gorilla. There are multiple species of gorilla. This giant animal, despite its imposing presence, is almost exclusively an herbivore. When it does add animals to its diet, it eats mainly ants and termites!

5. Orangutan — In the trees of Southeast Asian rain forests lives the **orangutan**, another relatively large primate. The orangutan has reddish brown fur. The females generally stand about three feet tall and weigh around 110 pounds, while the males are usually about four feet tall, weighing around 220 pounds. Orangutans eat mostly fruits, but will dine on insects and even birds occasionally.

6. Chimpanzees are primates that live in the trees of Africa. However, unlike most other tree-dwelling primates, they usually forage for food on the forest floor. Chimps eat mainly fruits, leaves, and insects, but will sometimes feed on birds and other animals, even small monkeys.

This chimpanzee is eating fruit. Their main diet also includes leaves and insects.
Image by Ikiwaner

7. Howler Monkey — In the trees of South American rain forests swings the **howler monkey**. These creatures are the largest monkeys of the Americas and are known for swinging through the trees grasping not only with their arms, but also with their tails. They are even better known for their loud hoots and cries, which gave them their name.

Howler monkeys make loud hoots and cries that can be heard for miles.
Image by Steve Hersey

8. Golden Lion Tamarin Monkey — One of the smallest monkeys, also found in South America, is the **golden lion tamarin monkey**. This little monkey, weighing only one to two pounds, is also one of the most endangered of the monkeys. It has a beautiful golden mane, which makes it a popular target for hunters, and its small size means it has many natural predators.

9. Boto — In some of the rivers that run through South American rain forests lives one of the most unique mammals, the **boto**. This river dolphin, a fish-like mammal with a fin on its back, is known for its pink color and the flexibility of its body. It can touch its nose to its tail, resembling a large, pink donut!

10. Bats — Even in rain forest skies, mammals can be found. The **many species of bats** are among the most common rain forest mammals. Some bats in the rain forest eat insects, others eat fruit, and the infamous vampire bat feeds on blood!

Review Questions

1. What is the top predator found on the forest floor in South American rain forests?

_____

_____

2. What elephant can be found in a rain forest ecosystem?

_____

3. Name a mammal that lives in the trees of the rain forest.

_____

4. Name a mammal that lives in the rivers of the rain forest.

_____

VII. Mammals of the Tundra

So far you've studied mammals of three different biomes: the deciduous forest, the taiga, and the tropical rain forest. You may think that God's creation couldn't possibly get more stunning! The Arctic Tundra, however, is a beautiful and fascinating biome. The ability of the resident mammals to survive life in the tundra is itself a reason for awe and admiration of God's creation.

The tundra is found mostly at the top of the world, in the Arctic. It is a harsh, frozen land that is inhospitable to most species of animals. There is a layer of frozen ground called **permafrost** (permanently frozen ground) just under the topsoil, which keeps trees from growing in the tundra. Temperature in the tundra averages 10 to 20 degrees. The tundra gets very little rain, making it a bit like a frozen desert.

Arctic tundra is treeless due to the permafrost, a layer of permanently frozen ground.

Image credit: unknown

Because of the lack of thick plant life, herbivores in the tundra <u>need to eat grasses, moss, and lichens</u>, which are small plants that grow on rocks. The **arctic hare**, also known as the polar rabbit, eats grass, leaves, and berries in the short arctic summer. In the winter, it eats moss, lichen, and even twigs. The fur of these rabbits acts as a camouflage to protect them from predators. Their fur is white in the winter, to blend in with the snow and ice. In the summer, their fur changes to brown or gray, the color of soil or rocks.

The arctic hare uses camouflage to avoid being seen by predators.
Image credit:unknown

A. Mammals in the Arctic Tundra

1. Caribou — One large herbivore living in the arctic tundra is the **caribou**, sometimes called the **reindeer**. Caribou are different from other deer because both males and females get antlers, though the males' antlers are thicker. Caribou are an important resource for the people who live in the tundra. These people use caribou for milk, meat, and to pull their sleds. The people even use deer hides for material to make clothes and other items.

Caribou, or reindeer, can be found in the tundra.
Image credit:unknown

2. Arctic foxes are omnivores that live in the arctic tundra. These small white foxes are only about the size of a house cat. Arctic foxes are scavengers that have been known to follow larger predators like polar bears to eat what the bears leave behind.

3. Polar bears are predators that eat mostly seals, although they will feed off whale and walrus carcasses, and will sometimes hunt other animals, like the arctic fox. A polar bear's fur is actually clear, which allows sunlight to reach its black skin. The light reflecting off the fur is what makes it look white. Mother polar bears make dens in the snow, so that they can give birth to their cubs in a safe place.

Polar bears hunt for seals from ice chunks floating in the partially frozen sea.
Image credit:unknown

4. Gray Wolves, Grizzly Bears, and Wolverines — Some species from the taiga, which you have already learned about, also make their homes in the tundra. **Gray wolves, grizzly bears, and wolverines** all can be found in the tundra.

B. Marine Mammals

Because the <u>tundra encircles the Arctic Ocean</u>, there are marine mammals living in this ecosystem as well. **Seals, walruses, and beluga whales** are all common marine

Gray wolves are closely related
to the domestic dog.
Image credit:unknown

Mountain goats have large power muscles
for climbing steep terrain.
Image credit:USFWS

mammals of the tundra. They have a thick layer of <u>blubber or fat</u> under their skin to keep their internal organs from freezing.

6. Mountain Goat — Occasionally, tundra ecosystems can be found at the tops of mountains, even if the feet of these mountains are located in warm climates. One interesting mammal found on mountains is the mountain goat. This animal has a thick layer of fur, covered by a shaggy layer of hair. The mountain goat's fur helps to protect it from

the cold. The goat's excellent climbing ability allows it to navigate the challenging terrain of mountain tops.

It truly is incredible that in the harsh, frozen tundra ecosystems, life can thrive. Even some people make their homes in the tundra. <u>Eskimos and some Indian tribes</u> make a living by hunting and fishing in this seemingly inhospitable biome.

Review Questions

1. What is permafrost, and how does it affect plant life in the tundra?

_____

_____

2. Describe a polar bear's fur.

_____

_____

3. What does God provide marine mammals in the tundra for protection from freezing?

_____

_____

VIII. Mammals of the Desert

The fifth biome that we will examine is the desert. Deserts are found throughout the planet, especially in Africa, Asia, Australia, and North America. Most deserts are very hot. All deserts get very little rainfall. The plants and animals in the desert must survive extreme temperatures with very little water. God has given the mammals of the desert the ability to do just that.

In the desert, animals must live with very little water.
Image credit: unknown

The desert biome gets very little rainfall.
Image credit: unknown

One of the common behaviors of desert mammals is to be **nocturnal**. An animal that is nocturnal is active mainly at night. It sleeps during the hot daytime hours, and comes out at night when it is cooler.

Most deserts have long summers with little or no rain. How do animals survive with so little water? Most desert animals must be able to obtain water from the food they eat, since they will often go a long time without finding a place with water. Because God has made many desert plants that can store water, some animals can obtain the water they need by eating the plants.

Shelter from the desert sun is necessary for survival in the hot desert. Many desert animals make their shelter underground to escape the hot temperature. Prey animals can escape predators by hiding in underground dens or burrows.

A. Desert Kangaroo Rat

One of the desert mammals that uses many of the above strategies is the desert kangaroo rat. This little rodent is about the size of a mouse. It is called the kangaroo rat because it hops around on its hind legs using its long tail for balance, like kangaroos do. The kangaroo rat lives in deserts in North America

A kangaroo rat can get all of its need for water in the process of digesting its food.
Image credit: unknown

and makes its den at the base of shrubs. It burrows underground below a shrub, and is nocturnal. As you might remember, this mammal's diet consists mainly of seeds, and, amazingly, it can get all the water it needs in the process of digesting its food!

B. Black-Tailed Jackrabbit

Another North American desert prey mammal is the black-tailed jackrabbit. The jackrabbit is nocturnal. Instead of burrowing underground, it finds <u>shelter among bushes</u> above ground. This herbivore has long ears that help it hear predators coming. The <u>long ears also give off heat</u>, helping keep its body temperature under control.

The black-tailed jackrabbit gives off heat through its long ears.
Image credit: unknown

C. The Meerkat

The meerkat is another prey animal which weighs only one-and-a-half pounds. The meerkat is a social animal; it lives in a large group of meerkats. A meerkat eats mainly insects, although it will sometimes also eat lizards, rodents, and even scorpions! Unlike many other mammals, the meerkat is **diurnal**, meaning it is active mainly during the day. Meerkats also have elaborate systems of underground tunnels to protect them from both heat and predators.

Meerkats sit upright to rest and watch for predators.
Image by Charles J. Sharp

D. Fennec Fox

The fennec fox is a predator in the African desert. The fennec fox averages only about two pounds! The fennec fox is a unique-looking animal because, like the jackrabbit, it has large ears to help it maintain its body temperature. The fennec fox is a nocturnal animal that makes underground burrows and eats mainly berries, lizards, and birds. If it were not a fox, you might think it is cute!

The fennec fox has large ears for controlling its body temperature.
Image by Drew Avery

E. Desert Bighorn Sheep

North American deserts in the United States and Mexico are home to desert bighorn sheep. They are huge animals with 3-foot curling horns! These herbivores thrive on steep hillsides. How does an animal this large survive in the harsh desert where there is little grass and little water? The bighorn sheep, along with other mammals like goats and cows, is a **ruminant**, which means its stomach is divided into four compartments. This kind of stomach allows ruminants like bighorn sheep to get the maximum amount of moisture and nutrients from their food, somehow even from dry grass. Thus, the bighorn sheep can go long periods without water. Even during the hot desert summers, it can go three days without drinking at a waterhole! Another characteristic that helps the bighorn to survive is that, unlike most mammals, its body temperature can safely go up or down several degrees.

Bighorn sheep have large curling horns.
Image by Jwanamaker

F. The Camel

The camel has special meaning for us Christians. We know that the three kings traveled on camels to see the Baby Jesus and to present their gifts to the King of kings. St. Mark and St. Matthew wrote in their Gospels that St. John the Baptist was clothed in camel's hair. Camels are mentioned throughout the Old Testament about 75 times. Camels transport not only people but also transport supplies. Job in the Old Testament owned 3000 camels. Job was obviously a wealthy man!

Camels have either one or two humps.
Image by J. Patrick Fisher

The camel is not a predator nor a prey animal. He is really a transportation and carrier animal for people who live in the desert. Some camels have one hump, some have two humps. They like to eat hay and other desert bushes. They can walk slowly or run very quickly. Patrol police in some African nations ride camels instead of horses!

Unlike the other animals we have studied, the camel is almost a necessary pet and means of transportation for many of those who live in the desert.

Review Questions

1. What does it mean to say that an animal is nocturnal or diurnal?

_____

_____

2. How do desert animals get water?

_____

_____

3. How do the shelters of many desert mammals protect them from heat?

_____

4. Why do the jackrabbit and the fennec fox have large ears?

_____

5. What is a ruminant?

_____

_____

IX. Africa and Australia Grasslands (Plains or Prairies)

You have learned about mammals from five of the world's biomes. The last biome that we will learn about is the Grasslands. In the United States, we usually call grasslands *plains* or *prairies*. The central United States is made up of a large grassland ecosystem known as the Great Plains.

One of the most famous grasslands in the world, however, is on the continent of Africa, and is known as the **savannah**. A savannah grassland has trees, but they are fewer and spaced farther apart than in forests. Many people take safari vacations to the savannah grassland in Africa to see all the animals.

As with all ecosystems, the animals must be able to meet their basic needs to survive. The savannah has a <u>wet season</u>, in which there is lots of rain. During the <u>dry season</u>, however, water can be scarce, and many different types of animals may share the <u>drinking holes</u> that are available.

As you might imagine, a grassland is full of grasses. This provides a major food source for plant eaters. Carnivores (meat eaters), however, dramatically compete to eat the herbivore animals! Because the savannah has large, open spaces, it is easier for prey animals to see predators coming, and they learn to run away very quickly. For safety reasons, it would seem, large herds of antelope, buffalo, zebra, and other prey animals gather together to roam the savannah. Predators see their food walking and running every day!

Predators like lions, leopards, cheetahs, and wild dogs need camouflage in order to sneak up close enough to launch an attack on a herd. Large herds provide protection for the prey, so the predators will usually attack a young or sick member of the herd which can easily become separated from the herd in a fast chase.

A. Lion

The apex, or top, predator in the African grassland is the lion. Lions live in groups called prides. Females of the pride do the hunting, while the dominant adult male in each pride defends the group from rivals. Though lions have no natural predators, some of their prey have quite powerful weapons for their defense. For instance, lions are sometimes killed by the horns of a water buffalo during an attack!

Lions use camouflage to approach prey unseen in the savannah.
Image credit: unknown

B. Spotted Hyena

Another mammal found in the African grassland is the spotted hyena, sometimes called the "laughing" hyena because of a noise it makes that sounds like laughter. Although spotted hyenas are omnivores with skill at hunting a variety of animals, they are well-known scavengers, eating the remains of what other carnivores have left behind. The spotted hyena lives in groups called clans. Hyena clans

Hyenas make a noise that sounds like laughter.
Image by Liaka

often can chase more solitary predators, like cheetahs, away from their kills, so the hyenas can enjoy a free meal!

C. African Elephant

The African elephant is a massive inhabitant of the savannah. African elephants are the largest living land animals. Young elephants are sometimes killed by lions, but adult African elephants have no natural predators. They are, however, targets for poachers, that is, people who kill them illegally for their ivory tusks.

Elephants live in groups of about 10 to 15 animals, which are led by a dominant female. During droughts, elephants sometimes dig their own waterholes, which other animals also can use to get a drink! Elephants can live as long as 70 years. Their teeth constantly wear down from chewing tough vegetation, but unlike humans, they have several sets of adult teeth that replace their old, worn-down teeth. After their sixth or seventh set of teeth wears down, old elephants sometimes die of starvation.

The African elephant is the largest land animal. This one is a juvenile.
Image credit: unknown

D. Hippopotamus

The third largest land mammal, behind elephants and rhinoceroses or rhinos (another inhabitant of the African savannah) is the hippopotamus. Hippos live in groups called schools. Although they are herbivores, hippos are highly territorial and aggressive, making them very dangerous to humans. Hippos escape the hot sun by spending most of the day, up to 16 hours, in water. They come out of the water at dusk to forage for food on land. They are good swimmers and amazingly fast runners for such huge animals! It used to be thought that hippos sweated blood. Actually, however, the glands of hippos give off an oily red substance that moistens their skin and protects them from the sun, like red sunscreen lotion!

Hippos give off an oily red substance that moistens and protects the skin.
Image by Kabacchi

E. Giraffe

One of the most recognizable animals of the African grassland is the giraffe. Giraffes are truly a marvel of God's creation! With males standing at around 18 feet tall at the top of the head (nearly 8 feet of this being its neck), giraffes are the <u>tallest living land animal</u>. This amazing height allows the giraffe to reach leaves well above what other mammals can reach. Giraffes have <u>21-inch tongues</u> to assist in grasping their food! Although the neck is so long, a giraffe's neck has only seven vertebrae! These seven vertebrae can be as long as ten inches and are connected with ball-and-socket joints, the same type found in your shoulder.

The giraffe is a true marvel of God's design.
Image credit: unknown

To get blood from the heart all the way up to the giraffe's brain, the powerful heart is capable of <u>producing very high blood pressure</u>. This high blood pressure would seem to pose a problem for the giraffe when it lowers its head for a drink, and the blood rushes down to the head rather than up. However, around the giraffe's brain, God has provided a series of expansive blood vessels that can absorb the blood pressure and protect the animal's brain.

F. Kangaroo

South of eastern Asia is the island continent of <u>Australia</u>. Australia is covered mostly by desert and grassland, but there are <u>forests along the coast</u>. There are interesting and unique species of mammals that can be found there. Australia is home to many of the world's marsupials. Unlike monotremes (the two mammals that lay eggs) and placental mammals (who give live birth to fully developed babies), **marsupials** give live birth to tiny babies who, after birth, continue to develop in a pouch on the outside of their mother's body.

Marsupials, like this kangaroo, carry babies in a pouch for a time.
Image by Jenny Bee

A well-known marsupial of Australia is the kangaroo. There are many species of kangaroos, and it is estimated that there are over 50 million kangaroos in Australia. Kangaroos have powerful hind legs that can propel them in jumps up to 25 feet long and six feet in the air. They are also fast runners, traveling up to 35 miles per hour.

G. Wallaby and Wallaroo

A marsupial similar to kangaroos, also found in Australia, is the wallaby. In fact, the only significant difference between a wallaby and a kangaroo is the size; wallabies are smaller than kangaroos. Wallaroos refer to those animals whose size is in between the wallaby and the kangaroo.

H. Koala

A koala is a popular marsupial from eastern Australia. "Koala bears" may be popular stuffed animals, but koalas aren't really bears. When a baby koala, a "joey," is born, it is only the size of a jelly bean! It crawls along its mother's fur to the front pouch in which it will develop for the next seven months. Koalas eat

primarily the leaves of eucalyptus trees. God has given them a special digestive system able to digest the tough eucalyptus leaves and not be affected by the poison in those leaves! God has provided those leaves especially for koalas; very few other animals can eat them. Koalas are nocturnal, coming out only at night. They don't need to drink much, but obtain most of their moisture from the leaves they eat.

Koalas eat primarily the leaves of eucalyptus trees.
Image credit: public domain

I. Duck-Billed Platypus

The **Duck-Billed Platypus** (PLAT-i-puhs) is also a unique species found only in Australia. The platypus is a monotreme, an egg-laying mammal, instead of producing live

The duck-billed platypus has webbed feet and a bill like a duck.
Image credit: Peter Scheunis

babies. Laying eggs is not the only strange characteristic of this mammal. It has <u>webbed feet and a bill like a duck</u>; it has a tail like a beaver, and the feet and body of an otter; and males have venomous stingers on their rear feet!

In exploring the relationships between the various animal populations of the African savannah, and the amazing unique creatures

for which Australia is known, one can truly appreciate the creativity of God and His benevolence in caring for these animals. He has given all animals to mankind for our use and enjoyment. God calls us to be good stewards of these animals and the whole of material creation.

Review Questions

1. What is a savannah?

_____

_____

2. Why can hyenas sometimes steal a kill from a cheetah?

_____

_____

3. With what special adaptations has God blessed the giraffe?

_____

_____

_____

_____

4. What is a marsupial?

_____

_____

5. What is special about a koala's digestive system?

_____

_____

6. Describe the duck-billed platypus.

_____

_____

X. Marine Mammals

In this chapter, you have studied mammals from all around the world, animals that live in different biomes. These mammals have been given the bodily features or tools they need to survive in their environments. Most of the mammals studied so far have been land mammals. There are many mammals, however, that spend most or all of their lives in the water. In this lesson, we will be studying marine mammals.

A. Whale

The largest marine mammals are whales. Different species of whales vary in size, but the largest animal on the planet is the blue whale, reaching 105 feet long and weighing as much as 200 tons. An elephant, by comparison, weighs about 8 tons! Commercial airplanes can weigh 100 tons, half the weight of a single blue whale!

The whale lives exclusively in water. However, it is a mammal. It has lungs and breathes air. The whale comes to the surface to breathe using the blowhole located on the top of its head. Unlike most land mammals, marine mammals like whales have very little hair. Some whale species migrate between summer feeding waters closer to the poles and winter waters nearer the equator, where they give birth.

Whales' diets vary widely depending on their species. All whales fall into one of two categories: **baleen whales** and **toothed whales**. Baleen whales do not have teeth. Instead, they have long bristles called baleen, which is made of keratin, the same protein found in your hair and fingernails. The baleen filters food out of the water for the whale to swallow. Baleen whales eat mainly plankton, small fish, and shrimp-like krill. Most larger whales are baleen whales, including blue whales, gray whales, and humpback whales.

The largest **toothed whale** is the sperm whale, which can reach 60 feet in length and 45 tons in weight. Toothed whales eat fish, squid, and other marine mammals, sometimes including other whales!

B. Dolphin and Porpoise

Similar to whales are dolphins and porpoises. Scientifically, these are considered toothed whales. However, they are generally smaller than other whales and are classified in their own sub-groups. Did you know that the killer whale is actually the largest species of dolphin? Dolphins and porpoises can be confused. The two main differences between the two groups are that dolphins are longer and leaner with longer snouts, and porpoises have more flattened teeth.

C. Seal and Sea Lion

Two other marine mammals that are sometimes confused with each other are seals and sea lions. These two animals, along with walruses, make up a group of marine mammals known as **pinnipeds**, which means

This female sperm whale is swimming with its calf.
Image by Gabriel Barathieu

"fin footed." Sea lions are actually considered "eared seals," while "true seals" or "earless seals" are what we generally call seals.

One of the primary differences, of course, is the presence of ears on sea lions. Seals have holes through which they hear, but no protruding ears. Sea lions have long front flippers and can rotate their back flippers. This allows sea lions to walk on land, whereas seals wriggle like caterpillars when they come ashore. Seals, however, are very efficient swimmers and often travel far from land to hunt. Sea lions spend more time on land than seals do, and they are more social, moving together as groups. One other obvious difference is that sea lions are much louder. Many people are familiar with the loud "barks" of the sea lions.

Seals are more comfortable in water and less social than sea lions.

Image credit: unknown

D. Walrus

The other pinniped, the walrus, can be distinguished from seals and sea lions by its long tusks. Walruses are larger than seals and sea lions. They live near the Arctic, so they have a thick layer of blubber to help keep them warm. Walruses are very loud and social, gathering in groups, and often can be seen lying around on land or ice.

Walruses can be distinguished from the other pinnipeds by their long tusks.

Image credit: unknown

E. Manatee

One unique marine mammal is the manatee. Unlike the pinnipeds, manatees always stay in the water. However, they are mammals and so must surface to breathe. Manatees live along coastal waters from Florida to Brazil, and also along the coast of western Africa. Manatees can be found in some African rivers and even in the Amazon River in South America.

Manatees are large herbivores that can reach lengths of up to 13 feet and can weigh up to 1300 pounds. Although they can swim gracefully, manatees usually glide along at a slow five-mile-per-hour pace. Because they move so slowly and swim near coastal waters,

Manatees often glide slowly through coastal waters.

Image credit: unknown

manatees are sometimes wounded by boats
that run into them. Manatees are sometimes
called "sea cows."

Review Questions

1. What is the largest animal on the planet?

_____

_____

_____

2. What are the differences between baleen and toothed whales?

_____

_____

_____

_____

_____

3. What are the differences between dolphins and porpoises?

_____

_____

_____

_____

4. What are pinnipeds?

_____

_____

_____

5. What are the differences between seals and sea lions?

_____

_____

_____

_____

Chapter Review Activity

SECTION A

Use the words in the word box to complete the sentences:

blubber	camouflage	canines	hibernation
marsupial	migration	monotreme	nocturnal
omnivore	pinniped	ruminant	savannah

1. _____ are sharp teeth useful for stabbing and tearing into meat.

2. An _____ eats both plants and meat.

3. During _____, an animal's temperature and heart rate decrease.

4. A mammal that lays eggs is called a _____.

5. A mammal with a stomach divided into four compartments, allowing it to get the maximum moisture and nutrients from its food, is called a _____.

6. _____ is a behavior in which an animal moves from one area to another for a period of time and then comes back again.

7. Marine mammals' internal organs are often protected by a thick layer of _____.

8. A _____ animal is active primarily at night.

9. _____ refers to a grassland ecosystem with some trees, but fewer than in a forest.

10. A _____ gives birth to a live, tiny baby that continues developing in a pouch on the mother's body.

11. A sea lion is an example of a _____.

12. An animal with _____ can blend in with its surroundings and avoid being seen.

Chapter Review Activity

SECTION B

Fill in the table below with the words in the box:

baleen	blue whale	duck-billed platypus	jaguar
rain forest	sperm whale	hippopotamus	walrus

EXOCRINE GLAND	DESCRIPTION
13. _____	Biome with the most diversity of life
14. _____	Apex predator of the South American rain forest
15. _____	Monotremes
16. _____	Produces a fluid that helps protect it from the sun
17. _____	Toothed whale
18. _____	Long bristles made of keratin that filter food for some whales
19. _____	Largest animal on Earth
20. _____	Pinniped

SECTION C

Circle the correct answer.

21. What system is commonly used to classify living things?

  A. Linnaean system

  B. Newtonian system

  C. Physiological system

  D. Alphabetical order

22. Which is **not** found in a rain forest?

    A. Howler monkey

    B. Boto

    C. Meerkat

    D. None of the above

23. Which biome is likely to have mostly nocturnal animals?

    A. Deciduous forest

    B. Taiga

    C. Grassland

    D. Desert

SECTION D

Answer the following questions.

24. What characteristics do mammals have in common?

    _____

    _____

    _____

25. How do mammals meet their need for oxygen?

    _____

    _____

    _____

Birds

Falcon

Flamingos

Penguin

Owl

Image credits (from top): unknown, unknown, Liam Quinn, unknown

I. Birds

A. Basic Traits

In the last chapter, we studied one of the classes of vertebrates, mammals. Another class of vertebrates is birds. Remember that **vertebrates** are animals with backbones. Like mammals, birds are **endothermic**, or warm-blooded. This means that their bodies normally maintain a constant temperature.

1. Feathers — Some things are common for all birds. We know that all birds have **feathers**, but perhaps we have not thought about how important feathers are for the birds. A bird's feathers are unique features that aid in flying but also are essential for protecting the bird's body. Of course, we all know that birds **lay eggs**. Birds do not give live birth.

2. Variety — Though all of these characteristics are common to birds, there is an amazing **variety in different species of birds**. Did you know that <u>some birds cannot fly</u>? Though most birds eat plants and insects, did you know that some birds are powerful hunters? So let's look at different varieties of birds.

Birds come in all sorts of sizes and all sorts of colors. The <u>largest bird</u> is the ostrich. Male ostriches average about 250 pounds, and incredibly, some ostriches have occasionally reached almost 350 pounds! The bird with the <u>longest wingspan</u> is the wandering albatross, whose wings can be up to 11.5 feet long. The <u>smallest bird</u> is the bee hummingbird, weighing in at less than a tenth of an ounce, and with a length of less than three inches.

If you live in the city, you have probably seen plenty of pigeons. Although they can have a pretty sheen in their feathers, many

There are many different types of birds, but the presence of feathers is common to all.

Image credit: unknown

Toucans have beaks that look like a living rainbow.

Image credit: dollarphotoclub.com

JMJ

pigeons are gray in color. Have you ever seen a toucan? This colorful bird, found in the South American rain forest, looks something like a living rainbow!

3. Useful — Birds are very useful to people. Many people have parakeets or other birds for pets, and birds like chickens provide food, both as a source of meat and of eggs. The eggs we consume are not fertile eggs. This means that there never was a baby bird inside. However, egg laying is the method through which birds give birth to their baby birds or chicks.

4. Hard-Shelled Eggs — Rather than developing inside a bird's body, the **young develop in hard-shelled eggs** that the bird lays. How long it takes for an egg to hatch depends on the species of bird; usually the larger a bird is, the longer it takes for its eggs to hatch. The eggs must be kept at a temperature close to the parent bird's body temperature, so eggs must be **incubated** or kept warm. Most birds do this by sitting on their eggs. Once the eggs are ready to hatch, the baby birds inside use their beaks to break their way out of the shells.

B. The Divine Pelican

Did you know that Our Lord has been called the **Divine Pelican**? St. Thomas Aquinas made reference to this in his beautiful hymn *Adoro te Devote*. The reference is based on how the pelican feeds the baby pelicans. Some birds carry food to their young with their claws or in their beaks. Some birds regurgitate food, that is, the parent swallows the food but does not digest it completely, and instead "coughs" it up to feed the chicks.

In medieval times, pelicans reminded people of the immense love that Jesus has for all of us.
Image credit: public domain

However, in medieval times, people believed that, if a pelican's young were very hungry and the mother did not have food, the mother pelican would pierce her own chest and feed her chicks with her blood. This belief reminded people of the immense love that Jesus has for all of us. When we are spiritually in need of Him, some people even "starving" for His help and love, we are reminded that Jesus sacrificed Himself on the Cross. After He died, the soldiers wanted to make sure He was dead. A soldier pierced His Heart, and His Blood poured forth from His Heart. We relate this fact to how Jesus "feeds" His Body and His Blood to us in the Holy Eucharist. The following is a verse from a poem by St. Thomas Aquinas. (It likely rhymed in the original language.)

Adoro te Devote
Lord Jesus, Good Pelican,
wash me clean with your blood,
One drop of which can free
the entire world of all its sins.

Review Questions

1. Name four characteristics common to birds.

_____

_____

2. Describe how birds give birth to their young.

_____

_____

3. Why is Jesus referred to as the Divine Pelican?

_____

_____

_____

_____

II. Meeting Basic Needs

Like mammals, birds have basic needs for oxygen, water, food, and shelter, as well as the proper climate. There are many similarities and differences among the various species of birds as to how these needs are met.

A. Obtaining Oxygen

Like mammals, birds have lungs and meet their need for oxygen by breathing air. However, flying requires a great deal of energy, and so birds need an especially efficient way of getting oxygen to their body cells. **Birds' lungs** are connected directly to a series of <u>air sacs</u>. These air sacs help supply birds with much more oxygen from each breath than other animals receive.

B. Obtaining Water

Like most mammals, birds get most of their water through drinking. Birds are often found drinking from ponds, lakes, rivers, and even little puddles. Many people have bird baths in their yards that provide water for birds, giving the people a chance to view these beautiful creatures.

C. Obtaining Food

Birds' diets are quite varied, depending on the species of bird. God has given each species a special beak, designed to allow those birds to eat their own particular food. For example, the hawk is a bird of prey. This means that it eats meat. Birds of prey have **strong, sharp beaks** for tearing meat.

Other birds get food from the blossoms of flowers. These birds, like the hummingbird, have **long, slender beaks** to draw nectar from the inside of flowers. Birds like the vermilion flycatcher have **short, wide beaks**. These are

A bird's beak is perfectly designed to meet its dietary needs. This peregrine falcon has a strong, sharp beak for catching small animals like rats, rabbits, and bats. The peregrine falcon can fly over 200 miles per hour in a mid-air dive!

Image credit: unknown

perfect for their diet of flying insects. Many birds, such as sparrows, feed on seeds, and have **short, stubby beaks**.

One of the most unique beaks is that of the pelican. The pelican's beak is **long and sharp**, enabling it to catch fish when it dives into water. The pelican also has a sort of "pouch" in its throat that can expand to accommodate a large meal.

Birds do not chew their food like most mammals do, but many birds have a **crop**, or a storage tank, near the throat. The crop allows these birds to store food after swallowing, before the food reaches the stomach. **Birds' stomachs** are divided into two sections. The long first part of their stomachs contains digestive enzymes, which begin chemical breakdown of the food. The food then reaches the muscular part of the bird's stomach called the gizzard, which squeezes and mechanically breaks down food.

D. Obtaining Shelter

Most birds build **nests** to lay and hatch their eggs. There are many different styles of nests. Often they are built with sticks, leaves, and mud in trees. However, not all birds build what we traditionally think of as nests. Some birds burrow underground for a "nest". Other birds use hollowed-out cavities of trees for nests. Some species of birds in Australia will make a mound out of decaying vegetation; as the vegetation decays, heat is produced,

This blue-throated warbler has made a nest of bark and twigs, perfect for those hungry little nestlings.
Image credit: public domain

which incubates the bird's eggs! These birds continually cover the mound to keep the eggs warm.

Some birds don't make nests at all, such as the **emperor penguin** of Antarctica. It is far too cold for a nest to be effective in Antarctica! So, to keep its egg warm, an emperor penguin holds the egg on top of its feet and covers it with a flap of skin.

E. Birds' Sense of Sight

Birds have a finely-tuned, excellent sense of sight. Some birds must spy their meals from high in the sky! So, God has given them very powerful eyes. Birds also have very quick reactions. They often fly quickly, and make precise landings, such as on a narrow tree branch or on their prey. As you continue to study birds, pay attention to the abilities, body parts, and behaviors that God has designed for these beautiful and fascinating creatures!

Review Questions

1. What is a bird's crop?

_____

_____

2. Explain some unique designs of birds' lungs and stomachs.

_____

_____

_____

_____

3. Why do birds have different types of beaks? Briefly describe some types of beaks.

_____

_____

_____

4. Why are nests important?

_____

5. How does an emperor penguin incubate its egg?

_____

III. Flight

Birds are most commonly associated with flight. Have you ever looked up and seen a bird floating effortlessly through the sky? Have you seen hundreds of birds flying together in a pattern? Perhaps you have even thought about how it must feel to fly like a bird! Many of us have flown in an airplane. The development of flying machines was an incredible technological advance. However, before Orville and Wilbur Wright took their historic first flight in 1903, people had made other attempts. Early attempts at flight included people strapping feathers to their arms. They soon learned that there is a lot more to flight than just feathers!

A. How Birds Fly

So how do birds fly? The key has to do with <u>air pressure</u>. As you read this book, your body is surrounded by air. Although you don't feel it, the air is applying a certain though small amount of pressure. Move your hand swiftly in front of you, and you will feel air pressure. By flapping their wings, birds push their wings down on the air so fast, it is fast enough to cause them to rise.

Imagine you are doing pushups. You push against the floor and the pressure of your push causes your arms to extend, pushing you up.

A bird needs thrust and flapping wings to take off from the ground.

Image credit: unknown

The same principle is at work in water, when you swim. A bird's wings pushing against the air pushes the bird up.

B. Wings of Birds

Birds do not always flap their wings when they fly, however. A bird's wings are designed to help keep them aloft. The shape of a bird's wings causes air to move more quickly over the wing than under it. Air that moves more quickly exerts less pressure on the wings than the air beneath that moves less quickly. This causes the air beneath the wings to keep the bird up. Airplanes use the same principle.

Birds use air currents to fly as well. Birds can rise even without flapping their wings by riding on top of warm, rising air. The way the birds angle their wings also affects how birds fly.

Birds can use air currents to soar effortlessly in the sky.
Image credit: unknown

C. Helps to Fly

God has given birds other important body parts that help them fly as well. Birds have very hollow bones, making them extremely light, which helps the birds fly. Feathers, of course, are a key ingredient to bird flight.

1. Feathers

Most feathers are classified as either contour feathers or down feathers. **Contour** feathers are the large feathers usually seen on the outside of a bird's body. Contour feathers are important for flight. Contour feathers "catch" air for the bird. Wing and tail feathers are essential for balance and steering.

Down feathers are short, fluffy feathers found against the bird's skin. Down feathers are important for trapping heat and keeping a bird warm. Some birds have **filoplumes** (FIL-o-plooms), hair-like feathers found among the down feathers. If a bird has filoplumes, they are mostly invisible to us, although occasionally they can be seen along the neck.

Besides helping with flight and insulation, feathers help protect the bird's skin from water, and the coloring can be useful for everything from camouflage (to hide for protection) to attracting a mate.

2. V Formation

If you have ever seen a fairly large group of birds flying overhead, you may have noticed them flying in a **"V" formation**, with a leader, followed by rows of birds just behind and to the side of the preceding birds, so the pattern

Birds use "V" formation to save energy on long flights.
Image credit: Dnrivera

looks like the letter V. This God-given flight formation actually helps the birds save energy on long flights. The birds are positioned perfectly for each bird to catch updrafts, that is, air currents created by the bird in front of it. Airplanes flying in a group use the same strategy to save fuel.

How did the birds figure this out? They don't hold graduate degrees in physics, after all! No, but God knows everything about physics. The birds didn't need to figure it out; this behavior is an instinct that God has created in them. This bird flight formation is yet another marvel of His loving design. Instincts allow birds and other animals to exhibit behaviors that they could not learn, but are automatic and which help them survive.

Review Questions

1. Name three important functions of feathers.

2. How does the shape of a bird's wings help keep it aloft?

3. What are the three types of feathers?

4. Why do birds fly in a "V" formation?

5. Why are instincts an important part of creation?

IV. Flightless Birds

When we think of birds, flight is one of the first things that comes to mind. But not all birds fly. In fact, there are about 40 species of flightless birds. Many flightless birds are large, with bodies too massive and wings too small to fly. However, flightless birds come

in all sizes. There are flightless ducks and, of course, penguins are flightless. There is even a flightless parrot.

A. Ratites

There is a group of flightless birds called the **ratites**. Ratites include all the species of ostrich, emu, rhea, cassowary, and kiwi. Most ratites are large birds and live in grassland ecosystems. They have no keel on their sternum. The keel is a ridge on the breastbone of flying birds to which the flight muscles are attached.

1. The Ostrich

You already know that the **ostrich** is the world's largest bird. It also lays the world's largest egg. Ostriches cannot fly, but they can run very fast, up to 43 miles per hour! It would be hard to catch one! Their legs are so strong that a kick from an ostrich can kill a lion! Ostriches also have a very powerful immune system, which means they seldom get sick. Ostriches live in Africa.

The ostrich cannot fly, but it can run up to 43 miles per hour, and its kick is powerful enough to kill a lion. It uses its wings as brakes and for balance when it runs.

Image credit: unknown

2. Emu, rhea, cassowary

Emus, rheas, and cassowaries are all similar to ostriches in some ways. They are large ratites. The emu is the second tallest bird in the world, and the cassowary is the second heaviest bird in the world. They are all very good runners, and although their wings are not used for flight, ratites' wings can be essential tools for helping them balance and

stop when they are tired of running. Emus are found in Australia. The colorful cassowary lives in Australia and New Guinea.

The rhea is found in South America. One interesting fact about the rhea is that after the female lays the eggs, it is the male that incubates them and cares for the young, certainly a reversal of responsibilities!

3. The Kiwi

The kiwi is not as large as the other ratites. The kiwi is New Zealand's national bird. The kiwi is about the size of a chicken, although it lays large eggs that weigh about one pound! Kiwis are nocturnal and spend the day sleeping in underground burrows.

Though only the size of a chicken, kiwis lay eggs that weigh about one pound.

Image credit: Glen Fergus

B. The Kakapo Parrot

Ratites are not the only type of flightless bird. One other flightless bird that is unique is the **kakapo**. This large, green, flightless parrot lives on two islands off the coast of New Zealand. The story of how they got there is an interesting one. Kakapos had become almost extinct. They give off a strong smell, which attracts predators. The kakapo parrot males do not help to care for the young, which left the little kakapos easy prey when the mother left them to find food. Scientists wanted to save the kakapo parrot, so they captured them and moved them to two islands on which there were no predators! There were so few kakapos left that each kakapo was given a name by the scientists!

There are so few kakapos left in the world that each one has been given a name!
Image credit: unknown

Penguins are flightless birds that live only in the Southern Hemisphere.
Image credit: Liam Quinn

C. The Penguin

Almost everyone is familiar with the penguin, another type of flightless bird. Did you know that there are seventeen species of penguins? Although most people associate penguins with Antarctica, not all penguins inhabit that southernmost continent. However, they all live in the <u>Southern Hemisphere</u>. Most penguins live in very, very cold climates. Penguins are built to withstand extreme cold well. Penguins' outer feathers are dense and coated with oil. This protects them from

freezing in cold water. Underneath the outer feathers, they have soft "down" feathers. In addition, penguins have a protective layer of fat under their skin. Although penguins cannot fly like most birds, and they cannot run well like the ratites, they are <u>expert swimmers</u>. Their wings serve as excellent flippers in the water.

Penguins' diet consists of seafood, such as krill, fish, and squid. However, penguins themselves can be prey for other animals, both on land and in the water. The leopard seal is the most common predator of penguins. The largest penguin is the <u>emperor penguin</u>, found in Antarctica. The emperor penguin stands about 45 inches or almost 4 feet high, and weighs 90 pounds! The smallest penguin, the <u>fairy penguin</u>, lives in southern Australia and New Zealand. It is only 10 inches tall and weighs only two and a half pounds!

Review Questions

1. What are ratites?

2. Tell three interesting facts about ostriches.

3. What is a kakapo?

_____

4. How did God design penguins to protect them from extreme cold?

_____

_____

V. Birds of Prey

Some of the most fascinating birds are the birds of prey. These birds are <u>skilled hunters</u> which catch their meals. Many birds, such as penguins, eat animals. Many birds are fish eaters, and many birds are insect eaters, which many of us have seen! To be included in the official group commonly called "birds of prey," however, there are certain characteristics a species must have.

The birds of prey, often called raptors, are defined by scientists as those which generally eat animals or vertebrates. Their prey are usually rather large compared to the bird's own size. Birds of prey have exceptionally <u>keen vision</u> even compared to other birds, <u>razor-like claws</u> called talons, <u>strong leg muscles</u> for carrying their sometimes heavy prey, and strong, <u>sharp beaks for tearing</u> into solid meat.

The birds of prey include hawks, eagles, falcons, harriers, kites, vultures, buzzards, owls, ospreys, and the secretary bird of Africa. Let's take a closer look at a few of these birds.

A. The Hawk

The **hawk** is a bird of prey that people often see circling overhead, looking for food. This is because, although hawks prefer open areas for hunting, they have adapted to populated areas in many places. The red-tailed hawk is the most common hawk in the United States. It can be found throughout almost

all of North America, with the exception only of the Arctic north. Its most distinctive feature is its brick-red tail. In February 2005, Dr. Louis Lefebvre, a Canadian scientist studying innovative feeding behaviors of birds, proclaimed hawks among the most intelligent birds.

The red-tailed hawk is the most common hawk in the United States.

Image credit: unknown

B. The Eagle

Most **eagles** are found in Europe, Asia, and Africa, but two species of this bird of prey—the golden eagle and the bald eagle—are found in the United States. The bald eagle, <u>the national symbol of the U.S.</u>, is actually not bald; its head is covered with white feathers. The bald eagle is much larger than the red-tailed hawk and, like the hawk, its range covers virtually the entire continental U.S. The bald eagle is most common in Alaska. At one point, the bald eagle was in grave danger of becoming extinct, but its population has rebounded

This bird of prey, the bald eagle, is the national symbol of the United States.

Image credit: unknown

thanks to conservation efforts. Although the bald eagle will eat numerous animals, its <u>diet consists mainly of fish</u>. It is also well known for stealing the kills of other birds or animals, which led Benjamin Franklin to argue against the bald eagle becoming the national symbol!

C. The Vulture

Vultures are a family of birds of prey that are primarily scavengers. They rarely hunt healthy animals and are famous for <u>feeding off the remains of other animals' kills</u> or feeding off decaying flesh of dead animals. The two species of condors are included in the vulture family. A common vulture in the United States is the turkey vulture, so named because it resembles a wild turkey from a distance. The turkey vulture has no feathers on its red head, and has an interesting way of defending itself. When it feels threatened, the turkey vulture will vomit strong stomach acids and partially digested meat. The strong smell sends most challengers on their way, and the acid mixture will sting the face of a rival animal that gets too close!

D. The Owl

Owls make up the only <u>nocturnal family of birds of prey</u>. All birds of prey need exceptional eyesight to see prey from far away and construct a successful attack, but owls have exceptionally large eyes that allow them to see well with very little light. Thus, owls are able to hunt at night. The <u>great horned owl</u> is the most common owl of the Americas. It is named for the feather tufts on its head that resemble horns. The great horned owl is a powerful hunter that often kills and carries prey heavier than itself! Its amazing digestive system allows it to eat its prey whole and later regurgitate bone and other unwanted parts. These owls are fiercely protective parents and have been known to attack humans who have wandered too close to their young.

The turkey vulture is so named because it resembles a wild turkey from a distance.

Image credit: M Jobling

The great horned owl is named for the tufts of feathers on its head. Owls are the only nocturnal birds of prey.

Image credit: public domain

Like all birds, God has given birds of prey incredible adaptations that allow them to meet their needs. They serve to help get rid of weaker animals as well as dead animals. Many people consider these aerial predators to be some of the most majestic of all birds.

Review Questions

1. Name three physical characteristics particular to birds of prey.

_____

_____

2. Why did Benjamin Franklin argue against the bald eagle becoming the United States' national symbol?

_____

3. Compare and contrast vultures and hawks.

_____

_____

4. Which are the only nocturnal birds of prey?

_____

VI. Record-Setting Birds

You have read about some unique and fascinating birds in the past couple of lessons, such as flightless birds and birds of prey. In this lesson, you will be introduced to some other unique birds as well as some record-setters. These birds give us a small picture of the incredible complexity and amazing designs of God's creatures, which He has given for us to care for, observe, and learn from. Studying these creatures can help us find ways to improve our own lives.

A. Largest Bird's Nest

You already know that the ostrich is the largest bird and the bee hummingbird the smallest. But did you know that the **largest bird's nest** ever recorded was created by a pair of bald eagles? The nest, which was created near St. Petersburg, Florida, was nine-and-a-half feet wide and 20 feet deep, and weighed more than two tons!

B. Highest Flying and Fastest Dive

Flight is one of the most amazing abilities of birds. The **highest flying bird** is the bar-headed goose. This bird flies over the Himalaya Mountains to migrate and reaches altitudes of 21,120 feet. The record for the **fastest dive** by a bird in flight is held by the peregrine falcon. This bird of prey can dive faster than 215 miles per hour, making it the fastest animal on the planet!

C. Deepest Recorded Dive

Not all birds dive in the air, though. The emperor penguin is a **record-holding diver in water**. The deepest recorded dive for any bird was made by an emperor penguin in the waters off of Antarctica. It dove to a depth of just over 1,853 feet. The emperor penguin also holds the record for the longest dive: 22 minutes.

D. Longest Migration

The Arctic tern holds the record for the **longest migration**. In the summer, it nests north of the Arctic Circle. Then it migrates south for the winter to hunt fish in the waters off Antarctica, before returning north again. This 44,000-mile round trip is the longest of any migration. It also makes the Arctic tern the animal that spends the most time in daylight on the planet. The tern is in the Arctic during the northern summer, and it is in Antarctica during the northern winter, which is summer at the South Pole. During summer, these places have almost constant daylight. Thus, the bird maximizes its time in the light.

The Arctic tern makes the longest migration in the animal kingdom.
Image credit: unknown

VII. Unique Birds

Some birds stand out as being particularly unusual, even unique; that is, they have something about them that is a one-of-a-kind feature.

A. The Flamingo

Though many people find the **flamingo** interesting, what is unique is its mouth. The flamingo's bill contains <u>rows of bony plates that act like filters</u>, much like baleen in some whales. The bony plates in its mouth trap food as the flamingo spits out the muck it takes in from the bottom of its watery environment. Another unique feature is that, unlike other birds, it is the <u>upper part of the flamingo's jaw</u> that moves up and down when it eats, not the lower part of the jaw.

The flamingo has one of the most unique beaks of all birds.
Image credit: unknown

B. The Woodpecker

The woodpecker is another bird with a unique feature: an amazing bill. The **woodpecker's bill** hammers into wood to pick out the critters inside a tree for food. But it's not the woodpecker's bill that is most intriguing. If you have ever heard a woodpecker pecking, it can sound like a rapid-fire machine gun. The <u>pressure exerted on the bird's head by the banging</u> is four times greater than the force that would leave a person with a concussion or other brain injury! How does the woodpecker perform this repeated head-bashing without terrible consequences?

The answer lies in the woodpecker's incredible design. The woodpecker's tail and toes are specially designed by God to allow the bird to keep its grip on trees as it pecks away. The woodpecker's tongue is unusually long, allowing it to slurp out hidden bug meals living within a tree trunk. But it is <u>an amazing series of shock absorbers</u> that protect the bird's brain. The woodpecker's beak and head-support muscles help absorb some of the shock and allow for perfectly straight strikes of the pecking into the tree trunk.

Scientists are studying God's incredible design of the woodpecker to develop safer headgear for people in the military and those involved in football and in other sports.

Image credit: unknown

The woodpecker also has a spongy bone located behind the beak that acts as a shock absorber and protects the bird's brain. These are only some of the parts that work together to keep the woodpecker's brain safe. Scientists and doctors have studied God's design for the woodpecker in attempts to develop better safety equipment for the heads of soldiers and of football players.

C. The Hummingbird

One unique and beautiful group of birds is **hummingbirds**. Hummingbirds can fly forward, backward, sideways, and even hover, all because of the <u>speed with which they beat</u> <u>their wings</u>. They beat their wings so fast it makes a humming sound. Hummingbirds can beat their wings more than <u>80 times per second</u>.

Hummingbirds are important pollinators.

Image credit: unknown

The heart rate of the hummingbird can reach more than 1,250 beats per minute, and the hummingbird can take 250 breaths per minute! All this activity requires an incredible fast-paced metabolism, which burns up energy. Consequently, hummingbirds must <u>eat more than their body weight in nectar every day</u> to fuel their incredibly fast-paced physical activity. Nectar is a sugar liquid produced by plants.

D. The Swallow

One of the most beautiful, unique events in the world of birds is the **migration of the swallows** in San Juan Capistrano, California. The swallows stay in Southern California for the summer, many at Mission San Juan Capistrano. They leave the Mission each year on October 23, the feast day of St. John of Capistrano, for whom the Mission is named, to spend the winter in Argentina in South America. Then, each year on the feast of St. Joseph, March 19, the swallows return to San Juan Capistrano, to the celebration of numerous tourists and locals. The migration of the San Juan Capistrano swallows has inspired parades, a hit song ("When the Swallows Come Back to Capistrano"), and the wonder of countless people over the years.

The swallows of San Juan Capistrano mark important feast days with their migration.

Image credit: Don DeBold

   Learning the facts about these unique birds should make us grateful to our Creator for the beauty and the diversity of His creatures. God takes such good care of birds, and we know that people are much more important than birds. We can be confident that God always will take care of us. As Jesus told His disciples, "Are not two sparrows sold for a penny? And not one of them will fall to the ground without your Father's will. But even the hairs of your head are all numbered. Fear not, therefore; you are of more value than many sparrows."

Review Questions

1. What records does the emperor penguin hold?

_____

2. How does the Arctic tern spend more of its life in daylight than any other animal?

_____

_____

3. What makes the woodpecker's design so remarkable?

_____

_____

_____

4. Why is the study of nature's marvels useful for the development of new technology?

_____

_____

5. How do the swallows help celebrate important feast days in Southern California?

_____

_____

VIII. Birds and People

St. Bonaventure, in his biography of St. Francis of Assisi, tells an interesting story of a falcon who was of particular help to St. Francis. St. Francis would get up in the middle of the night for prayer, and the falcon would cry out to waken him each night, a miraculous favor for which St. Francis was very grateful. However, when St. Francis was sick, the falcon would not call out in the middle of the night, but would wait until daybreak to wake him.

A. Birds as Food

While we do not have a falcon with such a God-given miraculous instinct, many people do rely on birds for a variety of things. For example, birds are an **important source of food**. People use birds, especially chickens, for both meat and eggs, both excellent sources of nutrition. Turkeys have pride of place at Thanksgiving, and many other birds, such as ducks and geese, are common food items. All of these are not only considered excellent eating, but are at the top of the list for good health and nutrition. Chicken, however, is the most popular meat being eaten in the United States. In fact, the chicken is the most popular bird in the world. Raising chickens has even become popular among rural home schooling families!

B. Birds Protect Plant Life

Birds are important for distributing and **protecting plant life**. Many small birds like the hummingbird are important pollinators, helping to carry seeds from one plant to another. In addition, birds can be important for keeping pests away from food plants. Many gardeners build special bird houses to attract birds as a primary means of pest control for their gardens and fruit trees.

C. Birds Trained for Hunting

People in the past would train birds to be of great use. Many hunters today use dogs to help them with their hunts, but in some places, it used to be common to hunt with birds. Falconry refers to the ancient practice of using birds of prey to assist with **hunting animals**, such as deer. Today, hunters need to be licensed for using birds to hunt. Traditionally, falcons are used, but hawks are another common bird used for the practice, in which case it is sometimes referred to as "hawking."

Hunting birds, like this kestrel, are trained to land on the gloved hand of the falconer.

Image credit: unknown

Carrier pigeons were used during wartime to relay secret messages.

Photo Credit: National Archives

D. Carrier Pigeons in Wartime

Pigeons have been trained to **carry messages** to desired locations. Carrier pigeons often have been employed as a method of communication during war. Pigeons were used in both World Wars. In World War II, carrier pigeons sometimes flew as many as 600 miles! For their service in World War II, the United States awarded 32 pigeons the Dickin Medal, which is an honor reserved for animals that provide important military service.

E. Birds as Pets

Finally, birds are **common pets**. Many people enjoy the lively chatter of their pet parakeets, whose small size makes them convenient pets. Others prefer larger parrots, which can learn to make a variety of sounds. Parrots often mimic sounds they hear, including human speech. The African gray parrot can mimic more human words than any other animal. Of course, bird-watching is a popular hobby among people who just enjoy the natural beauty of birds.

F. Thanksgiving Turkey

Did you know that the American tradition of Thanksgiving has roots in Catholic Europe? November 11 is the feast day of St. Martin of Tours. It was customary in Europe to celebrate with a feast thanking God for the harvest. This traditional thanksgiving feast survived in many places and was brought to the United States with the Pilgrims, who shared it with the Native Americans.

Traditionally, goose was the main dish for St. Martin's feast. This was part of the Pilgrims' Thanksgiving, along with some of the abundant wild turkey in the area. In the United States, at least, turkeys have taken the holiday away from the geese. President Abraham Lincoln proclaimed Thanksgiving a national holiday in 1863, stating: "I do therefore invite my fellow citizens in every part of the United States, and also those who are at sea and those who are sojourning in foreign lands, to set apart and observe the last Thursday of November next, as a day of Thanksgiving and Praise to our beneficent Father Who dwells in the Heavens."

Review Questions

1. Name important ways birds are used by people.

_____

_____

2. Explain two ways that birds assist plant life.

_____

_____

3. How have pigeons been useful during war?

_____

_____

4. Explain the Catholic roots of Thanksgiving.

_____

_____

IX. Extinct Birds

You have learned about birds and have studied some of the many species of birds that God has given us. The world is full of beautiful, incredible birds, but some of the birds that once inhabited the planet do not exist anymore. They are <u>extinct</u>. When the last individual of a species dies, and there are none of that species left alive, we say that species is extinct. In this lesson, you will be introduced to some of the birds that are extinct.

A. The Elephant Bird and the Moa

Two large extinct ratites are the **elephant bird** and the **moa**. These two flightless giant birds each lived on an island. The elephant bird lived on the island of Madagascar off the east coast of Africa, and the moa lived in New Zealand. The elephant bird is believed to be the largest bird ever to have lived, standing at <u>ten feet tall and weighing as much as 1,000 pounds</u>. Marco Polo is said to have investigated these birds during his travels. The moa could

The elephant bird is believed to be the largest bird ever to have lived.

Image credit: unknown

stand as high as 13 feet, but the bird was not built as solidly as the elephant bird, so it had a lighter weight. The elephant bird went extinct in the mid-1600s, and the moa went extinct in 1773.

B. The Great Auk

The **Great Auk** was also a flightless bird, but it resembled a penguin. It was a powerful swimmer that lived around the waters of the North Atlantic Ocean. As its numbers began to dwindle, a conservation effort was launched, but it was not enough to save the great auk, which went extinct in the mid-1800s.

The great auk once inhabited the waters of the North Atlantic Ocean.

Image credit: unknown

C. The Dodo

In 1865, Lewis Carroll wrote *Alice's Adventures in Wonderland*. This book contained a **dodo**, an extinct flightless bird. It sparked popular interest in the dodo. The dodo bird stood <u>three feet tall and weighed about 40 pounds</u>. It lived on the island of Mauritius, about 500 miles east of Madagascar, an island country in the Indian Ocean, off the coast of southeast Africa.

When human settlements came to Mauritius Island, the dodo fell prey to hunting by humans and by the animals that humans brought to the island. The dodo went extinct in the late 1600s.

The dodo went extinct
in the late 1600s.

Image credit: unknown

D. Passenger Pigeons of North America

One of the strangest extinction stories is that of the **passenger pigeon** of North America. When the Americas were discovered, it is estimated that North America contained five billion passenger pigeons, one-third of all birds in North America. These birds were so plentiful that they often had to stand on each other in trees to have enough room. Flocks of passenger pigeons would blacken the sky for hours.

The American people began to see passenger pigeons not only as a nuisance but also as a cheap source of meat. Hunting was encouraged, and many people believed the vast number of pigeons negated any need for protection or regulation. However, passenger pigeons could lay only one egg a year, and their population was in more danger than people realized. Much of the late 1800s still saw encouragement for hunting, but by the end of the century, the birds were almost gone. The last living passenger pigeon, "Martha," died in the Cincinnati Zoo on September 1, 1914.

E. California Condors

Some conservationists are currently trying to save the California condor. **California condors** are a species of vulture and are the largest flying land bird in North America. Their numbers began to decline from the time of the Gold Rush in the 1850s for a variety of reasons. By the 1980s, there were very few California condors left.

The once-plentiful passenger pigeon
was hunted to extinction.

Image credit: unknown

Captive breeding programs have brought hope to
the future of the California condor.

Image credit: unknown

The last California condors were removed from the wild in 1987 for a captive breeding program. There were only 22 California condors left at the time. However, through successful programs led by the San Diego Wild Animal Park and the Los Angeles Zoo, the first California condors were able to be reintroduced into the wild in 1992. Some of these have begun breeding in the wild, and in 2014 there were 127 wild California condors in existence.

As of 2017 it appears there are 463 total, with 290 in the wild and 173 in captivity—the U.S. Department of the Interior has an official report online.

The lessons of the passenger pigeon and other extinct birds are important for all of us. Animals have been given to people by God and, although they are a valid food source, we are responsible for protecting species from extinction when they are in jeopardy.

Review Questions

1. Compare and contrast the elephant bird and the moa.

_____

_____

_____

_____

2. What sparked popular interest in the dodo bird in the 1800s?

_____

_____

_____

_____

3. Contrast the stories of the passenger pigeon and the California condor.

_____

_____

_____

_____

Chapter Review Activity

SECTION A

Use the words in the word box to complete the sentences:

bird	contour	crop	down
filoplumes	incubate	nests	ratites
talons	Thanksgiving		

1. A _____ is a warm-blooded vertebrate that has feathers and lays eggs.

2. A bird's _____ is a storage tank near its throat that allows it to store food after swallowing.

3. _____ are flightless birds with no keel, such as the ostrich, emu, and kiwi.

4. St. Martin's feast day was the original occasion for _____ in Catholic Europe during the Middle Ages.

5. _____ feathers are visible and useful for flying.

6. Birds often _____ their eggs by sitting on them.

7. Birds have fluffy _____ feathers that keep them warm.

8. Birds of prey have razor-like claws called _____.

9. Birds often build _____ in trees, underground, or even as large mounds.

10. Some birds have hair-like _____ that often cannot be seen.

SECTION B

Fill in the table below with the birds in the box:

dodo   elephant bird   emperor penguin
hummingbird owl   passenger pigeon
pigeon   swallow   vulture
woodpecker

11. _____ Holds its egg on its feet and covers it with a flap of skin to incubate

12. _____ Only nocturnal bird of prey

13. _____ Scientists are studying its incredible head design to develop safety gear for people

14. _____ Consumes more than its body weight in nectar each day to fuel its amazing metabolism

15. _____ Returns to Mission San Juan Capistrano yearly on St. Joseph's feast day

16. _____ Awarded the Dickin Medal for service in World War II

17. _____ Condors are a type of

18. _____ Believed to be the largest bird ever to exist

19. _____ The last individual, "Martha," died in 1914

20. _____ Popular interest in this bird was inspired by the book *Alice's Adventures in Wonderland*

SECTION C

Please circle the correct answer.

21. Which birds are excellent swimmers?

    A. Ostriches

    B. Peregrine falcons

    C. Owls

    D. Penguins

22. What used to wake St. Francis of Assisi nightly for prayer?

    A. St. Bonaventure

    B. A falcon

    C. A raven

    D. An alarm clock

23. What do the air sacs connected to a bird's lungs do?

    A. Help it stay airborne

    B. Keep the lungs from "popping" at high altitudes

    C. Prevent the bird from crashing

    D. Supply it with extra oxygen from each breath

SECTION D

Answer the following questions.

24. Explain how the design of birds' bodies helps them fly.

_____

_____

25. Name two ways wings are important for flightless birds.

_____

_____

Reptiles and Amphibians

Snake

Tuatara

Salamander

Turtle

Image credits (from top): public domain, public domain, Cristo Vlahos, unknown

Reptiles and Amphibians

I. Reptiles

When we think about reptiles, we think about snakes and lizards and other creatures we would just as soon not run across when we are out walking on a sunny day in the woods! Since we know that God has a good reason for creating all His creatures, we also know that He has a good reason for creating reptiles. While we cannot think of any reasons offhand, we find that military scientists, who work with soldiers and teach them about surviving off the land, have good reasons for us to learn that reptiles are important for our good health.

That seems surprising, but the reason the military scientists give us is that reptiles keep the rodent population under control. Rats and mice, squirrels and beavers, even chipmunks, carry serious diseases and are often harmful to people, especially to children, or even to soldiers walking in an unfamiliar land.

Reptiles not only eat rodents, they eat insects which also can carry serious diseases which are harmful to people, especially soldiers walking through forests, or children playing in the woods. God's plan, evidently, is to keep

a moderate number of rodents and insects to do their jobs, but not to let reptiles become so many as to be dangerous to humans.

As we study the features of reptiles, let's remind ourselves which creatures we are discussing. The class of reptiles includes a wide variety of the following: alligators, crocodiles, lizards, snakes, and turtles. Okay, so we wouldn't mind finding a turtle if we are out walking in the woods!

A. Ectothermic

Reptiles are vertebrates, that is, they have backbones. However, unlike birds and mammals, reptiles are **ectothermic**, or cold-blooded. (The prefix "ecto" means outer; thermic means pertaining to temperature.) Ectothermic means that reptiles' bodies do not maintain a constant warm internal temperature. The body temperature of reptiles is affected by their surroundings or environment. If the temperature around them changes, even several times a day, their body

Because reptiles are cold-blooded, they often need to bask in the sun to keep their temperatures up.
Image credit: unknown

temperature changes just as often. For this reason, you may sometimes see reptiles basking on a rock in the sun to warm themselves! Protection from too much sun, however, is important as well. A reptile has more energy when its body temperature is warmer, but if the reptile gets too hot, it can overheat, slow down, and even die!

B. Need for Oxygen

Like mammals and birds, reptiles have <u>lungs</u> and meet their need for oxygen by breathing air. Even reptiles that spend a good amount of time in the water, like turtles and alligators, need to breathe air to obtain oxygen. Have you ever noticed—from afar, of course—that alligators and crocodiles often keep only <u>their heads</u> above water? It is not just because they are looking for something to eat, but also because they need to keep their noses out of the water to breathe! Do you know that crocodiles keep their "snout" out of the water even while they are "sleeping" so they can continually take in oxygen?

Crocodiles periodically
rise to the surface to breathe.
Image credit: public domain

C. Reptiles lay eggs

Reptile eggs are similar to birds' eggs in many ways. Unlike the hard eggshells of birds, however, reptile egg shells are soft and leathery. It is safer, however, not to attempt to find a reptile egg for breakfast! Those reptile mothers are sometimes not too friendly! Some Louisiana farmers, however, in order to protect alligators from extinction, often collect alligator eggs and protect them until they hatch. Then the farmers return the baby alligators back to their home in the marshes or rivers. Florida even offers an Alligator Hatching Festival for children to come, observe the hatching, and even hold some of the baby alligators!

Alligators hatch from eggs.
Image credit: shutterstock.com

D. Reptile Scales Useful

Reptiles have scales or hard plate-like shells on the outside of their bodies. The scales are made from the protein called <u>keratin</u>, the same protein that makes up our fingernails. Scales are important to reptiles for a variety of reasons. First, scales are a tough covering to <u>provide protection</u> from predators who would like to eat them! Second, scales are essential for reptiles because they <u>prevent reptiles from losing moisture</u> through their skin. Some reptiles live in very dry areas, and their scales help them to retain moisture underneath. Some reptiles, like snakes, use their scales <u>to help with movement</u>. Lacking legs, for example, snakes must slither along the ground to move. Their movable plate-like scales provide the necessary friction for the snakes to pull themselves along the ground.

Reptiles have scales that provide protection from predators, conserve moisture, and sometimes aid movement.
Image credit: Gruzd

For some reptiles, scales take on a very unique role. In rattlesnakes, for example, the specialized scales at the tail make a rattling noise when shaken. Rattlesnakes shake their rattles as a warning to scare off predators or other potential dangers.

Scales are used in different ways for some reptiles. The feet of some geckos have unique plate-like scales called lamellae (luh-MEL-ee). These lamellae scales allow the gecko to grip surfaces in a way that makes the scales appear to defy gravity and "cling" to things the gecko is climbing.

E. Classification System

In the Linnaean classification system, the class of reptiles is divided into four orders. One consists primarily of **snakes and lizards**.

Another consists of **crocodilians**, such as alligators and crocodiles. A third is made up of **turtles and tortoises**. And the fourth contains the two species of a reptile called the **tuatara**, found in New Zealand.

F. St. Patrick and the Snakes of Ireland

One saint commonly associated with reptiles is St. Patrick. St. Patrick was born in Britain around the year 387. As a boy, he was kidnapped and taken to Ireland, where he lived as a captured slave for six years. During this period, he became very close to God and spent long hours in prayer. He became known as the "holy youth." In time, he escaped from Ireland and returned home. After a while, Patrick had a vision of the people of Ireland calling him back to bring the teachings of Jesus Christ to them. Patrick then studied in a seminary and became a priest, traveled back to Ireland, converted many of the Irish people, built many churches, and eventually was appointed bishop of Ireland. It is believed he died about the year 460.

St. Patrick is famous for eliminating paganism from Ireland. There were many miracles as a result of St. Patrick's prayers and work among the Irish people. He was known for his sufferings but also for his devotion to prayers and saying daily Mass. While it is an ancient traditional belief that St. Patrick was responsible for eliminating the dangerous snakes of Ireland, it is believed by historians that the "snakes" were actually the pagans who ruled the land before St. Patrick converted them.

Review Questions

1. What does ectothermic mean?

2. Compare and contrast reptiles with birds and mammals.

_____

_____

_____

3. How are reptile eggs different from bird eggs?

_____

_____

4. Name three reasons reptiles' scales are important.

_____

_____

_____

II. Snakes, Lizards, and Tuatara

Snakes are some of the most amazing and yet most polarizing reptiles. Polarizing here means that some people automatically run to see them, and some people automatically run to get away from them! Some people are snake lovers and keep them as pets. Others are terribly afraid of snakes. Some snakes can be dangerous to humans, and they are responsible for numerous deaths each year, especially in the rural communities of Africa and Asia. We Catholics are aware that the devil is often represented as a snake, such as the devil-snake that tempted Adam and Eve. Consequently, most of us don't have "good" thoughts about snakes. Nevertheless, we need to study these creatures of God to learn why He made them!

A. Snakes

1. Have No Limbs — Snakes are distinct from other reptiles because they have no limbs. Their long, tubular bodies slither along the ground. Because of its unique shape, a snake's internal organs are often positioned differently than other reptiles' organs. For example, one of the kidneys is located before the other in a row, rather than across from it.

2. Swallow Food Whole — Snakes do have teeth, but they swallow their food whole. Often a snake will eat something wider than the diameter of its own body! How can it do that? Can you imagine eating something whole that was bigger than your head? Well, your jaw cannot do what a snake's jaw can do! The two

This snake has eaten an egg.
Image credit: unknown

sides of a snake's lower jaw are very flexible, allowing it to open its mouth much wider than its own body. Talk about a big mouth! It then engulfs its meal and the two sides of the jaw move alternately, pushing the victim prey down its throat. Once the snake has swallowed its prey, it digests it. Often a bulge can be seen in the middle of a snake that has just consumed a large meal. Check out the snakes the next time you are visiting a zoo!

3. Snakes are carnivores, so they **eat meat**. Many snakes eat small insects, snails, spiders, or fish. Other snakes eat birds, small mammals, and reptiles, as well as their eggs. Some snakes, however, can bring down prey as large as a deer! Some overanxious or very hungry snakes will simply grab prey with their mouths and swallow it alive. There are other ways a snake may catch a meal.

4. Some Are Constrictors — Some snakes, such as <u>boas and anacondas</u>, are **constrictors**. Constrictors grab their prey and then wrap their muscular bodies around it. Then these snakes begin tightening their grip. This is not a friendly hug! Every time the prey breathes out, the snake's grip gets a little tighter. Eventually, the animal suffocates. Then the snake eats its dead prey. These constrictor snakes find it safer to suffocate their prey

rather than trying to swallow a live animal, especially an animal which might have sharp teeth or long claws or a powerful kick!

5. Some Are Venomous — Some snakes are **venomous**. <u>Rattlesnakes and cobras</u> are two examples of venomous snakes. These snakes bite their prey and then **inject their catch with venom**. Then the snake waits for the venom to kill the prey so it can be safely eaten. Soldiers and others who visit warm desert areas need to learn about these dangerous snakes.

Rattlesnakes can be found in the United States. They are venomous and sometimes deadly to humans.
Image credit: public domain

A boa is a constrictor.
Image credit: unknown

Snakes and lizards have forked tongues that pick up scents and tell them about their environment.
Image credit: unknown

6. Snake Tongues — If you have spent any time looking at snakes, you may have noticed them <u>flicking their tongues out</u>. Is this just because snakes have really bad manners? No, snakes use their tongues to investigate their surroundings. In fact, <u>snakes "smell" with their tongues</u>! The snake picks up tiny scent particles from the air, water, or ground with its flicking tongue. When the tongue retracts back into the mouth, the snake gets important information about its environment from the particles.

7. Snake Reproduction — Some snakes give birth to live young, while other kinds of snakes lay eggs. For example, boas and pythons are similar types of snakes, yet pythons lay eggs and boas give birth to live young. Most sea snakes give birth to live young in the water, but some, such as the sea kraits, go to the land to lay their eggs.

B. Lizards

1. Have Legs — In the same order as snakes are lizards. **Lizards** have some obvious differences from snakes, and some that are not so obvious. The most obvious difference is the presence of legs. <u>Most lizards have legs</u>. Another difference is that most lizards have <u>moveable eyelids</u>. Lizards can blink their eyes, whereas snakes do not have eyelids; snake eyes are covered with a transparent scale. Because lizards generally do not have the tubular shape that snakes do, the <u>lizards' internal organs are arranged a little differently</u>, usually equal on both sides.

2. Shed Skin — <u>Both snakes and lizards shed their skin</u>. As lizards grow, their old skin comes off and is replaced by new skin. Snakes usually shed their skin in one long piece. It begins to come off by the head, and the snake simply slithers out of it. In contrast, lizards' skin is usually shed in patches.

3. Most Lay Eggs — Most lizards lay eggs; however, about 20 percent of lizards give birth to live young.

4. Lizard Meals — Unlike snakes, <u>some species of lizards are herbivores</u>, non-meat eaters. Other lizards eat animals, and a few are omnivores, eating both plants and animals. Some lizards swallow prey whole like snakes do, and some lizards snatch meals with quick strikes of their tongues. Chameleons, for example, can shoot their tongues farther than their own body length to catch insects! Lizards, like snakes, <u>use their tongues to smell</u>.

5. Few Are Venomous — <u>Only three lizard species</u> are known to be venomous: the Gila monster, the Mexican beaded lizard, and the Komodo dragon. Unlike venomous snakes which inject poison through needle-like fangs,

Mexican beaded lizard is akin to the Gila monster, but up to three times larger.

Image credit: public domain

Gila monsters make up one of only three known venomous lizards.

Image credit: public domain

The Komodo dragon is the largest of all venomous lizards, growing up to 10 feet in length.

Image credit: Mark Dumont

these venomous lizards fill their mouths with venom, which seeps into their prey through wounds made by the lizards' teeth.

Probably the most dangerous lizard to humans is the <u>Komodo dragon</u>, found in Indonesia, pretty far from the USA! These massive reptiles can grow as long as 10 feet and weigh 300 pounds! The Komodo dragons' mouths have sharp, serrated teeth and, along with their toxic venom, contain bacteria that is also toxic. We are still learning about these giant lizards, whose existence was recorded first in 1910 by Western scientists.

C. Tuatara

Although they inhabit a scientific classification order all their own, **tuatara** look very similar to lizards. The two species that exist of this endangered <u>burrowing reptile live in New Zealand</u>. It is believed that they can live 100 years!

Tuatara have crests of spines running down the center of their backs. Males can grow up to two-and-a-half feet long; females are a little smaller. Tuatara lay eggs, and it

Tuatara may look like lizards, but they are classified in a separate order.
Image credit: unknown

takes as much as 15 months before they hatch, the longest incubation period of any reptile. Another thing that is unique about the tuatara is that regardless of its food – insects, lizards, or small birds – the tuatara chews its prey thoroughly before swallowing it!

The tuatara is almost extinct, but several scientists in New Zealand are doing their best to keep the few alive, to keep them in a wild yet protective environment, and to protect them from their natural predators.

Review Questions

1. How is a snake able to swallow prey that is wider than its own body?

_____

_____

2. What is a constrictor?

_____

_____

3. Compare and contrast snakes and lizards.

_____

_____

4. Why do snakes and lizards stick out their tongues?

_____

_____

5. What is unique about the eating habits of the tuatara?

_____

_____

III. Turtles and Tortoises

A. Common Needs

Turtles are especially interesting and popular for children to observe. While little turtles can be easily purchased, larger ones can be found in gardens, fields, and forest areas. They are fun and educational to watch. Turtles and tortoises, with their telltale shells, are easily recognized. What is the difference between a turtle and a tortoise? Actually, tortoises are types of **turtles**. Unlike many other turtle species, however, **tortoises** live exclusively on land.

1. Shelter

Although turtles take shelter with them wherever they go, they often use forms of shelter besides their shells. Tortoises often dig burrows, and sea turtles use the water for shelter. Because sea turtles can be such excellent swimmers, diving into the water can be their best strategy for escaping a predator. On land, turtles face danger from mammals, birds, snakes, and alligators. In the water, turtles face danger from fish, such as sharks, and mammals, such as killer whales.

A turtle's shell is really an incredible form of shelter. Most turtles have hard shells, covered with plates made from the protein keratin. Some turtles have soft shells. When a turtle is threatened, it will pull its head and legs inside its shell. Some species, such as

the box turtle, can completely close the top shell against the bottom shell, making them especially well protected.

Turtles' shells provide protection against predators.
Image credit: unknown

2. Oxygen

Turtles have lungs and meet their need for oxygen by breathing air. Some water turtles, in addition to breathing air, can actually obtain oxygen from the water through their skin! Some species of turtles live exclusively on land, others are comfortable in the sea, and still others inhabit fresh water ponds. However, all turtles lay their eggs on land. They do not sit on their eggs to incubate them like birds do. Usually the female turtle digs a hole in which to lay her eggs and covers them with dirt. When they hatch, the baby turtles dig their way out and must fend for themselves.

Turtles bury their eggs, and their young
dig out after hatching.
Image credit: unknown

Tortoises are turtles that live
exclusively on land.
Image credit: unknown

3. Food

With over 250 species of turtles, their diet can be quite varied. Turtles do not have teeth; instead, turtles tear their food with sharp beaks. Some are omnivorous, eating plants as well as animals like insects, worms, and slugs. The snapping turtle eats fish, frogs, and even other turtles!

B. The Galapagos Tortoise

The largest <u>tortoise</u>, the Galapagos tortoise, is an herbivore that eats cactus plants. In contrast, the largest of all <u>turtles</u>, the leatherback sea turtle, which can weigh more than 1500 pounds, is a carnivorous turtle that eats jellyfish. Amazingly, the poisonous, stinging cells of the jellyfish, though powerful enough to kill some animals, do not harm the leatherback turtle!

Review Questions

1. What is the difference between a turtle and a tortoise?

_____

_____

_____

2. Besides their shells, what can turtles use as shelter?

_____

_____

_____

3. How do turtles incubate their eggs?

_____

_____

IV. Crocodilians

The fourth order of reptiles, **crocodilians**, includes the species of alligators, crocodiles, caimans, and gavials. For many people, crocodilians can be scary creatures. One can imagine coming down to the water's edge for a drink, not noticing the nostrils and eyeballs of a crocodile resting just barely above the surface. Then, suddenly, up jumps his head! In truth, crocodilians rarely attack people, but in many places, we share the same habitat, so in those areas, be careful and watch the water's surface!

Crocodilians are the largest living reptiles. The largest crocodile, the salt water crocodile, can grow as long as 24 feet! Crocodilians are at home both on land and in water, but they prefer to hunt from the water, and usually at night. They use their powerful tails for swimming and have webbed hind feet. Most crocodilians live in fresh water, but a few species can be found in salt water.

A. Crocodiles as Predators

Adult crocodilians can hunt massive prey, as large as a water buffalo! Crocodilians often wait patiently for their meals to come to the water's edge for a drink. Then the crocodile suddenly lunges, snatching its prey with powerful jaws and sharp teeth. A crocodilian will then drag its victim into the water and perform a "death roll," in which it spins around and around while holding its prey in its jaws. This maneuver is how they bite off chunks of meat to swallow.

Although the crocodile muscles that snap the jaw shut are incredibly powerful, the muscles that open the jaw are weak! People who remove alligators from residential neighborhoods in Florida, for example, can hold the gators' mouths shut with their hands, and tape them closed as they are transported. The opening jaw muscles are too weak to break the tape!

B. Differences in Teeth Between Crocodiles and Alligators

How do we tell the difference between an alligator and a crocodile, the two most familiar crocodilians? The best way is to look at the head. **Crocodiles** have more pointed snouts, whereas **alligators'** snouts are more rounded. Also, with their mouths closed, some of the lower teeth are exposed on a crocodile. On an alligator, the lower teeth fit into a pit in the upper jaw and cannot be seen on the outside of the mouth.

Crocodiles' snouts are more pointed than alligators. All crocodilians have mouths full of sharp teeth.

Image credit: unknown

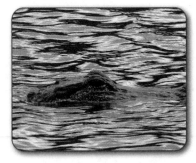

Only this alligator's eyes and nose are exposed above the surface of the water, making it very difficult for potential prey to see the alligator.

Image credit: unknown

Alligators often can be found lurking near the water.

Image credit: unknown

C. Caring for the Young

Crocodilians are unusual among reptiles in that they <u>care for their eggs and care for their young</u>. After preparing a nest and laying eggs on land, a female crocodilian will stay nearby until they hatch. Then the mother will gather her young in her mouth and carry them to an area of the water where they will be safe. A mother crocodilian may stay with her young for more than a year, and is attentive to their little "squawks" that might signal the presence of danger.

D. Caimans and Gavials

Caimans (KAY-mans), found in Central and South America, are very <u>similar to alligators</u>, but are smaller. It is actually a crocodilian, however. Several caimans are endangered, in danger of becoming extinct.

They like to live in freshwater and to bury themselves in mud! While they like to eat insects, as they grow bigger, they will eat fish, birds, turtles, and snakes. They are nocturnal, that is, they are more active at night.

Gavials of India and Pakistan have very <u>unique snouts among crocodilians</u>. The snouts of the gavials are long and slender, with a strange round "knob" at the end. The Gavials have many teeth, which are exposed when the mouth is closed. They like to live in swamps and catch fish. However, they are endangered species because their natural habitat is disappearing and they are hunted for food by natives.

Caimans like to bury
themselves in the mud.
Image credit: Lea Maimone

Gavials have a slender snout
with a large knob on the end.
Image credit: Bo Link

Review Questions

1. What animals are included in the crocodilian order?

_____

_____

_____

2. Describe the differences between alligators and crocodiles.

_____

_____

3. How do people take advantage of the differences in the strength of crocodilians' different jaw muscles?

_____

_____

4. What is unique about the parenting of crocodilians?

_____

_____

V. Amphibians

At one time, scientists classified **amphibians** (am-FIB-ee-ans) in the same class as reptiles, but as their knowledge of each type of creature grew, they found that amphibians are very different from reptiles. Now amphibians are identified by scientists as a distinct class. Basically, amphibians start out life in the water, but their bodies change with the growth of legs and lungs so they can live on land. Frogs and salamanders are good examples of amphibians.

A. Basic Traits

1. Basic Characteristics — Not all amphibians fit perfectly into their amphibian class. However, there are some basic characteristics common to most amphibians. First, amphibians are vertebrates, meaning they have a backbone. Second, they are cold-blooded, like reptiles. However, unlike reptiles, amphibians' have smooth skin, not scaly skin. In addition, the amphibians' skin is very thin. Because of their thin skin, most amphibians cannot inhabit dry environments. Without scales to prevent water loss, amphibians need to inhabit moist ecosystems to keep their skin moist.

2. Most Lay Eggs — Most amphibians lay eggs like most reptiles do, but amphibian eggs lack outer shells, so most amphibians lay their eggs in water. The term "amphibian" means "double life." The term is fitting for this class of animals because usually amphibians spend their early life in the water but move to land as adults. Many adult amphibians, however, can be found both on land and in water.

3. Need Oxygen — Because they are born in water, baby amphibians meet their need for oxygen by obtaining it from the water through their gills. Most amphibians develop

Baby amphibians meet their need for oxygen by obtaining it from the water through their gills.
Image credit: shutterstock.com

lungs as they mature, and as adults, they breathe oxygen from the air. One unusual detail about amphibians is that they can obtain oxygen from the air but they also can obtain oxygen from water through their thin skin. Now that is rare!

B. Metamorphosis

It is a big change for little amphibians to go from having gills to having lungs. Most amphibians go through a process of called metamorphosis (met-a-MOR-fo-sis). Metamorphosis is a process by which an animal goes through major body changes after birth, so that the adult of a species does not look at all like the juvenile. A caterpillar, for example, goes through metamorphosis as it develops into a butterfly.

terrestrial environment

aquatic environment

5. Developing from gills to lungs is not the only major change that happens during an amphibian's metamorphosis. Let us examine the stages of a frog's life. The frog begins life in an egg. When the egg hatches, the "baby" is a tadpole. A tadpole has a long tail, eats algae, and gets its oxygen through gills. As the metamorphosis progresses, the gills begin to be covered over and disappear as lungs develop. The tadpole then will develop legs. As the body changes continue, the tadpole will turn into a froglet. This is a small frog that still has its tail. About 12 weeks after hatching, a frog, with legs, lungs, and no tail or gills, will emerge.

Image credit: unknown

Review Questions

1. Compare and contrast reptiles and amphibians; that is, show the similarities and the differences.

_____

_____

_____

_____

2. Why is "amphibian" a good name for this class of animals?

_____

_____

_____

3. How do amphibians meet their need for oxygen?

_____

_____

_____

4. Explain metamorphosis.

_____

_____

_____

VI. Frogs and Toads

Amphibians are divided into three orders in the Linnaean system. One order consists of <u>frogs and toads</u>. Another order contains <u>salamanders</u>. A third order is made up of <u>caecilians</u> (see-SIL-ee-uns).

A. Frogs and Toads

God created frogs and toads with special physical characteristics to suit their environment and behavior. Both frogs and toads have powerful hind legs that can propel them in long leaps. They have skeletons designed to absorb shock, so their bones do not break when they come down from high leaps. Many species have webbed feet that help them swim, while tree frogs have sticky pads on their feet that keep them from falling as they leap from tree to tree.

B. Tadpoles, Frogs, and Toads

Tadpoles are the beginning stage of life for frogs and toads. They have a round body and a tail. They live in the water until they are more developed. They breathe oxygen through tiny organs called gills. Although most tadpoles feed on algae in the water, after metamorphosis, when the tadpoles develop into adults, almost all frogs and toads are meat eaters. Some of their favorite foods are insects. Frogs and toads flick out their sticky tongues and snare insect prey. Some large frogs eat amphibians, reptiles, and even small birds and mammals.

C. Camouflage

Camouflage is an important element allowing frogs and toads to approach their prey and hide from predators. If a predator does see a frog or toad, and the frog or toad cannot escape, the little frog or toad may play dead and try to blend in with the nearby leaves. Another defense of a frog or toad is to bloat itself up with air so it appears too big to eat!

D. Difference Between Toads and Frogs

Toads are a type of frog. There are visual differences that allow people to distinguish between toads and other frogs. Toads have some distinguishing traits that put them in the

This frog's feet are designed to keep it from falling when it leaps.

Image credit: unknown

Through the process of metamorphosis, these tadpoles will become frogs.

Image credit: public domain

Frogs have powerful hind legs for hopping.

Image credit: unknown

subgroup of frogs known as toads. First, toads generally have <u>drier, bumpy skin</u> compared to other frogs. Toads have <u>weaker legs than other frogs</u>. Toads would never win frog jumping contests, for either grace or distance! Often toads have <u>lumps behind their eyes</u>. These lumps are glands that secrete a poison when the toad is attacked by a predator. Finally, unlike most other frogs, most <u>toads don't have teeth</u>.

Toads have dry skin covered
with wart-like bumps.
Image credit: unknown

E. Frogs: Environment, Nocturnal, Lay Eggs

There are more than <u>4,000 species of frogs</u> in the world, and their behaviors are quite varied. Although most prefer wet, tropical environments, they are found all over the world. Some live in trees, some in water, some on the ground, and others burrow underground. Most species are <u>nocturnal</u>, but some are more active during the day. Most frogs <u>lay eggs</u>, usually in water, although not all. A few species give live birth to miniature frogs.

F. Frogs in the Bible

If you remember the story of the Exodus in the Bible, when Moses was sent to Pharaoh in Egypt, a series of plagues was visited upon Egypt to persuade Pharaoh to allow the Hebrews to leave. The second plague was the plague of the frogs. The Book of Exodus tells us the frogs overran the land. At first it seemed to have worked, for Pharaoh agreed to allow the Hebrews to leave and offer sacrifice to God. However, once the frogs were gone, the Pharaoh changed his mind.

The Bible tells us that frogs were everywhere in Egypt, even in their beds and in their kitchens. One other thing that may have made this plague difficult for the Egyptians to bear was the noise. Male frogs make a variety of noises, not just the standard "ribbit." The female frogs of each species know the vocalizations of the male frogs of their own species. The females of some species vocalize as well.

Frogs are amazing creatures. Many people enjoy watching them playing as pets. Frogs play an important role in their ecosystems. But none of us would enjoy a plague of them!

Review Questions

1. How are frogs' bodies well suited to their environment?

_____

_____

_____

_____

2. What might a frog or toad do when threatened by a predator?

_____

_____

_____

3. How are toads different from other frogs?

_____

_____

_____

VII. Salamanders

Salamanders are amphibians and have thin, smooth, moist skin.
Image credit: Cristo Vlahos

Salamanders are a group of amphibians. Remember that amphibians begin their lives in water with gills for breathing, but they develop lungs and legs for their lives on land.

A. Salamanders as Amphibians

Although many salamanders outwardly resemble lizards, lizards are reptiles and have scaly skin. Salamanders are amphibians and have thin, smooth, moist skin. Salamanders do not have claws on their toes, as lizards do.

A salamander may look a bit like a lizard, but it does not have scales.
Image credit: public domain

B. Characteristics of Salamanders
1. Keep Tails

Salamanders are sometimes referred to as "tailed amphibians" because they are amphibians that keep their tails (as they had in water) even as adults. Nonetheless, most salamanders do go through metamorphosis, a physical change from the very young to the adult stage.

2. Usually Lay Eggs

Almost all of the salamander species lay eggs. Some of the young begin as larvae in water and grow to adult salamanders. There are, however, some species of land salamanders that give birth to babies that do not go through metamorphosis.

3. Living Areas

Some species of salamanders spend their lives exclusively in the water, others spend their lives exclusively on land, and others frequent both land and water. Some species even make their homes in trees or in burrows underground!

4. Need Oxygen

Like all animals, salamanders need oxygen, but the way different species of salamanders meet that need is very interesting. Like frogs, many species of salamanders begin life with gills and, after metamorphosis, lose their gills and develop lungs. Some adult aquatic (water) salamanders have both gills and lungs. These salamanders sometimes use their lungs to breathe, but also use their lungs to help maintain their position in water. When their lungs are full of air, they will float; when the air is expelled, they can sink and search for food in the water below, using their gills to breathe.

Because of their thin skin, salamanders can get oxygen through their skin as well. In fact, some land salamanders never develop lungs, and "breathe" exclusively through their skin!

Unlike other salamanders, siren salamanders grow only two legs.
Image credit: USGS

5. Four legs

Most species do have four legs, though not all. One type of salamander is called the **siren**. Sirens are aquatic salamanders that never develop hind legs. Sirens grow only the front two legs, which are quite small.

6. The Newt

The **newt** is another type of salamander. The newt looks like most other salamanders, but its skin is typically not as smooth. Most newts are semi-aquatic as adults, meaning they spend part of their lives on land and part in the water.

Newt skin is not as smooth as that of other salamanders.
Image credit: public domain

7. Nocturnal

Salamanders are generally nocturnal, that is, they tend to be active at night. Their main food sources are insects, worms, and spiders. Some larger salamanders eat fish, small mice, and even other salamanders.

8. Usually Small Size

Most salamanders are small, six inches or less, but many grow six to eight inches. However, a few salamander species grow quite large. The biggest salamander, the Japanese giant salamander, is the largest amphibian, and can reach lengths up to five feet!

The Japanese giant salamander is the largest amphibian, which can reach five feet in length.
Image credit: J. Patrick Fisher

9. Defenses against Predators

Salamanders are timid animals, but they have some interesting defenses against predators. Camouflage, blending in with the environment, is an important defense. Salamanders spend most of their time hidden under leaves or branches so that predators cannot find them. One unusual defense tactic is by the fire salamander, which can shoot poison from its skin glands at an attacker!

Camouflage, blending in with the environment, is an important defense.
Image credit: public domain

10. Regenerate Limbs

Amazingly, God gave salamanders the ability to regenerate lost limbs! A fascinating behavior is called **tail autonomy**. When a salamander is confronted by a predator, its tail can fall off and continue wiggling! This often attracts the attention of the predator, allowing the salamander the opportunity to make a quick escape. God has arranged for the salamander to be able to grow another tail!

A salamander's tail can fall off when it is confronted by a predator.
Image credit: Metatron

God has given salamanders some truly amazing adaptations that help them to survive. Different salamander species have been given unique and powerful defenses. You might want to visit a pet store and observe the variety of colors of salamanders.

JMJ

Review Questions

1. How can a person tell the difference between a salamander and a lizard?

_____

_____

2. What are some ways salamanders meet their need for oxygen?

_____

_____

3. Compare and contrast salamanders and frogs.

_____

_____

_____

_____

4. Describe the unique characteristics of sirens and newts.

_____

_____

5. What is tail autonomy?

_____

_____

VIII. Caecilians

The strangest order of amphibians is the **caecilians** (see-sil-ee-uns). The caecilians are <u>legless</u> amphibians that are rarely seen by people and are still a bit of a mystery to scientists.

A. Size

Caecilians range in length from a few inches to more than four feet, though most are close to a foot in length. They can <u>resemble</u> <u>earthworms</u>, especially because their skin has ring-like folds called annuli. However, caecilians are vertebrates, meaning they have backbones.

B. Most Live Underground

Some caecilians live in water, but most <u>live underground</u>, which is why people seldom see them. They have very poor eyesight, but they have two retractable tentacles on their heads. Tentacles are long, slender organs which usually proceed from the head. These tentacles help caecilians explore their environment by detecting sound or motion. Caecilians are the only vertebrates with tentacles.

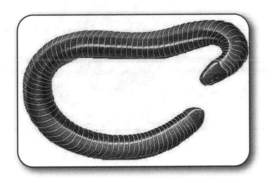

Caecilians can be mistaken for large worms.
Image credit: unknown

C. Tubular Shape

The design of caecilians' bodies resembles the bodies of snakes. For example, due to their tubular shape, the caecilian's internal organs are arranged differently than those of other amphibians. Caecilians <u>have lungs</u>, but their left lung is either very small or non-existent.

D. Skin Glands

Caecilians' skin is slimy because it is covered in mucus. Their skin <u>glands can secrete poison</u> when attacked by predators. Unlike other amphibians, caecilians have small <u>scales under their skin</u>.

E. Catching Prey

Caecilians come close to their meals, bite with their jaws, and hold on with their teeth. Caecilians eat mainly <u>worms, termites, shrimp, and insect larvae</u>, depending on whether they burrow into land or live in water.

F. Locations

Caecilians inhabit <u>swampy areas</u> of central Africa, Southeast Asia, and Central and South America. They are not found in the United States.

In studying caecilians, their unique design and how they live, you can recognize the immense creativity of God. If He takes such care in the creation of these little amphibians who live in swamps, how much more does He care for and love all of us?

Review Questions

1. How do caecilians resemble snakes and earthworms?

_____

_____

_____

_____

2. Why are caecilians rarely seen?

_____

3. How do caecilians explore their environment?

_____

_____

Chapter Review Activity

SECTION A

Use the words in the word box to complete the sentences:

amphibian	caecilians	constrictor	crocodilians
ectothermic	metamorphosis	reptile	sirens
tail autonomy	tailed amphibians		

1. A cold-blooded vertebrate with scales is a _____.

2. A cold-blooded vertebrate with smooth, thin skin is an _____.

3. A snake that squeezes the life out of its prey before eating it is a _____.

4. Alligators, crocodiles, caimans, and gavials are _____.

5. Many amphibians go through _____, a process by which an animal goes through major body changes after birth, so that the adult of a species does not look at all like a juvenile.

6. When threatened, a salamander can lose its tail, which can wiggle and distract a predator. This is called _____ _____.

7. _____ are aquatic salamanders that do not develop hind legs.

8. Salamanders are sometimes referred to as _____ _____ because they keep their tails as adults.

9. _____ are the only vertebrates with tentacles.

10. Reptiles and amphibians are _____, meaning they are cold-blooded.

Chapter Review Activity

SECTION B

Mark the following statements (#11-18) "true" or "false." If false, tell why:

11. All turtles are types of tortoises. _____

_____

12. Toads are types of frogs with moist skin, teeth, and exceptional jumping ability. _____

_____

13. Sirens and newts are both types of salamanders. _____

_____

14. Crocodilians are unique reptile parents because they abandon their young shortly after

   birth. _____

_____

15. Most lizards have legs and moveable eyelids, both of which snakes lack. _____

_____

16. Gila monsters, Mexican bearded lizards, and Komodo dragons are the only known venomous

   lizards. _____

_____

17. Lung-less salamanders breathe through their skin. _____

_____

18. Turtles lay their eggs in water. _____

_____

SECTION C

Circle the correct answer.

19. Which amphibians have poor eyesight, are rarely seen by people, and do not snatch their prey with sticky tongues?

    A. Salamanders
    B. Caecilians
    C. Toads
    D. Tortoises

20. Which is not an amphibian?

    A. Salamanders
    B. Turtles
    C. Frogs
    D. Caecilians

21. Which is not a lizard?

    A. Tuatara
    B. Komodo dragons
    C. Iguanas
    D. Skinks

22. Which is true of tuatara?

    A. They have the longest incubation period of any reptile.
    B. They live in New Zealand.
    C. It is believed they can live 100 years.
    D. All of the above

SECTION D

Answer the following questions.

23. What does it mean for an animal to be cold-blooded?

    _____

    _____

24. Describe the different ways frogs might defend themselves from predators.

    _____

    _____

25. How is a snake able to swallow prey that is wider than its own body?

    _____

    _____

Fish

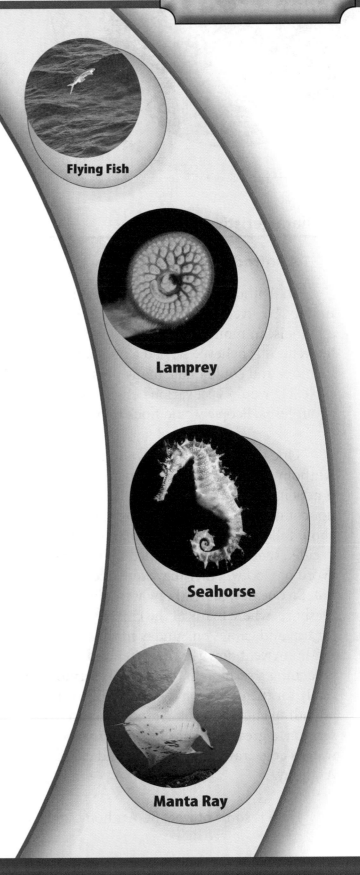

Flying Fish

Lamprey

Seahorse

Manta Ray

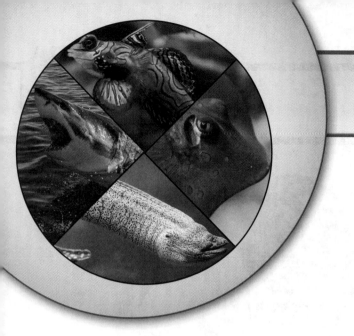

"To you [fish] was it granted, by God's command, to conserve the life of the Prophet Jonah, and then after three days, to throw him back, safe and sound, on dry land. It was you that gave the tribute-coin to Our Lord Jesus Christ when, because of His poverty, He had not wherewith to pay it. Finally, by a singular mystery, you [fish] served as nourishment of the eternal King Jesus Christ, before and after His Resurrection."

St. Anthony then pleaded with the fish to glorify God. Suddenly, the fish opened their mouths and bowed their heads, to which St. Anthony responded, "Blessed be the eternal God, for the fishes of the sea glorify Him more than men without faith."

Needless to say, the people of the town were astounded, and many realized their lack of Faith and disobedience to God's commandments. God used this incredible miracle to touch the hearts of the townspeople and, thereafter, many people in that town were converted.

I. Characteristics of Fish

A. Introduction: St. Anthony

St. Anthony of Padua was a great preacher in Italy. He lived from 1195 to 1231. He became a Franciscan monk and gave talks wherever he went. It is believed he had a photographic memory and could quote many passages in the Bible. He would visit various towns to teach about Jesus. People would flock to hear him.

One time, in a small town in Italy, St. Anthony realized the townspeople were not practicing their Catholic Faith. People were not coming to church to listen to the truth about following the Ten Commandments. He decided that the people needed to hear the Word of God whether they were in church or not. So one day, St. Anthony went down to the seashore, where many of the citizens gathered for fun and games on Sunday morning. St. Anthony went down to the water and began preaching a sermon to the fish! His sermon was really for the people on the shore who were not attending church. As St. Anthony began his sermon, a great number of fish approached the water's edge, raised their heads, and gazed at St. Anthony.

Here is some of what St. Anthony said:

Saint Anthony with Mary and the Christ Child.
Image credit: von Deschwanden

B. General Characteristics of Fish
1. Classes of Fish

In our study of vertebrates, we have explored mammals, birds, reptiles, and amphibians. The last group of vertebrates is fish. There are three classes of fish: **jawless fish**, **cartilaginous fish**, and **bony fish**. These classes are distinguished by the structure of their mouths and the types of skeletons they have. We will study each of them in depth in this chapter.

2. Definition of a Fish

What defines a fish? As we've seen with some other animals, not every species fits perfectly into its category, but there are some characteristics that are present in the vast majority of fish. Fish are vertebrates, so they have a backbone. Fish typically have scales. Because fish live in water, they have structures called gills with which they can obtain oxygen from the water. Most fish are ectothermic (ek-tow-ther-mik), or cold-blooded. Remember that cold-blooded animals do not have a constant internal body temperature. Their body temperature depends on that of their environment. Most fish reproduce with eggs that hatch outside their

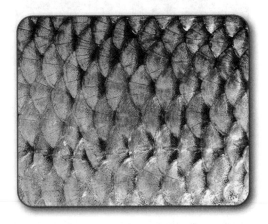

Fish typically have scales. They are layered like shingles on a roof. They protect the skin and allow more graceful movement through water.
Image credit: Kallerna

bodies. Some fish live in fresh water, some fish live in salt water, and some fish can survive in both fresh and salt water.

3. Gills on Fish

How do the gills work on a fish? As you know, water contains oxygen. A fish opens its mouth and gulps in some water. Gills contain many blood vessels. As water passes over the gills, oxygen from the water passes into the fish's bloodstream through those blood vessels in the gills. Carbon dioxide passes out of the bloodstream and into the water, which exits the fish through slits beneath the gills.

Fish use gills to obtain oxygen from the water.
Image credit: shutterstock.com

4. Diets of Fish

There are so many types of fish that their diets are quite varied. In fact, there are so many species of fish that they make up nearly half of all vertebrate species that exist! Most fish have teeth, but some have comb-like structures on their gills with which they filter food, similar to the way whales do.

5. Fins on Fish

Fish swim using water pressure. They pump their tail fins, called **caudal fins**, to propel themselves through the water. **Dorsal**

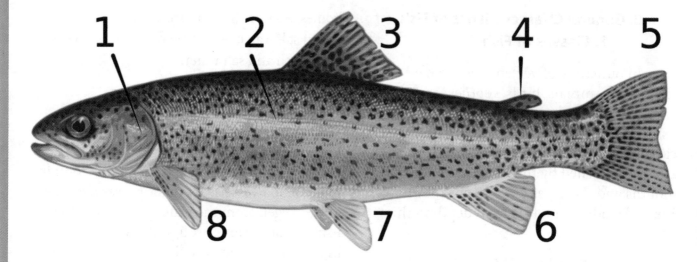

(1) - gill cover, (2) - lateral line; (3) - dorsal fin; (4) - adipose fin;
(5) caudal fin; (6) - anal fin; (7) - pelvic fins, paired; (8) - pectoral fins, paired
Image credit: Rainbow trout – USPS

fins are on the fish's back and are useful for balance. Some fish also have **pectoral fins**, on the sides of their bodies, behind their heads, and **pelvic fins** on the sides of their bodies closer to their tails. Pectoral and pelvic fins are called **paired fins** because there are two of them. Though these fins can sometimes aid in propulsion, they are mainly useful for steering.

Typical fins are bones or cartilage, covered with membranes that allow fish to push against the water much like the paddle of a canoe. Remember, though, that there are many different types of fish, with different types of fins.

6. Senses of Fish

Fish have powerful **underwater senses**. Many can see and smell very well under water. Sharks can smell just one drop of blood in the water. Many fish have a sense organ called a lateral line that runs from head to tail and allows the fish to detect vibrations and pressure changes in the water.

C. Schools of Fish

Often fish will be found in **groups called schools** or shoals. The difference refers to whether the fish are swimming in the same direction in a coordinated manner or not. If they are swimming in a coordinated manner, it is called schooling. Otherwise, the group is a shoal. This group behavior is important for fish because it can provide protection against predators.

These bluestripe snappers are schooling. They are swimming in the same direction in a coordinated manner.
Image credit: Jim and Becca Wicks

Review Questions

1. What are the three classes of fish?

_____

_____

2. What are some characteristics common to most fish?

_____

_____

3. How do fish use gills to get oxygen from the water?

_____

_____

4. How do fins help fish to swim?

_____

_____

5. What are the different types of fins?

_____

_____

II. Jawless Fish

A. Introduction

Of all the classes of fish, the jawless fish are the strangest. Although classified as fish, they are different in many ways from the other two classes of fish. There are fewer species of jawless fish than either of the other two classes of fish. All jawless fish are classified as either lampreys or hagfish.

B. Characteristics of Jawless Fish
1. No Scales

These odd, jawless fish creatures do not have scales like other fish do. The jawless fish skeletons are made of cartilage, but they do not have paired fins, only caudal fins (or tail fins),

and some have dorsal fins, on the back of the fish. Their elongated shape resembles that of an eel, but unlike eels, they do not have jaws.

The jawless hagfish lives deep on the ocean floor. It uses slippery slime as a defense against predators. Image credit: NOAA

2. Digestion

Jawless fish have mouths through which they eat, but they cannot open and close their mouths to bite! Jawless fish stab, scrape, and suck their food into their mouths. These fish do not have internal organs resembling those of other fish. They do not have a true stomach, just one long digestive tube that runs nearly the length of their bodies. These jawless fish have gill pouches that are different from the gills of other fish.

C. Types of Jawless Fish
1. Hagfish

Hagfish are a type of jawless fish. Hagfish are sometimes called slime eels (although they are not really eels) because their smooth bodies contain slime glands that coat their bodies in a slimy mucus. This is a useful defense because the slime can gag or choke predators and make hagfish difficult to eat. Hagfish live deep on the ocean floor. They eat marine worms and also scavenge the decaying flesh of dead fish or marine mammals.

Because jawless fish are cold-blooded, their very cold deep-water environment keeps their metabolism low, so they do not need to eat often! Hagfish are nearly blind, but one interesting skill they do have is that they can tie their bodies into a knot and then slide in and out of the knot! This ability can help them escape from predators, remove excess slime from their bodies, and provide extra leverage for tearing chunks of meat off prey.

2. Lampreys

Lampreys can live in salt and fresh waters. Many lampreys are found in fresh water rivers and lakes, but also in coastal salt-water seas. Some lampreys are parasites, which gives them a nasty reputation. A parasite establishes a relationship with a "host" organism through which the parasite benefits while the host suffers and often dies! A parasitic lamprey will latch onto another fish with its teeth. Its mouth has rings of sharp teeth which puncture the host fish's skin. The lamprey latches onto the fish and feeds off the blood of its host. Although lampreys do not feed off human blood, in some places, people have so disturbed the fish populations that the lampreys have bitten and latched onto people's skin!

The jawless mouth of a lamprey. Some lampreys attach to and feed off the blood of their hosts.
Image credit: unknown

Review Questions

1. Name three ways jawless fish are different from most other fish.

_____

_____

_____

2. Compare and contrast hagfish and lampreys.

_____

_____

_____

_____

3. How do the slime glands of hagfish help them to survive?

_____

_____

4. Why are some lampreys considered parasites?

_____

_____

III. Cartilaginous Fish

A. Introduction

Cartilaginous (kar-til-AJ-uh-nus) **fish** have skeletons made of cartilage, like jawless fish do. However, this class of fish does have moveable jaws as well as paired fins. These fish also have scales, unlike jawless fish. The scales of cartilaginous fish are a little different than the scales of bony fish. Cartilaginous fish usually have placoid (PLACK-oid) scales, which are pointed, like teeth or thorns, and give the fish a rough feel. Placoid scales are sometimes called denticles because of the tooth-like shape of the scales.

With flattened bodies and wide pectoral fins, rays can be seen "flying" gracefully through the water.
Image credit: shutterstock.com

B. Rays and Skates

Probably the two best-known cartilaginous fish are rays and sharks. **Rays** have flattened bodies with wide pectoral fins that can look almost like wings. Rays often can be seen "flying" gracefully through the water at aquariums. **Skates** are cartilaginous fish that look similar to rays, although they differ in several ways. Rays are generally larger than skates. Many rays' tails have barbs on them, which skates' tails do not. Additionally, rays give live birth, whereas skates lay eggs.

Rays and skates live on the cold ocean floors and filter feed on invertebrates like oysters, clams, and shrimp. Rays and skates, as well as some sharks, have not only gills but **spiracles**, that is, openings in the tops of their heads, through which they can breathe. This is important so that these fish can rest on the ocean floor and get oxygen from water without ingesting a load of sand from the ocean floor.

Skates are an egg-laying, smaller version of rays.
Image credit: dollarphotoclub.com

C. Sharks
1. Characteristics

When people think of **sharks**, they usually think of man-eating great white sharks. Sharks have inspired movies, countless documentaries, and fear in swimmers and surfers alike. However, there are over 300 species of sharks, and only a few are dangerous to humans. Sharks can range in size from six-and-a-half inches long (the dwarf dogshark), to more than 40 feet long (the whale shark). Most sharks are found in seas and oceans, but they occasionally have been known to travel up rivers as well.

Sharks are skilled predators. Their hunting is aided by a special "sense" that detects electrical signals given off by prey. Inside a shark's mouth are rows of sharp teeth. When teeth in the front are lost, new teeth move forward to replace them! Although sharks are predators, their diet varies from plankton, which they filter out of the water, to a variety of fish, to large marine mammals like sea lions and seals. Most sharks give birth to live young, though some species lay eggs.

2. Kinds of Sharks
a. Whale Sharks

Whale sharks are the largest fish in the world. These giants can grow to more than 40 feet long and weigh 13 tons! Despite its size, the whale shark's diet consists of very small creatures, such as plankton, small fish, and squid. The food is filtered by tissue attached to its gills. Though whale sharks are very large, they are not dangerous to humans. They are a favorite of scuba divers, though, who like to "play" with them sometimes by hanging on to their fins to hitch a ride!

b. Great White Shark

The **great white** is the most famous shark. This large predator can grow to more than 20 feet long and weigh nearly two-and-a-half tons.

Though extremely large, whale sharks eat tiny creatures, such as plankton, small fish and squids.
Image credit: Derek Keats

Great white sharks have been known to leap completely out of the water in pursuit of prey.
Image credit: Terry Goss

Although great white shark attacks are rare, people have been killed by these animals. Seals are a favorite item on the menu of great whites. It is believed that the sharks occasionally mistake surfers for seals, as the surfers are lying and paddling on their boards.

C. Bull Shark

The **bull shark** is smaller than the great white shark, but the bull shark is the most aggressive of sharks. The bull shark can grow to more than 11 feet long, weigh 500 pounds, and is considered the most dangerous shark to humans! Bull sharks prefer <u>coastal waters</u> and

are known to sometimes swim inland up <u>fresh water rivers</u>, both of which bring the sharks into contact with people.

D. Chimaeras

The last group of cartilaginous fish are the **chimaeras** (ki-MER-as). Chimaeras resemble sharks in some ways. However, they do not have rows of sharp teeth; instead they have plates for grinding. Chimaeras also have only one gill opening on each side. The largest chimaeras grow to nearly five feet in length. Most species prefer deep waters and ocean floors.

Bull sharks are often found in the same coastal waters where people tend to congregate.
Image credit: Snelvis

Chimaeras prefer to live in deep water and on the ocean floors.
Image credit: unknown

Review Questions

1. Compare and contrast cartilaginous fish and jawless fish.

_____

_____

_____

2. Why are spiracles important to rays and skates?

_____

_____

_____

_____

3. Describe the "sense" that helps sharks hunt.

_____

_____

4. Compare and contrast the great white and bull sharks.

_____

_____

_____

IV. Bony Fish

A. Introducton

The vast majority of fish, about 95 percent of all fish species, are bony fish. Bony fish have jaws and their skeletons are made of bone, not cartilage. Bony fish include fish like salmon, trout, herring, and tuna, as well as more unusual fish, like seahorses and eels. Bony fish can be found in all types of waterways, from salt water oceans to fresh water lakes and rivers, even in estuaries that contain brackish water, a mixture of salt and fresh water.

B. Fins and Gills

Unlike jawless fish, bony fish do have paired fins. Their pectoral fins have more mobility than those of sharks, allowing them a greater range of swimming motions. Their gills are covered by a flexible flap called the operculum (oh-PUR-ku-lum). The operculum closes as water is taken in through the fish's mouth. Water passes through the gills, exchanging oxygen for carbon dioxide in the fish's blood, then the water pushes open the operculum as the water exits the fish's body.

C. Scales

Most bony fish have flat scales, which may be either cycloid (SIGH-kloid), ctenoid (TEE-noid), or ganoid (GAN-oid) scales. Cycloid scales, found on fish like salmon, are smooth to the touch. Bass are an example of fish with ctenoid scales, which are rough to the touch. Some fish, such as the gar, have ganoid scales, which are shiny and hard.

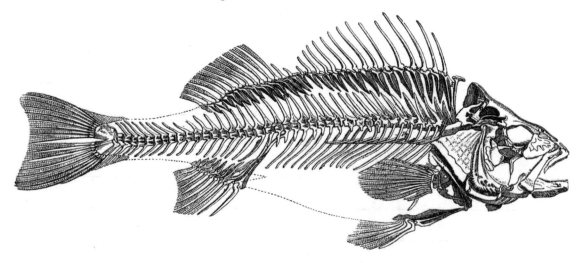

This is the skeletal structure of a bass, which is a type of bony fish.
Image credit: Terry Goss

D. Swim Bladder

Most bony fish have an amazing organ called a **swim bladder**, which is not found in jawless or cartilaginous fish. The swim bladder is a gas-filled sac that helps stabilize bony fish at different depths in the water. It works on the same principle as a submarine. When a submarine's tanks are filled with air, it is more buoyant, meaning it floats better and rises. When the air is replaced with water, the submarine submerges. A bony fish uses its swim bladder in a similar way. By controlling the amount of gas in the swim bladder, the fish can control its buoyancy. This allows the fish to float at different depths without expending too much energy.

The swim bladder of a rudd.
Image credit: Uwe Gille

E. Three Body Regions

The bones of bony fish are made up of three main regions. The **skull** protects the fish's brain. The **vertebral column** includes the backbone and ribs. The **fin skeleton** includes the bones making up the fish's fins. Strong bones are important to support the fish's muscles. For example, the sailfish, the fastest fish in the ocean, uses powerful muscles to stabilize and propel itself through the water at up to 68 miles per hour! Now that is a hard fish to catch!

Review Questions

1. Contrast bony fish with sharks.

_____

_____

_____

_____

2. What is a swim bladder and how does it work?

_____

_____

3. What are the three main regions of bony fish's skeletons?

_____

_____

_____

V. Unique and Amazing Fish

By now you have come to recognize the amazing variation in the animal kingdom. God has created animals with incredible beauty and adaptability. The fish in this lesson are only some of the most unusual in the water, as well as out of it, as you will see.

A. Out of Water Fish
1. African Lungfish

Pop quiz: Where do fish live? There are many ways you could have answered that question, but most likely your answer included water. That is true—almost always. Have you ever heard of the **African lungfish**? The African lungfish can survive the dry season out of the water! Usually, if a lake or pond dries out, the fish that live in it will die. However, during the African dry season, if the lungfish's watery home dries out, the African lungfish can survive.

Lungfishes have gills and lungs. The lungs are actually swim bladders lined with blood vessels that allow them to obtain oxygen from the air! Lungfishes can burrow in the ground, cover themselves with mucus, and breathe through openings in the tops of their burrows. When the drought is over and the water returns, they emerge from their burrows to their watery homes.

2. Mudskipper

The **mudskipper** is another fish you may sometimes find out of water. Its pectoral fins are large and muscular, and the mudskipper can use its fins to hop around the mud. Mudskippers spend more time out of the water than in it, but they don't have lungs, as lungfish do. They have amazing ways of getting the oxygen they need! Mudskippers have sacs around their gills and around their mouths in which they store water. They can use this stored water for oxygen when they are on land. Mudskippers can absorb oxygen also through their skin, tail, and the lining of their mouth and tongue! Amazingly, God has created mudskippers so they can adjust the shape of the lenses in their eyes to allow them to see well both on land and in the water!

3. Flying Fish

Some fish can live in water and on land, but what about in the air? Ask the **flying fish**. These fish are so named because of the leaps they make out of the water, especially when escaping predators. They have extremely large pectoral fins that look like wings. Flying fish can glide up to 650 feet in one leap! Then they can use their tails to "skip" across the water without submerging. Flying fish can stay above the surface of the water for 1,300 feet! A flying fish off the coast of Japan was recorded above the surface for 45 seconds!

Lungfish have both gills and lungs.
Image credit: by Uwe Gille

Mudskippers spend more time out of the water than in it.
Image credit: Webridge

Flying fish have very large pectoral fins that look and act like wings.
Image credit: shutterstock.com

B. Seahorse

The **seahorse** is one strange fish! It is so named because of the shape of its head, which looks somewhat like a horse's head. Actually, a seahorse resembles a knight on a chess board. Seahorses swim "standing up," propelled by their dorsal fin. They use their small pectoral fins to steer, and they have no caudal or tail fins. They may not have tail fins, but they do have a tail, a prehensile tail. This means the tail of most seahorses can grasp things!

Another unusual trait about seahorses is that it is the male of the species that "gives birth". Females lay the eggs, but the eggs are incubated in a pouch on the male's abdomen. When the eggs hatch, the baby seahorses emerge from the male's pouch.

The seahorse is so named because of the shape of its head, which looks somewhat like a horse's head.
Image credit: NOAA

C. Eels

One of the creepiest groups of fish may be **eels**. These "snakes of the sea" slither through water as snakes slither on land. The electric eel of South America is not a true eel, but it resembles eels. The electric eel has cells that can give off an electrical charge, up to 600 volts! This is powerful enough to kill a fish that the electric eel desires to eat, as well as fight off predators. Electric eels, as well as some true eels, sometimes slither across land to get from one body of water to another.

The electric eel has cells that can give off an electrical charge, up to 600 volts!
Image credit: Steven G. Johnson

D. Symbiosis

Many of the instincts that God has designed are wonders to consider! You have learned about hibernation, migration, birds' flying formations, and more. Sometimes,

An example of symbiosis, the smaller remoras clean the back of the larger nurse shark.
Image credit: Duncan Wright

animals of different species have instincts that work together. A long-term relationship between two different types of organisms is called **symbiosis** (sim-bee-OH-sis). Both organisms often benefit from this relationship, which can then be called **mutualism**.

Here is an example of symbiosis. Cleaner fish are the living toothbrushes of the sea. These tiny fish actually swim into the mouths of larger fish and pick parasites and bits of food from their teeth! These cleaner fish also clean other parts of the fish, such as the skin, gills, and fins. For example, little pilot fish can be seen swimming with large sharks. Normally you would not expect a fish to voluntarily swim among the teeth of a shark, but these little fish have been given the instinct to enter the mouths of their predatory companions, and the sharks have the instinct not to eat the little fish. Both species benefit. The pilot fish gets a free meal, while the shark gets a free dental cleaning. God's kingdom on planet Earth is truly incredible!

Review Questions

1. How are the methods for obtaining oxygen when on land different for the lungfish and the mudskipper?

_____

_____

2. How does a male seahorse "give birth"?

_____

_____

3. Explain the symbiotic relationship between a pilot fish and a shark.

_____

_____

_____

VI. Ecosystems for Fish

A. Introduction

What are the differences between salt water fish and fresh water fish? Why do some fish thrive in one environment, while other fish thrive in another environment? Simply by looking at a fish, you cannot tell whether it is a fresh water fish or a salt water fish. There is no distinctive physical marking on fish associated with any particular ecosystem. In fact, some fish can live in both fresh water and salt water. Some fish can live in a mixture of salt water and fresh water, which is called brackish water.

B. Fish in Various Ecosystems
1. Salt Water Fish

If you have ever been in the ocean and swallowed a mouthful of water, one of the first things you noticed was how salty it is! Oceans and seas are salt water ecosystems. Did you know that salt water covers more than 70 percent of the planet? We humans would have a hard time living in a salt water ecosystem. People cannot drink salt water in place of fresh water. However, these salt water ecosystems are teeming with life, including many fish.

Salt water fish bodies can process salt. Salt water fish have an internal (inside their bodies) salt concentration <u>less or lower</u> than that of their watery salty environment. Their salty surroundings constantly draw or pull water <u>from</u> the fish's body. Salt water fish, therefore, first, must drink lots of water, second, must produce little urine, and third, must expel excess salt from their bodies.

Brook trout is one example of a fresh water fish.
Image credit: US Fish & Wildfife Service

Tuna is one example of a salt water fish.
Image credit: NOAA

2. Fresh Water Fish

Some fish must live in a fresh water ecosystem. Fresh water ecosystems cover <u>only about one percent</u> of the planet's surface, but they contain approximately 40 percent of the species of fish! Fresh water ecosystems include rivers, streams, lakes, and ponds. Fresh water also comes from underground wells.

Fresh water fish have a higher salt concentration <u>inside their bodies</u> than their environment contains. Fresh water fish <u>draw in water</u> from their surroundings through their skin and gills. They have powerful kidneys that can process large amounts of water. Thus, these fresh water fish produce large amounts of urine, but they retain salt in their bodies.

Fresh water fish also tend to be hardier and more adaptable than salt water fish. This is because their environment is less stable, such as rushing rivers or evaporating ponds. Fresh water fish must be able to adapt to a changing environment. Although the different ocean zones are quite unique, the <u>salt water oceans are more stable</u> than fresh water environments for the fish that inhabit them. Fresh water fish experience changing conditions, such as a lake that freezes in the winter, or a lake that has changing nutrient levels throughout the year.

3. Fish in Different Ecosystems

Some fish are able to live in both fresh water and salt water environments. These fish constantly move between the two environments. Other fish, however, are born in one kind of water but spend their adult lives in a different kind of water. For instance, salmon are born in fresh water but spend their adult lives in salt water. These are called **anadromous** (ah-NAD-row-mus) fish. Other

Atlantic Salmon is one example of an anadromous fish.
Image credit: USPS

fish are born in salt water, but spend their lives in fresh water. For instance, some eels begin their lives in salt water but spend their adult lives in fresh water. These are called **catadromous** (kah-TAD-row-mus) fish.

4. Estuaries

Some ecosystems have brackish water, which is what we call a mixture of salt water and fresh water. These mixed fresh water and salt water ecosystems are called **estuaries**. Estuaries often occur where fresh water and salt water ecosystems meet, such as where a fresh water river empties into a salt water sea. The salt concentrations of estuaries can vary according to the tides. Fish that live in estuaries need to be able to adapt to those changes.

Clearly, God takes care of the fish He has created. He created fish so they are able to adapt to a changing environment. This

This estuary is formed at the mouth of Sri Lanka's Maduganga River and the Laccadive Sea.
Image credit: Julie Anne Workman

can remind us of the constant, loving care God takes of us even when we are faced with the unexpected. We should trust in God and know that when we are faced with unexpected, changing situations, He will help us to be strong.

Review questions

1. What are the differences between salt water fish and fresh water fish?

_____

_____

2. Why are fresh water fish often hardier than salt water fish?

_____

_____

3. What are estuaries?

_____

_____

4. What is the difference between anadromous fish and catadromous fish?

_____

_____

VII. Ocean Depths

"God created the great sea monsters and all kinds of swimming creatures with which the water teems" (Gen. 1:21a).

A. Introduction

Everything that God has made reflects His beauty, His wisdom, and His creativity. The ocean is no exception. The ocean is not just a single ecosystem, but is actually composed of many different ecosystems, consisting of many different types of life. God has created each organism with adaptations that allow it to survive in its particular environment.

B. Three Ocean Zones Out From the Shore

1. Intertidal Zone

The ocean contains three distinct zones moving out from the shore. The **intertidal zone** is the area where the breaking waves reach the shore. The intertidal zone is generally under water during high tide, and above water during low tide. The intertidal zone has plenty of oxygen and nutrients in the water and soil, and supports such animals as urchins, crabs, and starfish, which can live in both water and moist sand.

2. Nearshore Zone

Beyond the waves but close to shore is the **nearshore zone**. The nearshore water zone is characterized by its calm water and abundant sea life. Sunlight reaches much of the water in this zone, allowing the water to support plant life, such as algae. Algae provides food for many different types of fish.

This bay along the Mediterranean Sea is an example of the nearshore zone.
Image credit: public domain

3. Open Ocean Zone

The vast expanse of ocean that covers most of our planet makes up the **open ocean zone**. The vast open ocean itself is divided

Kalamitsi Beach along the Ionian Sea is an example of the intertidal zone.
Image credit: Ggia

There is no land visible for as far as the eye can see in this example of the open ocean zone.
Image credit: Tiago Fioreze

into different zones by the depth of the ocean: the sunlight zone, the twilight zone, and the midnight zone.

Many factors affect the types of life in different parts of the ocean. Such factors include <u>temperature, sunlight, pressure, and levels of oxygen</u>. The average depth of the ocean is <u>14,000 feet</u>! The deeper the water, the less sunlight and oxygen is available. Also, the temperature drops in deepest water and the water becomes very, very cold.

The <u>water pressure rises</u> in the deeper and deepest water. People need to wear special diving suits with helmets when they go on deep dives. Submarines can go much deeper than human divers, but they also must be specially designed to withstand the amazingly increased water pressure!

C. Three Ocean Zones Moving Downward
1. Sunlight Zone

The uppermost level of the open ocean, called the **sunlight zone**, is full of life. Because sunlight reaches this top zone, photosynthesis takes place here, resulting in abundant life. Remember that photosynthesis is the process by which plants, with the energy from light, convert water and carbon dioxide into food.

Tiny microscopic phytoplankton, drifting on the warm water's surface, make up the beginning of the ocean food chain. Many sea creatures, including large varieties of fish and marine mammals, eat this phytoplankton (fie-tuh-PLANK-ton) or they eat other sea animals that are swimming around looking for something to eat! Although the sunlight zone is the smallest zone in terms of size, the sunlight zone contains most of the ocean's living creatures.

2. Twilight Zone

Generally beginning at a depth of about 660 feet down, and extending to approximately 3,300 feet down, is located the middle layer, popularly called the **twilight zone**. Although this zone does receive some small amount of light during the day, there is not enough light for photosynthesis to take place. Thus the amount of food is scarce. The water in the twilight zone becomes very, very cold, and the water pressure can reach as high as 1,470 pounds per square inch! That is an amazing amount of pressure on any creature of the sea!

It would seem that nothing could live in these cold, high pressure conditions, but God has given the dwellers of the twilight zone incredible tools for survival. One of the most amazing tools for survival is <u>bioluminescence</u> (BIE-oh-loo-muh-NES-ence). God has

Sunshine fills the sunlight zone, making abundant life possible.

Image credit: public domain

Giant sunfish prefer the murky darkness of the twilight zone.

Image credit: public domain

Pyrosome jellyfish live at twilight zone depths and glow with bioluminescent light.

Image credit: Nick Hobgood

arranged that some sea creatures at this very low, cold level in the ocean, and even below this depth, incredibly, <u>can make their own light through chemical reactions</u>. Some sea creatures can have light from the presence of glowing bacteria on their bodies! This amazing gift of God allows these deep-ocean creatures to see in a dark world, helping them to find food or confuse their attacking predators.

Much of the food in the twilight zone comes from marine "snow," that is, organic material that <u>sinks down like snow from the sunlight zone</u> above. Also, some twilight zone creatures swim up toward the dark, less-cold ocean surface at night to feed, and then swim back down at dawn. The twilight zone has many different creatures, including plankton, species of crustaceans (sea creatures having hard shells like crusts), and other animals, such as the octopus.

3. Midnight Zone

Below the twilight zone is an even more extremely cold and dark environment, called the **midnight zone**. This zone is in total blackness! The sun's rays cannot reach the midnight zone. The water pressure is extremely high, and the water's temperature is near freezing. Like inhabitants of the twilight zone, many creatures in the midnight zone depend on marine "snow" for food. Other, bigger creatures eat the smaller creatures who have managed to survive by eating the "falling snow."

God has given many sea creatures in the midnight zone the ability to emit light and display bioluminescence. Bioluminescence is a chemical production of light from the bodies of creatures, such as lightning bugs or fireflies. Ask your parents to go on the Internet and look for "ocean creatures bioluminescence" to see videos of the most incredible ocean creatures God has created!

The midnight zone is home to Lanternfish, which are an important source of food for larger marine animals. Image credit: public domain

Creatures in the very cold ocean midnight zone tend to live relatively sedentary lives so as not to waste energy. Some animals of the midnight zone include types of slow-moving crabs, fish, and worms, among others. It is amazing that there is such a surprising variety of life in the dark, cold waters of the midnight zone.

D. The Ocean Floor

The ocean floor contains some incredible features. In places, ocean trenches can be found. These trenches are deep "pits" that can reach depths three times deeper than the average depth of the ocean floor. The water pressure can rise to 16,000 psi (pounds per square inch). Even here, in the very deepest part of the ocean, and of the planet, life can be found.

Have you ever heard of ocean floor volcanoes? Ocean floor volcanoes can support their own ecosystems, filled with life. The volcano vents expel heat that creates hot mineral-rich environments that are ideal for certain types of ocean bacteria. These bacteria, in turn, provide a valuable food source for many deep sea creatures.

The oceans offer us countless opportunities to marvel at the amazing wonders God has made for us. The beautiful and interesting diversity of ocean life can inspire us to meditate on the beauty, the power, and the creativity of God. The vast ocean ecosystem, supported in many ways by one of the smallest creatures God has made, plankton, can impress on us the wisdom of God's incredible designs.

With the majority of the oceans still unexplored, many ocean creatures and features remain in large part a mystery. Our Creator

gives the oceans and their creatures to us to care for them and to enjoy them. Even more amazing, God so loves us that He offers us an eternity to enjoy all the blessings and incredible things He has prepared for us in Heaven!

Review Questions

1. Why does the sunlight zone contain most of the

ocean's living creatures?

_____

2. What is bioluminescence?

_____

3. What creatures other than fish inhabit the different ocean zones?

_____

_____

VIII. Fish and People

A. Fish as Pets

Have you ever had a goldfish? Some children grow up with a goldfish bowl in their home, where they enjoy feeding the fish, watching the fish, and even cleaning the "home" or fishbowl for their pet fish. Although you cannot play with a fish, these beautiful and graceful swimming creatures are fun to watch. If you have never had a pet fish, perhaps your parents can take you to a pet store to see the various fish in the store aquarium.

A goldfish in a bowl is pretty simple. Some people, however, have elaborate tropical aquariums. The care of some fish can be difficult because their environment needs to be just the right temperature to allow them to survive. Other fish are simpler, but all fish need properly cleaned homes, food, and the correct type of water.

B. Fish for Good Health

Some doctors have a saying: "If more people ate fish, more doctors could go fishing." Fish is so nutritious and so healthy for people to eat, that doctors believe if people ate more fish, they would not have so many sick patients! This is, in large part, due to the Omega-3 oils that are found in many fish. People sometimes buy fish oil supplements to stay healthy when they do not eat enough fish.

Not all fish are equally healthy as food sources. People have found that some fish tend to contain mercury or other toxins, perhaps from chemicals emptied into rivers. Some people believe that wild fish is healthier than farmed fish. That may be, but the farm fish are likely free of chemicals from industrial waste. It is good to know the environment from which your fish has come. Since the

Fukushima nuclear disaster in Japan in 2011, for example, many samples of Pacific fish have shown elevated levels of radiation.

C. Fish as a Christian Symbol

The fish has been an important Christian symbol since the beginning of the Church. It has been found in the Roman catacombs. It is said that the Ichthus, or fish symbol, was used by Christians to secretly identify themselves during times of persecution of Christians. Christians would draw the symbol in the dirt on the ground when speaking to someone; if the other person did the same, it signified that it was safe to talk about the Faith.

So where did the fish symbol for Christianity come from? "Ichthus" is the Greek word for fish. It was used as an early abbreviation, for "Iesous CHristos THeou Uios Soter," meaning, "Jesus Christ, Son of God, Savior."

D. Fish in Sacred Scripture

We read about fish often in the Gospel readings. Remember when Jesus fed 5,000 people with a few loaves of bread and a couple of fish (Jn. 6:1-15)? In fact, the words "fish" as well as "fishes," "fisherman" and "fishing" appear in the Bible almost 100 times! Remember that the apostles Peter, Andrew, James, and John were fishermen. Jesus told them that they were to become "fishers of men." Jesus meant they would "catch" people to help bring them into the Kingdom of Heaven.

You might want to read the events in John 21:1-19. Jesus uses fish to teach a lesson about Heaven and eternity. The event happened after the Resurrection when Peter took some of the Apostles fishing. They suddenly saw Jesus on the shore. Jesus had a fire and fish cooking on the fire. Verse 11 tells us: "Simon Peter went over and dragged the net ashore of one hundred fifty-three large fish. Even though there were so many, the net was not torn."

The Fathers of the Church have seen the net as a symbol of the Church. Peter, the first pope, dragged the net ashore, filled with 153 fish. It is believed that at the time of this event, there were 153 known groups of peoples on the Earth. So we see a beautiful image of Peter, dragging the "Church" like a symbol with all known groups of people to the "shores" of eternity, to the shores of Heaven. The net symbolically contained "fish" or people from every nation on planet Earth, and yet the net is not torn. Jesus is teaching us that He wants the "net" of the Church to hold all people of the Earth and bring them to Heaven.

With that wonderful picture of the love of Jesus Christ for all the people on the Earth from the beginning of time to the end of time, we end this science book.

Review Questions

1. What are some health benefits and concerns about eating fish?

_____

_____

2. Why has the fish been a symbol of Christianity since ancient times?

_____

_____

Chapter Review Activity

SECTION A

Use the words in the word box to complete the sentences:

> anadromous   bioluminescence   catadromous   caudal
>
> paired   seahorse   spiracles   swim bladder
>
> symbiosis   fish

1. A _____ is a cold-blooded vertebrate, most of which have scales and obtain oxygen through gills.

2. _____ are openings in the tops of the heads of rays, skates, and some sharks through which they can obtain oxygen.

3. A _____ _____ is a gas-filled sac that helps stabilize bony fish at different depths in the water.

4. Some deep ocean fish can produce their own light through _____.

5. _____ is a long-term relationship between two different types of organisms.

6. A fish's tail fin is its _____ fin.

7. A _____ has a prehensile tail, swims upright, is propelled by its dorsal fin, and the males of the species "give birth."

8. Pectoral and pelvic fins are _____ fins.

9. _____ fish are born in fresh water but spend their adult lives in salt water.

10. _____ fish begin their lives in salt water, but spend their adult lives in fresh water.

Chapter Review Activity

SECTION B

Write the word *jawless*, *cartilaginous*, or *bony* to identify the following fish:

11. Do not have paired fins

_____

12. Includes lampreys and hagfish

_____

13. Have placoid scales

_____

14. Have no scales

_____

15. Includes about 95% of fish species

_____

16. Contains sharks and rays

_____

17. Do not have skeletons made of cartilage

_____

18. Have flat scales

_____

SECTION C

Circle the correct answer.

19. Which fish spends time out of the water?
    A. Mudskippers
    B. Flying fish
    C. Lungfish
    D. All of the above

20. Which shows the three levels of the open ocean in order from shallowest to deepest?
    A. Sunlight zone, Midnight zone, Twilight zone
    B. Twilight zone, Sunlight zone, Midnight zone
    C. Sunlight zone, Twilight zone, Midnight zone
    D. Midnight zone, Twilight zone, Sunlight zone

21. What is the largest fish in the world?
    A. Great white shark
    B. Bull shark
    C. Whale shark
    D. Blue whale

22. What dangerous shark inhabits coastal waters and fresh water rivers?

    A. Bull shark

    B. Great white shark

    C. Whale shark

    D. Electric eel

SECTION D

Answer the following questions.

23.   What are the differences between fresh water and salt water fish?

    _____

    _____

    _____

24.   Explain the miracle of St. Anthony and the fish.

    _____

    _____

    _____

25.   Why has the fish been an ancient symbol of Christianity?

    _____

    _____

    _____

Glossary

Adrenal glands: two glands, which produce three dozen hormones, located on top of the kidneys. Each adrenal gland is made of an outer cortex and an inner medulla. The adrenal cortex controls salt and water balance in the body. The adrenal medulla controls the body's response to stressful events and controls metabolism.

Adrenaline: the "fight or flight" hormone responsible for preparing the body to withstand stressful events. Adrenaline is the hormone responsible for the increased heart rate, blood pressure, and shakiness that a person experiences when frightened, nervous, or excited.

Aerobic: processes that require oxygen.

Aerobic exercise: exercise that stimulates and strengthens the heart and lungs, thus increasing the capacity of lungs to provide oxygen to the blood.

Airways: tube-like structures that carry oxygen-containing air into the respiratory system.

Algae: a plantlike organism that lives in water.

Allergy: the exaggerated response of a person's immune system to a foreign substance that would not trigger a response in most people.

Alveoli: tiny air sacs where gas exchange in the lungs occurs.

Amphibians: cold-blooded, vertebrate animals that live part of their life cycle in the water and part on the land. Amphibians include frogs, toads, and salamanders.

Antibiotics: powerful medicines that can destroy bacterial infections.

Antibodies: molecules that attach to infected cells in order to kill the germs.

Aorta: the largest artery of the circulatory system located on the top of the heart.

Aortic valve: allows blood pumped by the left ventricle to pass into the aorta and to the rest of the body, but does not permit blood to flow back from the aorta into the left ventricle.

Appendicular bones: the bones that make up the limbs of the human body, that is, the arms, legs, hands, fingers, feet, and toes.

Appendix: part of the immune system; assists with the maturing of B-cells.

Arteries: vessels that carry blood away from the heart.

Arterioles: the smallest arteries.

Atria: plural of atrium; the two smaller chambers at the top of the heart that pump blood into the larger ventricles.

Autonomic nervous system: part of the peripheral nervous system, which controls involuntary bodily functions such as heartbeat and food digestion.

Axial bones: the bones of the body's axis, that is, head, neck, chest, and backbone.

Axon: the extension from the nerve cell body at the bottom or end of the cell. An axon carries impulses away from the cell body and transmits impulses to other cells.

Bacteria: the simplest creatures that are considered alive; bacteria are small, single-celled organisms.

Ball and socket joint: like that of the shoulder or of the hip, this joint allows movement in a full circle.

Bile: fluid that is produced by the liver and aids in the digestion of fats and oils.

Birds: warm-blooded, egg-laying vertebrates with feathers, wings, and a beak, which usually have the ability to fly.

Blood pressure: the force needed to keep blood flowing through the vessels to the whole body.

Blood vessels: the "pipes" that carry blood throughout the body. The major types of blood vessels include arteries, veins, and capillaries.

Blood: a specialized tissue composed of living cells in a liquid environment.

Bone marrow: tissue inside the bones that produces red blood cells.

Bony Fish: comprise the vast majority of fish; have jaws and skeletons made of bone not cartilage.

Brain: the organ that controls most of the functions of the body.

Bronchi: the tubes at the end of the trachea that bring air into the lungs. The bottom of the trachea divides into two main bronchi; these divide again into smaller and smaller tubes.

Bronchioles: the smallest tubes of the bronchi.

Capillaries: small blood vessels with thin walls that connect the artery and vein systems. Oxygen and nutrients pass through the walls of the capillaries to the body's cells, and waste products are collected from the cells.

Carbohydrate: an important organic energy source for your body. All sugars and starches and fibers are carbohydrates.

Cardiac muscle: the specialized muscle of the heart.

Carl Linnaeus (li-nee-uhs): Swedish scientist who devised a system of classification and naming of organisms that remains the basic framework of the modern system used today.

Cartilage: firm rubbery tissue that serves as a cushion at the joints.

Cartilaginous Fish: fish whose internal structure is not bone but cartilage. Cartilaginous fish include sharks and rays.

Cell membrane: a biological membrane that separates the interior of all cells from the outside environment and protects the cell from its surroundings.

Cell: the basic unit of structure and function of all living organisms.

Central nervous system: includes the brain and spinal cord.

Cerebellum: an important part of the brain located at the base and back of the brain. The cerebellum is primarily responsible for balance and muscle coordination.

Cerebral cortex: the outer layer of the cerebrum. It is the location where most of the thinking and perception is done. The cerebral cortex is made up of what is called gray matter, which is responsible for storing and processing information.

Cerebrum: the largest part of the brain; the cerebrum is primarily responsible for voluntary activity. This is the area in which thought occurs. The cerebrum also controls our sensory perception (sight, hearing, smell), and controls our speech and memory.

Chemical digestion: the breakdown of food particles by chemical means, through the action of enzymes, into simpler substances.

Cholesterol: a type of fat found in human blood.

Cilia: the hairs in the trachea.

Circulatory system: includes the heart, blood vessels, and the blood. This system brings oxygen and nutrients to the cells in the body, and brings waste products, like carbon dioxide, to the lungs and other organs of waste disposal for elimination from the body.

Colon: another name for the large intestine. It is the final part of the digestive tract, where any remaining water is re-absorbed for use in the body.

Compact bone: the dense outer layer of a bone.

Connective tissue: tissue that supports and connects other tissue types within organs or connects bones to muscles.

Crustaceans: marine creatures that usually have a hard shell or crust. Examples of crustaceans include lobsters, crabs, crayfish, and shrimp.

Cuticle: part of the hair shaft; the thin protective layer.

Decomposers: organisms that break down dead materials in the soil and turn them into nutrients that go into the soil.

Dendrites: short, highly-branched extensions that help increase the surface area of the nerve cell body. Dendrites receive impulses from other cells.

Dermis: the middle layer of skin that contains the base of the hair follicles and the base of the sweat glands.

Diaphragm: a large muscle at the bottom of the chest cavity responsible for the work of inhaling and exhaling.

Diastolic pressure/number: measures the pressure in the arteries when the heart relaxes.

Digestion: the breaking down of complex food into the basic building blocks of carbohydrates, proteins, fats, vitamins, and other small nutrients.

Digestive system: the organ system responsible for breaking down food into carbohydrates, proteins, fats, vitamins, and other small nutrients which are used by the human body for energy to fuel all the life processes.

Ducts: tubes surrounded by tissue to conduct liquids, such as the tear duct.

Duodenum: the beginning of the small intestine, where bile and pancreatic fluid mix with food.

Ear: the organ of hearing.

Electrical impulses: part of the method that nerve cells use to send information from one end of the cell to the other. In the heart, electrical impulses make the heart beat.

Endocrine system: system of glands which releases fluids inside the body directly into the blood stream; responsible for maintaining health and guiding growth and development.

Enzymes: substances that make a chemical reaction in the body work faster, or better, like the digestion of food.

Epidermis: the outer layer of skin.

Epiglottis: a small flap of cartilage at the base of the throat. The epiglottis is a protective feature of the respiratory system. The epiglottis flap automatically covers the trachea when we eat so that food does not go down the trachea to the lungs.

Eye: the organ of sight.

Fats: the most energy dense nutrients. Some foods, like fruits and vegetables, have almost no fat; while others, like nuts, oils, butter, and red meat, have lots of fat.

Fatty acids: the building blocks of the fat in food and in the body. When we digest fats, they are broken down into fatty acids which are absorbed into the blood.

Fibrin: a protein in the blood that forms a blood clot to stop bleeding.

Fungus: (plural: fungi): a living thing that is generally beneficial in nature. Fungi are decomposers.

Gallbladder: organ that stores and releases bile into the duodenum to aid in digestion by breaking down fats.

Gastric juice: a thin, strong acid that is secreted by the glands in the lining of the stomach which contains hydrochloric acid and enzymes that break down proteins.

Genetic: inherited from a parent (for example, an allergy).

Gills: respiratory organ found in many water organisms which allows them to breathe by removing oxygen from water and excreting carbon dioxide.

Glands: produce hormones important for good health and development of the human body.

Gliding joints: two bone plates that glide against one another. The joints in your ankles and wrists are gliding joints.

Glucagon: the hormone that increases blood sugar levels.

Glucose: the sugar found in the blood, which is the primary source of energy for most of the body's cells.

Glycogen: an important source of energy for the body.

Gonads: glands necessary to have a baby.

Gray matter: composed of nerve cell bodies and is responsible for storing and processing information.

Growth: the gradual increase in size of an animal or vegetable body over time.

Heart Chambers: the four chambers in the heart: two atria and two ventricles.

Heart: the muscular organ at the center of the circulatory system that pumps the blood through the blood vessels to the body tissues.

Hemoglobin: iron compound in red blood cells of humans which allows the cells to carry oxygen.

Hinge joint: allows movement back and forth in only one plane; the elbow is a hinge joint.

Homeostasis: a state of internal stability.

Hormones: chemical messengers that affect the activities of other parts of the body.

Host cell or animal: an animal or plant cell on or in which a parasite or virus lives.

Hydrochloric acid: produced in the stomach; a strong acid that helps break down food, particularly proteins in food.

Hypothalamus: gland which regulates the body's temperature. It also controls other automatic functions and regulates the pituitary gland.

Immune system: the body system that fights germs.

Immunity: the body's ability to prevent or resist infection or illness caused by germs.

Insulin: the hormone that lowers blood sugar levels.

Invertebrates: animals that do not have a backbone.

Irregular bones: bones of a variety of shapes and sizes that do not fit into the other categories of bones; including the middle ear bones, the vertebrae, some facial bones, and the jawbone.

Joint: the location at which bones connect.

Keratin: a protein that makes up hair, fingernails, and parts of the skin.

Kidney: the pair of organs that filter wastes from the blood.

Lamprey: long, eel-like, jawless fish with smooth skin, no scales, and a sucker-like mouth without jaws.

Large intestine: the final part of the digestive tract, where water and nutrients are absorbed and waste is compacted so it can exit the body.

Larynx: a tube-shaped organ in the neck containing the vocal cords; also called the voice box.

Lateral line: a system of sensory organs unique to fish that detects vibrations and pressure changes in the water.

Left hemisphere: the left half of the cerebrum, it is largely responsible for logical thinking and mathematical computation.

Leprosy: also known as Hansen's disease; a terrible skin disease.

Leukocytes: white blood cells.

Lichen (lie·kin): small plants that grow on rocks.

Ligaments: tough bands of connective tissue that join two bones together.

Lipids: types of fatty acids.

Liver: organ that assists in digestion by producing bile.

Lungs: the organs responsible for getting oxygen from the air into the blood so it can be carried throughout the body.

Lymph fluid: circulates throughout the body, collecting waste to get rid of it, and carrying important vitamins to help different parts of the body.

Lymph nodes: small glands situated in different parts of the body, such as in the neck, the chest, and the abdomen. When the human body is fighting disease or infection, the lymph nodes filter enemy antigens out of the lymph, and lymphocytes destroy antigens at the location of the lymph node glands.

Lymph system: the system within the immune system that absorbs fluid from the body's tissues and returns it into circulation.

Lymph vessels: are similar to veins. Like veins, lymph vessels have valves that prevent the lymph fluid from flowing back towards the tissues. The lymph vessels empty lymph fluid into two lymph ducts.

Malaria: a serious illness in humans; people with malaria experience high fevers, shaking chills, and flu-like symptoms. Malaria is transmitted to humans through the bite of an Anopheles mosquito and is common in tropical and subtropical areas where these mosquitoes are found.

Mammals: warm-blooded animals that feed their young with milk produced in mammary glands.

Mammary glands: a unique trait of mammals; used by female mammals to produce milk to feed their young.

Marsupials: mammals that give live birth to tiny babies who, after birth, continue to develop in a pouch on the outside of their mother's body; examples include opossums, kangaroos, and koalas.

Mechanical digestion: the physical breaking down of larger pieces of food into smaller pieces.

Medulla oblongata: the portion of the brainstem that regulates breathing, blood circulation, digestion, and other vital involuntary functions.

Melanin: pigment responsible for skin color.

Melatonin: the hormone produced by the pineal gland that regulates the sleep cycle.

Metabolism: the rate at which a person obtains energy from the food he or she eats.

Mitral (my·trill) valve: separates the left atrium from the left ventricle to prevent blood from flowing backwards.

Molecule (mol·e·kyool): the functional substance of most of creation. A molecule is a combination of two or more atoms of either the same kind, or of two or more kinds.

Monotremes (mon-o-tremes): mammals that lay eggs.

Motor nerves: transmit information away from the central nervous system to the rest of the body, specifically to muscles and glands.

Muscle tissue: is made of interconnected, elongated cells that have the ability to contract and relax. Muscle tissues are responsible for movement in almost all animals.

Muscles: support and protect other body organs, but most importantly, muscles are the agents or the cause of movement for the body.

Mutualism (myoo·tyul·ism): a symbiotic relationship that helps both organisms.

Natural killer cells: kill abnormal cells like cancer cells.

Nephron (nef-ron): tiny, microscopic structures in the kidneys that filter the blood.

Nerves: bundles of special cells called neurons, which carry impulses between the central nervous system (the brain and spinal cord) and the rest of the body.

Nervous system: the part of an animal's body that coordinates its voluntary and involuntary actions and transmits signals between different parts of its body. The human nervous system includes the brain, the spinal cord, the sensory organs, and the nerves.

Neurons: or nerve cells, are the functional cells of the nervous system. Neurons have three functions: (1) to transmit sensory information to the central nervous system; (2) to process, integrate, and interpret incoming sensory information; and (3) to transmit motor impulses to muscles and glands to affect a change as a result of the sensory information.

Nose: the organ of smell.

Nutrients: used by the cells to keep us in good health.

Nutrition: the process by which all organisms take in nutrients from their environment and use the energy from the nutrients for life processes.

Olfactory: relating to the sense of smell.

Olfactory nerve: carries messages for our sense of smell.

Organisms: living things composed of various levels of cellular organization, such as human beings, animals, and plants.

Organs: groups of tissues that work together to perform a specific function, such as the liver, brain, and heart.

Pacemakers: specialized cells in the heart that control the electrical system of the heart to cause it to beat.

Pancreas (pan·cree·us): gland which produces pancreatic fluid which aids in the digestion of food.

Parathyroid glands: are located on the thyroid gland. They produce a hormone which is important for controlling the level of calcium in the blood.

Pathogen (path·o·jen): agent or living germ that causes disease.

Pepsin: one of the two enzymes found in gastric juice.

Plasma: the liquid part of blood. Plasma is composed of water but also carries nutrients.

Peripheral nervous system: nerves that come from the spinal cord and branch out to the different parts of the body.

Peristalsis (per-uh-stal-sis): the wave-like contractions of the esophagus.

Peyer's Patches: filter out harmful organisms from the digestive tract; also help B-cells mature.

Phagocyte (fag-o-site): white blood cell

Pharynx (fair·inx): the throat.

Photosynthesis (foh-tuh-sin-thuh-sis): the process by which plants convert water and carbon dioxide into food with the help of light.

Pineal (pi-nee-al) gland: gland, located within the brain, important in regulating the sleep cycle by releasing the hormone melatonin.

Pituitary gland: gland which regulates the body's hormones.

Pivot joint: type of joint that allows for rotation; for example, a pivot joint in the neck allows turning of the head from left to right.

Placental mammals: mammals who give live birth to fully developed babies.

Plankton: a variety of single-celled organisms, which live together in a body of water.

Platelets: cell fragments responsible for blood clotting to protect the body from excessive blood loss.

Pleura: a thin tissue layer that protects the lungs.

Pneumonia: an infection that inflames the air sacs in one or both lungs.

Pores: little holes in the skin which emit sweat.

Proteins: make up the muscles, and support growth and tissue repair.

Pulmonary circulation: brings deoxygenated blood to the lungs to discard carbon dioxide and to pick up oxygen.

Pulmonary valve: regulates the blood flow from the right ventricle into the pulmonary artery for the lungs and prevents blood from flowing backward to the heart.

Pupil: the part of the eye where light enters.

Red blood cells: carry oxygen throughout the body.

Reflex: an involuntary response of the nervous system to some stimulus.

Reproduction: the ability of living organisms to produce offspring similar to themselves.

Reptiles: cold-blooded vertebrates that have dry, scaly skin, and usually lay soft-shelled eggs on land; examples include snakes, turtles, crocodiles, and lizards.

Respiration (res-puh-rey-shuhn): the movement of oxygen from the outside air to the cells within tissues and the transportation of carbon dioxide in the opposite direction.

Right hemisphere: the right half of the cerebrum; it is largely responsible for creativity.

Roots: the organs that anchor the plants in the soil, and which absorb water and minerals from the soil.

Respiratory system: is composed of every organ and structure that is involved in bringing oxygen into the blood.

Saddle joints: joints where one of the bones forming the joint is shaped like a saddle, with the other bone resting on it like a rider on a horse; for example, the joint at the base of the thumb.

Saliva: produced by salivary glands in the mouth. The function of saliva is to moisten the food.

Sebaceous (see-bay-shus) glands: glands in the skin that secrete oil called sebum that protects the hair.

Sebum (see-bum): a thick substance secreted by sebaceous glands. Sebum consists of fat and cell fragments; it lubricates and waterproofs the hair in your skin.

Secretion: the process by which a substance, such as a hormone, chemical, or enzyme, is released from an organ or gland to perform a particular function.

Sense organs: take in information from the environment.

Sensory nerves: these transmit sensory information to the central nervous system.

Skeletal muscle: the striated muscles that move the bones in the skeleton.

Skin: the major organ of touch. Its main functions are protection, temperature regulation, and sensation.

Small intestine: the largest digestive organ of the human intestinal tract, where most digestion occurs.

Smooth muscle: the specialized muscles inside the organs. Smooth muscles move involuntarily.

Somatic nervous system: part of the nervous system that takes in sensory information such as touch, pain, or temperature from different parts of the body, such as the arms and legs, and transports that information back to the brain. The motor nerves of the somatic nervous system are used for voluntary movement.

Species: a group of organisms having common characteristics.

Spinal cord: a thick bundle of nerves that comes from the brain and runs down the spinal column.

Spleen: filters the blood to rid it of germs and other debris.

Spongy bone: has air pockets and may look like a kitchen sponge.

Starches: complex carbohydrates.

Stems: the organs through which the water and minerals are transported to other parts of a plant.

Strep throat: a bacterial throat infection that can make your throat feel sore and scratchy.

Striated (stry-ay-ted) muscle cells: meaning "striped" muscle. Because muscles are made up of fibers containing parallel bands of different material, muscles appear striped under a microscope.

Subcutaneous (sub-cue-tane-nee-us) layer (skin): the third and deepest layer of the skin.

Sugars: usually simple carbohydrates.

Symbiotic (sim·by·ot·ik) relationships: close and long-term relationships between two different species that benefits one or both of the organisms.

Synapse: a gap between the end of one nerve cell and the beginning of another nerve cell.

Synovial (syn-no-vee-ole) joints: joints that enable movement.

Systolic (sis·taul·ik) pressure: the force generated when the ventricles are contracting and pushing blood through the arteries.

Taste buds: contain taste receptor cells.

T-cells: directly kill germ-infected cells. The "T" in T-cells stands for the thymus gland where the T-cells are generated and "trained."

Tendon: a very strong band tissue that connects bone to muscle.

Thoracic (thor-as-ic) cavity: the chest cavity that contains the heart and lungs.

Thymus gland: important in the immune system; develops T-cells.

Thyroid gland: produces two hormones which regulate the body's metabolic rate, or the rate at which body cells use energy.

Tissues: groups of cells that work together to serve a specific function.

Tongue: the major organ of taste.

Toxin: a poison.

Trachea (tray·key·ah): a tube-like pipe supported by rings of cartilage and lined with cilia. The trachea connects the voice box to the lungs.

Tricuspid (tri-cus-pid) valve: separates the right atrium from the right ventricle to prevent blood from flowing backwards when the heart is beating.

Tuberculosis (TB): a potentially serious infectious disease that mainly affects the lungs.

Ureter (you-ree-ter): a thin muscular tube through which urine is transported away from the kidney.

Urethra (you-ree-thrah): the tube at the lower end of the bladder. When the bladder is full, urine passes through the urethra and finally out of the body.

Urinary (your-in-a-ree) bladder: a hollow muscular organ that stores urine until it is released from the body.

Urinary system: purifies the blood in the body and removes metabolic wastes from it.

Urine: a liquid that consists of the waste products filtered out of the blood.

Valves: fibrous flaps that control blood flow to keep it from going backwards.

Vegetable: any edible part of a plant.

Veins: vessels that carry blood back to the heart.

Ventricles: two large chambers that pump blood out of the heart to the lungs and to the body.

Vertebrates: animals which have backbones.

Villi: Tiny, finger-like projections on the wall of the small intestine, through which nutrients from food pass into the bloodstream.

Virus: a small, non-living, infectious pathogen that reproduces only inside the living cells of other organisms.

Vitamin D: is made in the skin with help from sunlight. Vitamin D helps the body to absorb calcium to keep bones strong.

White blood cells: are responsible for fighting infection.

White matter: composed of projections from the gray matter nerve cells called axons, which transmit information to different parts of the brain.